A Trying Time

Jim Wallace

A Trying Time

The North-West Mounted Police In The 1885 Rebellion

Bunker to Bunker Books
Winnipeg
1998

Canadian Cataloguing in Publication Data

Wallace, Jim, 1932-

A trying time

Includes bibliographical references and index.
ISBN 1-894255-00-3

1. North West Mounted Police (Canada) -- History.
2. Riel Rebellion, 1885.   3. Northwest, Canadian --
History -- 1870-1905.   4. Frontier and pioneer life --
Prairie Provinces. I. Title.

FC3216.2.W342 1998   363.3'09712   C98-920095-7
HV8157.W342 1998

Bunker to Bunker Books
34 Blue Spruce Crescent
Winnipeg, MB.
R3M 4C2

- Dedicated To -

Bruce & David

"The North-West Mounted Police
have a trying time before them."

Lord Lansdowne 1885

Contents

Preface

The North-West Rebellion in 1885 was, in every sense, "a trying time" for the North-West Mounted Police. The role of the force in the insurrection has been described by historians as "minor" and "insignificant" but this does not do justice to the part played by the relatively small number of members in the Mounted Police at that time. While they were not in the engagements at Fish Creek and Batoche with General Frederick Middleton, the Mounted Police were involved in Colonel Otter's march from Swift Current to Battleford, the attack on Poundmaker at Cut Knife Hill, General Strange's advance from Calgary to Edmonton and Fort Pitt and the engagements at Frenchman Butte and Loon Lake, as well as the initial engagement at Duck Lake.

The Mounted Police had a heavy casualty rate. While figures vary, depending on the source, the Mounted Police provided approximately 10% of the 5,456 men in the North-West Field Force and suffered more than 15% of the fatal casualties, despite not being involved in several major engagements. In the initial clash at Duck Lake there were 12 fatal casualties, or approximately 13% of those involved, while the total casualties, killed and wounded, including the Special Constables of the Prince Albert Volunteers, was 23% of those present. At Cut Knife Hill the Mounted Police provided approximately 20% of the force and suffered 37.5% of the fatal casualties. On this basis, it is hard to accept the role of the force as either "minor" or "insignificant."

General Middleton, Commander of the Canadian Militia, seemed to have an ingrained dislike of the Mounted Police prior to his arrival in the west and, up until the pursuit of Big Bear, he had no Mounted Police members serving in his column. His outspoken criticisms of the force were taken up by the soldiers under him and the press who accompanied them. In the columns commanded by Otter and Strange, there were no such problems and the men who fought side by side at Cut Knife Hill, Frenchman Butte and Loon Lake generally had a great deal of respect for each other.

A Trying Time

Few Canadians realize that the Rebellion almost saw the end of the North-West Mounted Police when General Middleton and Adolphe Caron, the Minister of Militia and Defence, decided the force should be abolished after the rebellion. Fortunately, the Mounted Police survived while Middleton, after his brief moments of glory, was involved in a scandal over stolen furs so the men he so badly maligned were able to feel some vindication.

This book describes North-West Mounted Police activities just before, during, and just after the rebellion. Before the rebellion and at the beginning of the insurrection the force was at a low point, poorly trained, ill equipped and badly paid. During the Rebellion the Mounted Police made a significant contribution, largely due to a number of experienced and resourceful individuals who, together with inexperienced but willing new members, rose to the occasion. At the end of the rebellion an infusion of new recruits and a number of changes in senior ranks set the stage for what would hopefully be better times.

As far as possible I relied on documents created at the time but, in some cases, I have also used later reminiscences and memoirs. Most records of events come in several versions, some with variations and some with contradictions. I have endeavored to flag those places where differing views are important. A great deal of care has been taken in identifying individual members associated with specific activities. Here, too, there were many contradictory sources and I hope that the margin of error has been kept to a minimum.

I received considerable assistance from the Hudson's Bay Company Archives/Public Archives of Manitoba, the Manitoba Legislature Library, the Glenbow-Alberta Institute Archives and Library, the Calgary City Library, the Winnipeg City Library, the University of Saskatchewan Library Special Collections, and the National Archives and National Library of Canada. I wish to specially acknowledge the kind assistance of Glenn Wright, of the Historical Section, Royal Canadian Mounted Police and Sarah Montgomery at the National Archives. The

Preface

cooperation of the Editor of the *RCMP Quarterly* in granting permission to use the photograph on the front cover of this book is greatly appreciated.

I would also like to give thanks to the many other people who assisted me in some way. Dr. Ruth Cooke read the first draft of this book, just as she did with *A Double Duty*, and hopefully has forgiven me for misspelling her name in the preface to that book. Susan Fonseca did proofreading/editing and made several helpful suggestions. Renata Jakubowicz once again cheerfully provided support and encouragement during research in Alberta. Jerry Holtzhauer assisted with research at the National Archives and Wayne Cline, John Thyen, and Mike Dorosz helped track an elusive and badly needed picture. Last, but not least, I would like to thank Geoff Todd of Bunker to Bunker books who made this all possible. While the assistance of these many individuals was appreciated, the responsibility for any errors or omissions remains mine.

Jim Wallace

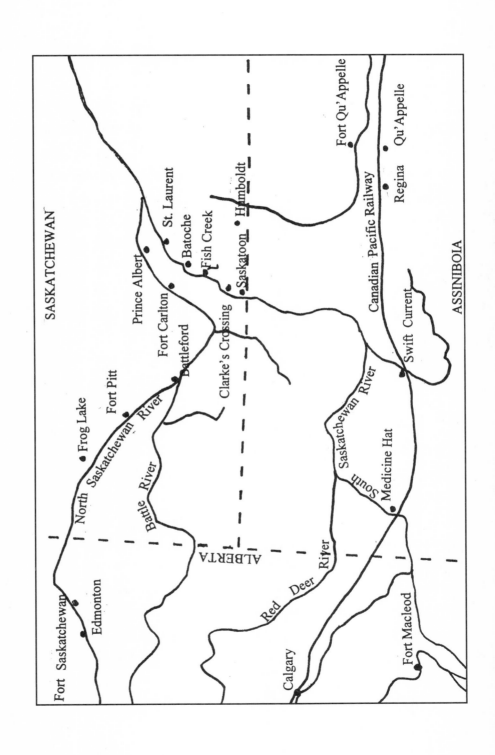

Changes On The Plains

In the 1880's Canada took pride in the peaceful settlement of the west in contrast to the bloody Indian wars and general lawlessness which accompanied the conquest of the "wild west" south of the border. After the arrival of the North-West Mounted Police in 1874, there was remarkably little conflict between the police and the Indians or Métis. This relative calm ended in 1885 with the outbreak of an armed insurrection on the South Branch of the Saskatchewan River. Citizens in eastern Canada were shocked at the news of a Métis rebellion but it came as no surprise to many in the west, especially to the Mounted Police, settlers, and some Indian Department officials who had been warning the government in Ottawa for some time that trouble was brewing. The failure of the Canadian government to recognize and deal effectively with the problems of the people of the North-West transformed manageable problems into inevitable conflict. To trace the origins of this crisis, one must look back to Canada's acquisition of the vast territory of Rupert's Land from the Hudson's Bay Company in 1869.

Following Confederation in 1867, Canada was a much smaller nation than it is now, consisting of Prince Edward Island, Nova Scotia, New Brunswick and parts of present day Quebec and Ontario. British Columbia was a well-established Crown Colony, while the area between Ontario and the Rockies and far to the north was controlled by the Governor and Company of Adventurers of England Trading into Hudson's Bay. The Hudson's Bay Company had no interest in encouraging settlement but had a clear incentive to maintain the trust and friendship of the Indians on whom their livelihood in the fur trade depended. When Canada acquired Rupert's Land from the Hudson's Bay Company, in exchange for £300,000 and more than six million acres of land, it increased the area of the nation by seven times. Ottawa was totally unprepared for the challenge of implementing sovereignty in this huge, newly acquired territory and the result was a vacuum in which there were no local government, no legal system and no means of exercising control in the area.

Without any consultation with those living in the territory, an Act was passed under which Rupert's Land would be governed as a single territory by a governor and an appointed council. At Red River, the only significant settlement in Rupert's Land at the time, the Métis inhabitants were deeply concerned about language rights, schools and title to the lands they occupied. These concerns could easily have been alleviated by consultation and a less arrogant approach by the government. When this did not occur, the Métis found a leader, Louis Riel, who they believed could represent their aspirations.

William McDougall, the governor-to-be, prematurely ordered surveys at Red River employing the system of sections and townships used in Ontario. This caused great apprehension among the Métis whose farms were laid out in river lots, as done in Quebec, so when the Métis and surveyors confronted each other, trouble started. The Métis concerns, aggravated by the intransigence of the Canadian government, led to an insurrection at Fort Garry in 1869 and formation of a provisional government under Louis Riel. A military force was sent to put down the rebellion and Riel fled to the United States. Negotiations, which were started during the uprising, led to the passage of the Manitoba Act and the creation of the new Province of Manitoba in 1870.

Following creation of the Province of Manitoba, the Métis at Red River found themselves becoming rapidly outnumbered by newcomers. Many Métis families then drifted off to the relatively unoccupied areas to the west where they formed small communities of buffalo hunters, a vocation with a very limited future. Some went to Wood Mountain, some to St. Albert and others to St. Laurent on the South Branch of the Saskatchewan River where they established themselves on traditional river lots.

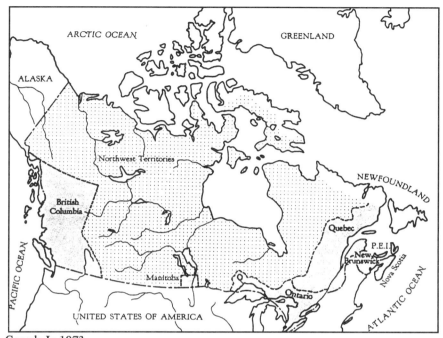

Canada In 1873

While national attention was focused on the problems at Red River, all was not well further west where Indian tribes had been decimated by diseases introduced by white men and then exploited by American whisky traders moving in from Montana. By the end of 1872, conditions were deteriorating rapidly. The activities of the whisky traders increased, hunting decimated the buffalo at an alarming rate, and the exploitation and debauchery of the Indians continued unabated.

The acquisition of Rupert's Land and the expansion of Canada was linked to Sir John A. Macdonald's vision of a country stretching from coast to coast, tied together by a transcontinental railway. The thing most likely to turn his dream into a nightmare would be the outbreak of an Indian war when settlers were arriving in

3

the west. A costly Indian war would not only disrupt the construction of the railway but also had the potential to derail his vision of a nation from sea to sea. He, therefore, considered it essential that law and order be established in the territory.

Although Sir John A. Macdonald recognized the need for a military or police force in the north-west to make it safe both for settlement and for construction of a transcontinental railway, he procrastinated while Lieutenant Governor Morris at Fort Garry kept up constant pressure on Ottawa to take action. Eventually, in 1873, an Act was passed authorizing the formation of a police force for the North-West Territories and the first men were hastily recruited and despatched to Lower Fort Garry for training. Just after approval for the force, word reached Ottawa of the murder of several Assiniboines in the Cypress Hills, in what has become known as the Cypress Hills Massacre and this accelerated the recruitment and training of the first members.

In 1874, the force moved west in an arduous march and established a base at Fort Macleod in what is now southern Alberta.[1] The following year posts were established at Fort Walsh in the Cypress Hills, Fort Calgary, Fort Saskatchewan, downstream from Edmonton, and Swan River Barracks near Fort Pelly in what is now Saskatchewan. In 1876, a post named Fort Battleford was built at the junction of the Battle and North Saskatchewan Rivers. The force was initially welcomed by the Indian tribes because it gave them the chance to get a new lease on life after they had been driven to a low ebb by disease and whisky. The Mounted Police worked to establish friendly relations with the various tribes and initially, built up a mutual trust due to fair and consistent application of what was called "the white man's law."

During their first years in the west, police strength was concentrated in the traditional hunting grounds of the Blackfoot Confederacy, whose members were considered the most warlike Indians on the Canadian plains. In 1876, when Sitting Bull and the Sioux crossed the boundary from the United States following their

4

victory at the Little Big Horn, the focus of police attention shifted to the Fort Walsh and Wood Mountain area. After the departure of the Sioux and the relocation of several bands away from the international boundary and Canadian Pacific Railway, the area around Fort Battleford became more important.

To ensure land was available for settlement and railway construction, the government entered into a series of treaties with Indian bands at Fort Qu'Appelle in 1874, Fort Battleford and Fort Pitt in 1876, and Treaty Number 7, the Blackfoot Treaty, at Blackfoot Crossing in 1877. These treaties were intended to extinguish aboriginal title to the land. By the time of the Treaty Six negotiations at Fort Carlton and Fort Pitt the buffalo were rapidly disappearing and it was obvious that the aboriginal people would undergo a major change in lifestyle.

During the treaty talks, Poundmaker raised the question of ensuring adequate support and assistance during the transition from hunting to an agricultural economy. Lieutenant Governor Morris, setting the party line officials would follow for years, told the chiefs that he could not promise all the Indians could be fed and supported since it would be very expensive and, given this assistance, some of them would never do anything for themselves.[2] When Morris eventually realized that all the chiefs were insistent on some kind of safeguard in times of trouble, he agreed to the inclusion of a famine assistance clause. This clause would become a bone of contention between the bands and the government for many years. Possibly because they were anxious to conclude the treaties, the government reluctantly agreed to give support to the Indians in time of need although, unfortunately, this promise was never fully honoured.[3]

The chiefs who signed Treaty No. 7 also depended on the government to help meet the rapid changes occurring around them. The government never liked the famine clause and, in any case, was not in a hurry to make what it considered unnecessary expenditures. Many officials believed the buffalo would still be around for some time so the Indians could learn to become farmers while sustaining

5

themselves in the interim by the buffalo hunt. For the first few years following the treaties, some bands attempted to start farming but there were long delays in surveying their reserves and providing equipment. The implements, animals and seeds eventually provided were found wanting, both in quantity and quality but, at this time, the government was mesmerized by the problem of Sitting Bull and the Sioux in the Cypress Hills and gave little thought to other Indian problems.

When the Mounted Police first arrived on the plains, they were the primary contact between the government and the aboriginals. Officials were appointed to be responsible for relations with the Indians, but they were few in number and the majority of face to face contacts continued to be between the Mounted Police and the Indians. By 1877, Ottawa created what was called the North-West Superintendency to look after Indian Affairs in the huge region from Manitoba to the Rocky Mountains. The organization was under Lieutenant Governor David Laird who, in addition to being Lieutenant Governor, was the Indian Commissioner. Laird was provided with a ridiculously inadequate staff and budget. M.G. Dickieson, a former recording clerk at treaty negotiations, was double-hatted as Assistant Indian Commissioner and Indian Agent for Treaty Six, while Allan McDonald, a former Army officer, was the Indian Agent for Treaty Four. Given the size of the territory and difficulties of travel, the Indian Agents could do little except distribute treaty payments, often with assistance from the Mounted Police.

There were some Indian leaders who signed the treaties reluctantly, while others flatly refused to do so. The bands that did not sign were left without a reserve, roaming freely on the plains and pursuing the dwindling herds of buffalo, on both sides of the international boundary. The leaders who refused to sign did not consider the terms of the treaties sufficiently generous and wanted to bargain for a better deal. The government officials, who had little actual authority to make changes, regarded those who would not sign as "troublemakers." The chiefs who were the greatest irritants to the Indian Department at this time were Big Bear, Beardy and Piapot. Poundmaker's name was later added to the list.

Big Bear, who was the leader of the largest band of Cree on the plains, refused to sign Treaty No. 6 at Fort Pitt because he realized that all the Cree bands would have to present a united front to deal with the government on an equitable basis. While the Cree saw Big Bear as possibly the only leader with the necessary skills to achieve their aims in a non-confrontational way, government officials only saw him as a problem. The harder Big Bear worked to bring the tribes together to present a united front to the government, the harder officials worked to thwart his efforts. Still refusing to sign the treaty and move onto a reserve, Big Bear and his followers continued to roam the plains, frightening settlers and annoying and frustrating government officials.

By 1878 there was widespread suffering among the tribes on their reservations and thousands of destitute and desperate Indians came to North-West Mounted Police posts such as Fort Walsh, Fort Macleod, and Battleford, seeking food. Starvation was widespread and the Indians looked to the government to meet the obligation, made during treaty negotiations, that food would be provided in times of need. The government was frequently warned of the seriousness of the situation by the North-West Mounted Police and by those Indian Department officials who were not afraid to tell the truth. M.G. Dickieson, the Assistant Indian Commissioner, warned "As I think we are on the eve of an Indian outbreak which will be caused principally by starvation, it does not do to scan the exact lines of a treaty too closely."[4] The *Saskatchewan Herald* reported that the chiefs of the Eagle Hills band told Edgar Dewdney, who had replaced Laird as Indian Commissioner, that they had never been so near to starvation.[5]

1879 should have been a year for consolidating gains and moving forward, since the way was now clear for the Canadian Pacific Railway to be completed and for settlers to move onto what had, until recently, been Indian hunting grounds.

7

Instead, the inexplicably rapid demise of the buffalo herds caught the government completely unprepared and in the face of the Indian Department's inability to cope with the starvation and destitution of the Indians, the major activities of the Police were watching the Sioux and providing humanitarian relief to starving aboriginals.

Edgar Dewdney, who became Lieutenant Governor as well as Indian Commissioner, was charged with implementing a policy of converting the Indians from nomadic hunters to self-sufficient farmers. On his arrival in the west, travelling with North-West Mounted Police Commissioner James Macleod, Dewdney was given a stark introduction to the realities of conditions on the plains when they found thirteen hundred Indians at Blackfoot Crossing, emaciated and weak, who had traded their horses and firearms, eaten their dogs and were now searching for gophers and mice.[6]

Taking advantage of the starving condition of the Indians, the government used food as a coercive tool to enforce its policies. Lieutenant Governor Dewdney wanted to bring the holdouts, such as Big Bear and Piapot, under treaties so he held back rations from them in order to force them to sign. The government planned to move the bands onto small reserves, separated from each other and well north of the international boundary and the Canadian Pacific Railway line. To weaken the influence of charismatic leaders who were attracting large entourages, Dewdney allowed anyone with a minimum of 100 followers who would sign a treaty to be regarded as a chief. This led to some loss of members by the recalcitrant chiefs such as Big Bear, who lost Little Pine, Lucky Man and Thunderchild. Those who departed were often the more moderate members of the band, while those who remained with Big Bear, such as Wandering Spirit and Big Bear's own son, Imasees, were usually the most militant.

Edgar Dewdney introduced a system of home farms, staffed with Farm Instructors, who were supposed to assist the Indians in becoming farmers, as well as raising crops to supplement the rations. Rather than teaching, the main role of the Farm Instructors soon became the distribution of rations, a role which brought them into frequent direct conflict with the Indians. The home farm program was unsuccessful for a variety of reasons, including the fact that those selected for appointment as instructors were often unqualified, did not speak the language of the band they were to teach and frequently had no knowledge of dry farming.

There was a difference in attitude between the Mounted Police and the Indian Department in dealing with the Indians. The Mounted Police had lived on the plains with the Indians before there were Indian Agents and settlers so many of them knew what life had been like for the bands prior to the demise of the buffalo and the institution of the reserve system. As Superintendent Lief Crozier pointed out in a report, ". . . it must be considered that to their minds the contrast between the life they led before the white man came among them and their present one is hardly favourable."[7] Many Mounted Police officers had been present at the treaty negotiations and their perception of what had been promised often appears to have been closer to that of the Indians than it was to the interpretation of the Indian Department.

Senior bureaucrats in the Indian Department were obsessed with the idea that everyone must work and the notion that the famine clause could justify feeding people without exacting labour from them was unthinkable. This led to the work for rations policy which was instituted despite the fact that it was contrary to treaty obligations. In addition, there was often no work to be done and in the winter the Indians frequently lacked the clothing and footwear to work outside, had work been available. When the remaining buffalo in Canada dwindled to numbers insufficient to feed the bands that traditionally depended on them for food, hunting parties started to move south of the boundary where the last of the large herds could still be found. In the fall of 1879, Lieutenant Governor and Indian Commissioner Dewdney encouraged the Blackfoot to follow the buffalo into Montana, thus ridding himself of the problem of feeding them. He later boasted that this had saved the Canadian Government an estimated $100,000.[8] By 1880, with widespread hunger among the Indians, every Mounted Police post was inundated with starving people seeking assistance and the force gave all the help possible. When Inspector Cecil Denny at Fort Calgary found Indians starving and even eating grass, he started to issue beef at the rate of 2,000 pounds a day to the Blackfoot, Stoneys and some Métis.[9]

In the fall of 1879, Louis Riel left his exile in the United States and travelled to Wood Mountain to see Sitting Bull, then went south to join the Métis camp on the Milk River in Montana. At that time, Riel attempted to form a native confederacy based on the Métis hunting community, whose members traded with or were related to all the Indian tribes in the region. He planned that when he succeeded in uniting the Indians and the Métis, they would attack the Mounted Police at Wood Mountain, Fort Walsh, Fort Macleod and Battleford, with the eventual aim of declaring a provisional government and negotiating a treaty with Ottawa.[10] Inspector James Walsh kept a close watch on Riel's activities and managed to dissuade several bands from joining his alliance.[11] A number of bands, including Crowfoot and his Blackfoot and Big Bear's Cree, were in Montana hunting buffalo and spent the winter in close proximity to Riel and the Métis on the Milk River. Riel's efforts to form an Indian confederation were unsuccessful, possibly because the chiefs had their own agenda which differed from that of the Métis leader. As Big Bear saw it they ". . . should not fight the Queen with guns. We should fight her with her own laws."[12]

By 1879, as starvation increased, relations between the Mounted Police and the Indians became strained and were never the same again. The Mounted Police, too few to force the Indians to do anything, had always relied on persuasion and were generally regarded as fair, firm and consistent in applying the law. When the government proved incapable of dealing effectively with the problem of starvation after the disappearance of the buffalo, Lieutenant Governor Dewdney and the Indian Department officials continued to resort to insensitive measures, usually involving control of food supplies or curtailing freedom of movement or expression. These measures often violated the law, treaty obligations and basic human rights. The Mounted Police were caught in the middle. They had to enforce bad policy and back up officials who were often uncaring and incompetent. As their role in enforcing coercive policies increased, what remained of the mutual trust and respect between the force and the Indians was sharply reduced.

In addition to Big Bear, another notable irritant or "troublemaker," in the eyes of the government, was Chief Beardy, who claimed that whites had been responsible for decimating the buffalo and should now provide for the Indians. In February 1879, settlers in the Duck Lake area complained that Beardy and his followers were likely to cause trouble. Following discussions with the Lieutenant Governor, it was decided to station a three-man Mounted Police detachment there for a short time but it was withdrawn to Prince Albert in 1880. When the 1880 treaty payments were being made at Duck Lake, Beardy refused to accept payment claiming his band had made better treaty terms than other bands, and demanded more money. When all the bands except Beardy's had received their treaty money and rations, the remaining government supplies were locked in the trading post of Stobart, Eden & Co. at Duck Lake and the Police departed to Prince Albert and Fort Carlton.

Word soon reached the detachment at Fort Carlton that some of Beardy's Indians had visited the trading post at Duck Lake and threatened to help themselves if the trader would not hand over the food. Inspector James Walker, with a sergeant and two men, immediately returned to Stobart's store in Duck Lake.[13] The Indians appeared, armed and in full war paint, riding in circles and firing into the air. When they dismounted and crowded into the stockade, Walker and his men appeared with revolvers and carbines. The Inspector told them he would shoot the first man to attempt to take supplies from the store. Beardy then relented and the Mounted Police paid treaty money and distributed food.

- 2 -
Deference to Defiance

By late 1880 and early 1881, as the impact of the reserve system started to take full effect, there were additional signs that the Indians were running out of patience, manifested in the anger and frustration vented on Indian Agents and Farm Instructors. Almost without exception, the altercations were over rations, causing the *Saskatchewan Herald* to comment that "he must be fed, if he does not get it he will take it; and he is in a position to do so. It is easier and cheaper to feed them than to fight them."[1] When John Delaney, a Farm Instructor, was horsewhipped for refusing to give rations to two Indians, the perpetrators were sentenced to two months imprisonment for the affair, but probably felt it was worth it. Another Farm Instructor, George Gopsill, a former Mounted Policeman, was threatened with a knife by Yellow Mud Blanket. Yellow Mud Blanket got off with a lecture, while Rattlesnake Dog received a sentence of two months hard labour for thrusting a knife at D.L. Clink.[2]

Frank Oliver in the *Edmonton Bulletin*, cautioned that "An Indian outbreak, if one occurs, will be entirely caused by the present mismanagement of affairs under Commissioner Dewdney and the local man."[3] The *Saskatchewan Herald* voiced similar concerns, noting ". . . it is certain that if any trouble arises it will be wholly due to the criminal negligence of the Indian authorities in Ottawa, who are responsible for the present muddle."[4] Warnings to Ottawa continued but those charged with responsibility for Indian matters seemed incapable of comprehending that anyone could possibly know more than they did about conditions in the west.

While Edgar Dewdney was theoretically responsible for Indian matters, he was, in real terms, able to exercise little independent authority. The position of Superintendent General of Indian Affairs was filled by the Prime Minister, Sir John A. Macdonald, but the day to day direction was in the hands of the Deputy

13

Superintendent, Lawrence Vankoughnet, who might well have been the most meanspirited and parsimonious civil servant to ever serve in Ottawa. He exercised firm central control on the conduct of Indian Affairs and allowed his subordinates no freedom of thought or action.

Although there were capable, devoted and honest men in some positions in the Indian Department, there were many who zealously followed the dictates of Vankoughnet and others of his ilk. At all levels there were some who were insensitive and unfeeling at best and corrupt and dishonest at worst, and relished the opportunity to exercise power over the Indians. When Lawrence Vankoughnet formulated policies that violated both the spirit and the letter of the treaties made with the bands, the agents and subagents were often equally overzealous in applying these policies, seemingly anxious to show just how tough they could be. Their actions often brought them into conflict with the Mounted Police, who were generally inclined to be more understanding of the problems of the bands than the Indian Department and often appeared to be more humanitarian.

As 1881 drew to a close, there were a number of ominous signs which Ottawa continued to ignore, despite the constant warnings of the Mounted Police. The previous year, Commissioner Irvine had pointed out in a report that, with the demise of the buffalo, the Indian population would "irrespective of the aid received from Government, be a starving one, a dangerous class requiring power, as well as care, in handling."[5] At this time large numbers of nomadic Indians still wandered the plains in search of food but conditions in the west were changing rapidly with the construction of the Canadian Pacific Railway which was moving steadily across the plains. As regressive policies took effect and the aboriginals realized that many of the promises made to them would not be kept, disillusion set in. The good relations between the Mounted Police and Indians, carefully nurtured from the first meetings at Fort Macleod, were placed under considerable pressure, both by the ineptness of government officials and by unfair and punitive policies. The Indians' initial respect for the Police and their faith and trust in them continued to be steadily eroded as policemen were often required to enforce unfair and unpopular measures. Where there had previously been deference, there was now defiance.

These changes also caused grave concern to the Métis, who saw the influx of settlers as a threat to those already settled in the country. At Fort Qu'Appelle, hundreds of Métis petitioned the Governor General expressing the opinion that they had received unfair treatment compared to the Manitoba Métis. They cited promises made during negotiations of the Fort Qu'Appelle Treaty that Métis rights would be recognized and respected.

As tensions increased, there were potentially dangerous clashes between officials and Indians. At Blackfoot Crossing on January 2, 1882, there was a serious confrontation between the Blackfoot and members of the Mounted Police. It all started with a quarrel between Charles Daly, an Indian Department employee and Bull Elk, a minor chief. Bull Elk said that a beef head was sold to him then given to someone else so he tried to take it back. He and Daly had a disagreement on the subject and after the argument shots were fired, with one shot passing close to Daly's head. Inspector Francis Dickens came from Blackfoot Crossing with Sergeant Joseph Howe and two constables to arrest Bull Elk.[6] The Blackfoot had spent long periods in the United States hunting the fast disappearing buffalo herds and several of their high-spirited young men formed a Soldiers Lodge while they were in Montana. Now, for the first time since the arrival of the North-West Mounted Police in the west, the Blackfoot resisted them. When Howe and Constable Gilbert Ashe arrested Bull Elk, the Blackfoot warriors surged forward and knocked Dickens down while firing their weapons in the air.[7]

Inspector Dickens, surrounded by 700 aggressive Indians, got a message to Crowfoot, who came to the scene. When Crowfoot said, he would like the accused man released in his custody on a promise to appear, Dickens surrendered the prisoner. When news of the incident reached Fort Macleod, Superintendent

15

Lief Crozier, who was considerably tougher than Dickens, took 20 men to the Blackfoot camp, re-apprehended Bull Elk and took him in for a preliminary examination. Crowfoot demanded for a second time that Bull Elk be turned over to him but Crozier refused. When Crowfoot, highly annoyed, asked if the Mounted Police intended to fight, Crozier replied "certainly not, unless you commence."[8]

Some time later another confrontation occurred on the Sarcee Reserve. When a band member by the name of Crow Collar damaged government property in the ration house, the Indian Agent called for help from the Mounted Police detachment at Fort Calgary. Sergeant John Ward went to the reserve to arrest Crow Collar who had been accused of doing the damage but the Sarcee Chief, Bull's Head, would not surrender him.[9] Superintendent John McIllree and ten men came from Fort Calgary and warned the chiefs that if they did not hand over Crow Collar the Police would arrest Bull's Head and take him to the guard room.[10] The chiefs refused and Bull's Head was duly arrested. The situation was very tense and the Sarcee, who were very angry and agitated, outnumbered the police by a large margin. Since night was falling, the police returned to the Indian Agent's house leaving Bull's Head with the band. When they returned the next day after reinforcements arrived from Calgary, Crow Collar was surrendered to the police. McIllree reported he put Bull's Head in jail from Saturday to Monday and when he ordered his people back to their reserve, they went quietly. Crow Collar was sentenced to ten days imprisonment and had to pay for the damages.[11]

These incidents were indicative of the growing reluctance of many bands to allow the police to come in and make an arrest with a few men, especially in any incident which involved an Indian Agent or Farm Instructor. In 1882, a journalist was quoted in the House of Commons as saying, "though so far the police have been able to make arrests of Indian predators in the face of overwhelming odds, the general impression is that the game of bluff is about played out, and that day when three red-coated prairie troopers, through sheer pluck and coolness can overawe a large band of Bloods, Piegan or Blackfoot is now nearly or quite passed by. . . ."[12] The attitude of Indian Department officials and the reduction or elimination of rations could be found at the heart of virtually every confrontation between the Police and the Indians at this time. Up until now the Police had sided with the Indians in almost every dispute with whites, but they were increasingly seen by the Indians as taking the side of the oppressive officials.

Despite the pressure to sign treaties and move onto reserves, a number of chiefs continued to hold out, especially Piapot and Big Bear. They roamed the plains, frequently returning to the Cypress Hills where they relied on the North-West Mounted Police post at Fort Walsh for rations. In the spring, to the annoyance of the Indian Department, large numbers of Indians who had already settled on reserves came to the Cypress Hills to join them. Following the buffalo herds, Big Bear and his followers went to Montana, despite having told Commissioner Irvine that they were not going to cross the international boundary. Irvine, somewhat exasperated at Big Bear's reluctance to settle down, kept the Americans advised of his movements and said "I hope if he crosses the line the Americans will catch him and give him a sound thrashing."[13]

Shortly afterward, the United States Army mounted the Milk River Expedition to expel Canadian Indians and Métis and push them across the border. Big Bear's band, warned in advance, disappeared from their camp and made a skillful retreat under their war chief, Wandering Spirit, reappearing at Fort Walsh with 130 lodges of starving Indians. Big Bear was reported to have threatened that if adequate supplies were not provided, his men would help themselves. The threat was taken seriously, supplies were moved into the fort, the local traders' stocks of ammunition were secured in the police magazine and two 7-pounder mountain guns were positioned in the bastions. Big Bear and 150 warriors delivered a message demanding food but were told there would be no rations for non-treaty Indians. The warriors rode around the stockade, making war cries and firing into the air in a

17

vain attempt to intimidate the occupants of the fort. Later, at the time of the full moon, they tried once more but were again unsuccessful.

Edgar Dewdney continued his attempts to persuade Big Bear to move north and settle on a reserve but the chief resisted even in the face of starvation. Officials in Ottawa became annoyed at the Police for feeding what they regarded as a band of troublemakers but, as Commissioner Irvine pointed out, ". . . we are sure to have a row here if these Indians are not assisted. They would rather be shot than starve to death."[14] While on a trip to the west, Frederick White, the Comptroller of the North-West Mounted Police, accompanied by Senior Surgeon Augustus Jukes, went to visit some of the Indians who would not make the move to a reserve in the north.[15] Jukes wrote a report describing the destitution, starvation and lack of adequate housing. He commented that "it would indeed be difficult to exaggerate their extreme wretchedness and need, or the urgent necessity which exists for some prompt and sufficient provisions being made for them by the government."[16] White reported to Dewdney that "They are very stubborn on the northern reserve question, still to allow them to starve would be a scandal."[17]

Slowly but surely the policy of not providing rations to those who refused to sign treaties took effect. Worn down by malnutrition and worried about the future of their children, the dissidents gave in, one by one. On December 8, 1882, Big Bear finally signed, although he maintained his objective of negotiating better terms and conditions and organizing a united front to deal with the government. Frederick White in Ottawa congratulated Commissioner Irvine for his "skillful and successful efforts to induce Big Bear to accept treaty."[18]

Conditions grew worse and worse and the Indians reached the end of their patience but instead of rebellion they first chose to appeal to Sir John A. Macdonald. Three chiefs wrote to him outlining conditions in the west, asking "why does not the head man of the Indians appear among us, he whom we call in our language the 'white beard' and by the whites called Dewdney? He took a rapid

18

run once through our country; some of us had the good luck or bad luck to catch a flying glimpse of him. He made us all kinds of fine promises, but in disappearing he seems to have tied the hands of the agents, so that none of them can fulfill these promises." They considered this the cause of their problems and said they were "reduced to the lowest stage of poverty. We were once a proud and independent people and now we are mendicants at the door of every white man in the country; and were it not for the charity of the white settlers who are not bound by treaty to help us, we should all die on government fare. Our widows and old people are getting the barest pittance, just enough to keep body and soul together, and there have been cases in which body and soul have refused to stay together on such an allowance."[19]

The government wanted the newly signed bands to move to the north and Piapot agreed to take a reserve near Qu'Appelle, while Lucky Man and Big Bear wanted to go to the Battleford area, where Big Bear could be near his friend Poundmaker. In the Spring of 1883, Piapot eventually agreed to move to a reserve near Indian Head. The Canadian Pacific Railway had reached Maple Creek so Piapot and 800 of his band were loaded into boxcars for the trip. En route, a boxcar filled with Indians derailed and rolled down a slope, stopping with the doors jammed shut. The boxcar had to be broken open to release them. The Indians, who, quite reasonably, probably viewed this catastrophe as part of a conspiracy to kill them, promptly returned to the Cypress Hills.

In June 1883, the Indian Department sent an agent, Thomas Quinn, to the Cypress Hills to assist in persuading the bands there to move to the north. Quinn, who was later killed in the Frog Lake Massacre, was a half-breed of Sioux ancestry and had once been employed by the Mounted Police in the Cypress Hills as an interpreter. The band chiefs were planning a Thirst Dance and did not want to move north until it was over. They asked for food for the ceremony but were refused by Edgar Dewdney. Piapot, angered by Dewdney's attitude, harangued him about broken promises then pulled down his treaty flag, removed his treaty medal, handed them to the interpreter and left.

Big Bear refused to move from the Cypress Hills unless his band was provided with food and transport for the journey. Eventually the move got underway, with his entourage of 550, many of them on foot, travelling north with a fifteen-man Mounted Police escort. Big Bear's band was supposed to go to Fort Pitt but he stopped en route near Battleford to visit with his friend Poundmaker. The citizens of Battleford were not overjoyed at the visit and "the relief felt in the south at their departure was equalled only by the apprehension of the settlers and authorities in the north at their arrival."[20] In defence of Big Bear the *Saskatchewan Herald* noted that ". . . it became the fashion to blame Big Bear for all raids and wrongs that they could not bring home to anyone else. . . ."[21]

While at Battleford, Big Bear held a Council with John M. Rae, the Indian Agent, who was a political appointee and a cousin of Sir John A. Macdonald. He was always uncomfortable meeting Indians, especially those who were trying to renegotiate treaties and obtain better treatment for their people. Rae told Big Bear to move on to Frog Lake. After a few weeks, Big Bear and his followers moved as far as Fort Pitt but would not continue to Frog Lake since they had not selected the reserve in that area. Concerned at his remaining in Fort Pitt, the government established a 25-man Mounted Police detachment there under Inspector Francis Dickens.

On October 17, 1883, in a retrograde move, the control and management of the North-West Mounted Police was transferred from the Department of the Interior to the Department of Indian Affairs when Sir John A. Macdonald became responsible for that Department as Superintendent General of Indian Affairs. This move signalled a major turning point in relations between the Mounted Police and the aboriginals since it was perceived as allying the force more closely with the coercive and punitive attitudes of the Indian Affairs Department and helped to further erode the trust with the Indians built up by the force over a decade.

As starvation continued to take its toll, the frustration of the Indians manifested itself in isolated incidents which were remarkably few, given the level of provocation. At Eagle Hills, Lean Man drew a pistol on Farm Instructor James Payne who had twice thrown him out of his house where he had gone to seek help.[22] The intervention of others saved Payne's life. In January 1884, after an unsuccessful hunting expedition, Big Bear's father-in-law, Yayakootywapos, was refused rations by John Delaney, who then ordered him out of the ration house. Yayakootywapos sat on a pile of frozen fish refusing to budge unless he was given food. When Delaney grabbed him to throw him out, the Indian drew his knife. Delaney ran out of the ration house and went for the Police. Yayakootywapos received a two-year sentence.[23] As the resistance to punitive and unfair practices increased, the Police were being called upon more frequently to use their powers to back up Indian Agents and Farm Instructors who were themselves often the cause of the trouble.

Big Bear continued his efforts to unite the Cree in order to strengthen their bargaining power and obtain better treatment from the government. He sent a message to the reserves in the area to inform them that he would be sponsoring a Thirst Dance and Council in the coming summer. This activity did not escape the notice of the Indian Department and Hayter Reed reported, "I am confident these Indians have some project in view as yet undisclosed and it would not be a source of surprise to find that they are making efforts to procure a large gathering from east and west, at Battleford or adjacent thereto in the Spring in order to test their powers with the authorities once more."[24] He was right.

21

- 3 -
Tension Rising

The winter of 1883-84 came early and was very severe. Across the plains, the Indians suffered terribly and there was anger, discontent and a sense of betrayal seething just below the surface and likely to break out at the slightest provocation. A continuous series of incidents increased the tension and came dangerously close to erupting into major clashes. One of these took place at Crooked Lakes near Broadview, about 80 miles east of Regina. To add to the widespread starvation and incredible suffering in Indian camps that winter, instructions came from Ottawa to reduce rations. In an unbelievably overzealous application of these orders, the Assistant Indian Commissioner, Hayter Reed, known to the Indians as "Iron Heart," decided that some bands could live on fish and game, thus requiring no rations. One of these, Yellow Calf's Band at Crooked Lakes, was told that their rations would be curtailed.[1]

At Crooked Lakes, the Indian Agent, James Setter, was fired for giving food to Indians who had not worked. His replacement, Hilton Keith, had firm instructions to provide rations only to the aged and those who worked. That winter there was no game, not even rabbit, so the band members were on the verge of starvation but Keith was instructed to reduce rather than increase rations. The local Hudson's Bay Company man, N.W. McKenzie told him, "Keith, for God's sake do not reduce their rations any lower, or there will be trouble."[2] His advice went unheeded.

On February 18, Hilton Keith had a confrontation with Yellow Calf and about twenty-five other band members who were seeking food. When Keith refused to give them rations, they helped themselves to 60 sacks of flour and 12 sacks of bacon from the warehouse. As McKenzie described it they "threw out as much flour and bacon as they wanted and threw Keith out on top of it."[3] Keith informed Hayter Reed, who was acting as Indian Commissioner in the absence of

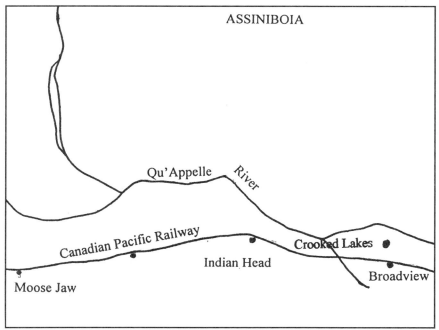

Location of Crooked Lakes

Edgar Dewdney. Reed immediately sent Inspector Richard Burton Deane and 10 policemen to the reserve.[4] For some reason which is difficult to understand, they were instructed to take only their sidearms, not their carbines.[5] Deane was told that ". . . he should at all hazards avoid any collision which might involve the shedding of blood."[6] This was an easy order to give but considerably more difficult to carry out.

When the police arrived at Crooked Lakes, an Indian named Louis O'Soup directed them to a house where those who had taken the food were dining and dancing. O'Soup warned that the dancers "considered themselves justified in their action in that they, or many of them, were in want of food at the time they took it, and that they had not had an opportunity of laying their grievances before the lieutenant governor."[7] Deane sent his men back to the Farm Instructor's house and went with Sergeant James Bliss to talk to the 60 or 70 Indians assembled in the house.[8] The Indians complained that reducing their rations had been a breach of faith and they had only taken what was rightfully theirs but agreed to consider Deane's request that they give up their leaders for trial. Things now seemed to be nearly under control but the next morning Superintendent William Herchmer arrived with more policemen and the reinforced party returned to the Indians' house.[9]

When the Indian Agent, Allan McDonald, arrived just ahead of Herchmer and his men, Yellow Calf informed him the men in the house would not allow themselves to be arrested. McDonald wanted to parley but Herchmer moved in quickly, forming the police in a line with their pistols drawn. Weapons immediately appeared in the windows and armed Indians came around the corners of the house. Deane recalled that McDonald "who was not about to take responsibility for the police action," said "I'll have nothing to do with it" and wisely left.[10]

The situation was a stand-off with the Mounted Police at a complete disadvantage and the possibility that any little error could have resulted in carnage. Rather than avoiding a confrontation, Superintendent Herchmer appeared to be precipitating one. Indian Agent McDonald returned while Herchmer was talking to Yellow Calf and suggested they adjourn to O'Soup's house to continue the discussion. Herchmer came to the conclusion that the young warriors "would fight to the death - that they were well armed, and might just as well die then as be starved by the government."[11]

Hayter Reed came to Crooked Lakes on February 24 to attempt to break the impasse but the Indians would not talk to him until the following day. When they met, with O'Soup acting as spokesman, Reed was able to reach a compromise by which the government would not press charges of resisting the Police in return for a guilty plea for theft which would be dealt with leniently. Under this plea bargain, Yellow Calf and three others were arrested. The charges against Yellow Calf were then dropped and the three others pleaded guilty and received suspended

24

sentences. Inspector Deane later said he did not know what "Herchmer proposed to do in the house even supposing the Indians had admitted us at all. We had no warrant to arrest anyone - no information had been laid, and neither of us knew who the guilty parties were." He concluded that they "were, in effect, provoking the Indians to commit wilful murder by threatening to thrust themselves into premises into which we had no right to force our way without the Queen's warrant."[12]

Following the trial of the three Indians, the magistrate, Colonel Hugh Richardson, called Herchmer and Deane into his office and demanded to know what they had been doing without a warrant. Deane fell back on the excuse of obeying orders and Herchmer said nothing. Deane later expressed the opinion that "the police had made a *faux pas*, and had lost their most valuable asset, their prestige."[13] Deane says the incident was covered up: Herchmer did not report it and Hayter Reed deleted any references to starvation in the report drafted for him by Deane. The Annual Report of the Commissioner of the North-West Mounted Police only noted briefly that ". . . a little trouble occurred with the Indians on the Crooked Lakes reserve near Broadview, which at one time bid fair to assume somewhat serious proportions but which happily passed off in due course."[14]

Looking back at the incident, McKenzie observed that "It was very lucky for the Mounted Police that the Indians had a good feed, so that their tempers were somewhat cooled off by their stomachs being full, or none of them [the Mounted Police] would have come out of that valley alive, hampered as they were with buffalo coats, deep snow and only sidearms. I shudder yet when I think of what might have occurred had a shot been fired even by accident."[15] Although this incident had all the signs of a fiasco that came perilously close to becoming a tragedy, Frederick White asked Commissioner Irvine to pass on to those who went to Crooked Lakes, "especially Colonel Herchmer, Sir John A. Macdonald's appreciation of the efficiency shown by them in connection with the matter."[16]

Forty-six years after this incident, a solicitor at Grenfell, Saskatchewan wrote to the Department of Indian Affairs seeking compensation for an Indian by the name of James Two Voices of Cowessess Reserve who claimed to have aided the government at the Yellow Calf Reserve. While there are some variations in details, his description of events is similar to earlier reports although he was more than one hundred years old at the time the letter was written. James Two Voices said the Indians had a Council and decided collectively to demand rations after two of their band members had starved to death. When Keith, referred to in this statement as Mr. Keep, refused them, an Indian called Cha-chi-ka-Kwan picked up an axe and smashed the store house door. O'Soup is then alleged to have told the Farm Instructor not to call the Police but Keith did and the Indians got ready to fight. James Two Voices says Indian Agent McDonald then asked him to help stop the Indians doing wrong, saying "the government will reward you some day." The Indians were said to have laid a stick six paces from the house and warned the Police that they would fire if anyone stepped past it. James Two Voices says he rode between the Indians and the Police, stopping them from firing. O'Soup is then said to have had both sides go to his house to talk.[17]

The Indians were not the only people on the plains who were unhappy with what was happening to them and with the continued inaction of the government in redressing their grievances. In addition to the Indian tribes, the major groups in the area were French half-breeds, English half-breeds and European settlers, each with its own axe to grind. The Indians had been dependent on the buffalo which had been largely exterminated and their traditional way of life had come to an abrupt end for this reason at the same time. The transition from nomadic hunters to self-sufficient farmers was plagued by a shortage of agricultural implements, the inferior quality of the wagons and implements that were supplied, poor quality cattle, and inexperienced (and, in some cases, dishonest) Indian Agents and Farm Instructors. Despite these drawbacks, many of the Indian leaders

26

recognized that the treaties were the only thing that would protect their cultural identity in the long term. They had an interest in improving the conditions of the treaties, not in rebelling against them.

Many of the French half-breeds or Métis had come from Red River in order to maintain their traditional way of life which centred around the buffalo hunt. The disappearance of the buffalo destroyed their livelihood. Even the ownership of the land on which they had settled was in jeopardy, just as it had been fifteen years previously in Red River. A number of the Métis became involved in carrying freight for the Hudson's Bay Company and new settlers, but the advent of the Canadian Pacific Railway and steamboats on the rivers reduced opportunities in these endeavours. They petitioned the government endlessly for help in resolving their problems but no help had been forthcoming. As they now saw it, their only hope lay in finding a leader who would look after their interests as Louis Riel had done in Fort Garry.

While not tied to the traditions of the buffalo hunt, the so-called English half-breeds and European settlers shared many of the same problems as the Métis. The term English half-breed is somewhat inaccurate since the majority appear to have had Scottish blood and no true Scot enjoys being referred to as English. This group was concerned with short term assistance to overcome famine and crop failure as well as representation in a constituent assembly. Many white settlers were also disappointed and suffered financial losses when the decision was made to build the Canadian Pacific Railway in the south rather than through Prince Albert and Edmonton. Contractors, who hoped for lucrative contracts, land speculators who hoped to make quick fortunes, and farmers who thought they would have a rail line to take their crops to market were all disappointed.

Prince Albert was a focal point for political activists and the populace was split into factions, usually on political grounds. The residents were prepared to actively protest anything with which they disagreed and when there was a dispute

27

over the proposed site for a telegraph station, an extra contingent of Mounted Police was sent there to maintain order. There was concern that the policemen were being co-opted and Sir John A. Macdonald advised Lieutenant Governor Dewdney that "all the policemen at Prince Albert have been or are to be changed and a new set placed there. Such changes should be frequent so as to prevent too close an alliance between the policemen and the rowdy element."[18]

The focal point for white protest was the Settlers' Union and two white men, William Henry Jackson and Thomas Scott, who took an active part in protest meetings and were considered spokesmen for the white settlers and English half-breeds. These white residents had also been actively agitating for change and Louis Riel is said to have been brought to Saskatchewan with money subscribed by the white settlers of Prince Albert.[19] Many of the whites involved in the return of Riel appear to have been speculators of one kind or another who hoped the half-breed farmers would be issued scrip which had been so profitable to those who bought it up at Red River in the 1870's.

The changes on the plains were reflected in two related but different initiatives - first, the vain search by the Métis for a solution to the problem of their disappearing lifestyle and second, the effort by aboriginal leaders to find a way to alleviate hunger and negotiate other improvements in the treaties. While many of their problems were shared, their eventual approaches to solving them were quite different. The Métis on the South Branch, in the settlements of Batoche and St. Laurent, recalled the success of their insurrection at Red River in 1870 and hoped, somehow, to emulate this. Because of their shared concerns, the English and French half-breeds held a general assembly, with representation from both groups, on March 6, 1884 at the Lindsay School House. Because not all of those present were fully conversant with the Manitoba Act on which they were basing their petition, it was suggested that they seek help from the person most familiar with the subject - Louis Riel. A resolution was passed to send a delegation "to said Louis

28

Riel, and have his assistance to bring all the matters referred to in the above resolution in a proper shape and form before the Government of Canada, so that our just demands be granted."[20] Gabriel Dumont and James Isbister were chosen as delegates and were joined for the trip by Dumont's brother-in-law, Moise Ouellette and Michel Dumas. Isbister was an old Hudson's Bay Company employee. Before he would go, he wanted to get the approval of somebody he viewed as having authority so he went to see Chief Factor Lawrence Clarke, who later claimed he sent him away.[21]

At this time Big Bear, Poundmaker, and some other Indian leaders wanted to unite the tribes in an effort to bring greater pressure on the government. Early in 1884, Big Bear sent messengers to the other chiefs inviting them to a Thirst Dance and Grand Council, to be held in the summer at Poundmaker's Reserve outside Battleford. Big Bear planned to visit Piapot near Qu'Appelle following this meeting, then meet with Dewdney in Regina, and go on to Ottawa where he thought there was a man called government. The *Saskatchewan Herald* noted that Big Bear "had seen and conversed with many of the chief officers of the Department but none of them seems to be the 'the head' - there is always someone higher. To settle who this higher power is has now become the one object of his life."[22] The same newspaper later commented that "If the old growler gets down to Ontario it is to be hoped he will be kept there."[23]

There was also concern that Riel was covertly attempting to influence the Indian bands throughout the west. A report came to Calgary from the Indian Agent at the Blackfoot Reserve expressing concern about the hostile attitude shown by what were termed previously friendly Indians. The Indian Agent said the problem started with the arrival of a half-breed who was now in Crowfoot's camp. Inspector Samuel Steele sent Sergeant Frederick Dann and a constable to Gleichen, near Blackfoot Crossing, where they managed to lure the wanted man to the railway station and arrest him.[24] When the two Mounted Police officers were taking the prisoner to Calgary on the train, they removed his shackles and he managed to slip out of his handcuffs. He grabbed Dann's rifle, jumped out of the train and headed back to the Thirst Dance being held at Crowfoot's camp.

When Sergeant Dann and the constable jumped out behind the prisoner, Dann injured his knee and the constable, in his high boots, was unable to catch up with the half-breed. They continued on to Calgary and reported to Superintendent William Herchmer and Commissioner Acheson G. Irvine, both of whom were there at the time. Herchmer sent Inspector Steele to Crowfoot's camp, with Constables John Walters and John Kerr, to arrest the escaped prisoner.[25] The policemen scouted the area and after picking up John L'Hereux, the interpreter, went to the Thirst Dance camp near the Peigan Sand Hills.

Inspector Steele entered Crowfoot's lodge at dawn, leaving L'Hereux outside, and found the wanted man sitting in a circle with Crowfoot and his head men. After a confrontation with Crowfoot, Steele seized the wanted man by the collar of his shirt and dragged him out of the lodge. Walters and Kerr secured the prisoner while surrounded by hundreds of disturbed and angry Indians. Steele lectured the Indians in general, and Crowfoot in particular, on the need to obey the law and cooperate with the police. He then arranged a rail ticket to Calgary so that Crowfoot could attend the men's trial and see that it was fair. When the charge was heard by Commissioner Irvine, Steele was not called to be present or give evidence and the charge was dismissed. As suspected, the man was later found to have connections with Louis Riel.

The Indian Department had an obsession about Indians gathering in large groups. Despite the bands having been assured of freedom of movement, Indian Department officials could not stand being unable to control them. The Deputy Superintendent General of Indian Affairs, Lawrence Vankoughnet, asked Frederick White to have the Mounted Police patrol the area between Victoria Mission and Battleford and between Fort Qu'Appelle and Broadview, to prevent such gatherings. Vankoughnet noted "there is, as the spring appears and the grass grows, a strong inclination among the Indians consequent upon their confinement in one locality, to wander from reserve to reserve and this spring it is feared that attempts will be made to congregate in large numbers near Indian Head, Broadview and Battleford, and possibly in moments of excitement to seize unprotected stores." He added that there would also be "strong inclinations on the part of the Indians to kill cattle when their rations are stopped on their leaving their reserves or on their refusing to work." He asked that, if possible, strenuous and immediate efforts be taken to prevent such gatherings.[26]

Sure enough, as spring came, the movements started. As part of his ongoing effort to organize a united front, Big Bear sent messengers in April to all the bands in the area inviting them to a Thirst Dance and conference, to be held in June on the boundary between Little Pine's and Poundmaker's reserves. This would provide the tribes an opportunity to air their grievances. The bands were united in that "all were experiencing the same problems of malnutrition, inadequate farming implements and a loss of faith in the government." [27]

In May 1884, Piapot grew so concerned about the increasing number of deaths on his reserve that he decided to abandon it and find a new home for his people. He also decided to hold a Thirst Dance and invited other tribes to a ceremony on Pasqua's Reserve where they would also discuss the treaties and the government's failure to live up to them, especially the famine clause. The sight of large numbers of Indians on the move alarmed the settlers, so when Piapot's band moved toward Pasqua's Reserve, Hayter Reed requested that the Mounted Police help dissuade them. Indian Agent McDonald wanted Piapot and his band followed. He arranged with Reed that a member of Pasqua's Band would lay a complaint about Piapot's presence on their reserve, thus providing the necessary excuse to have them arrested.

31

Commissioner Irvine and a party of policemen accompanied Hayter Reed to Indian Head where they found Piapot and Long Lodge camped on the plains. When asked why he had left his reserve, Long Lodge complained that there was no fresh meat and no source of fresh water. He said that a number of his people were dead and more would die if they remained on the reserve. Piapot voiced similar concerns. Irvine warned both chiefs that the government could not allow groups of armed Indians to roam about the plains. He left them to consider his advice and returned two days later with 56 men and a 7-pounder gun under Superintendent Herchmer. This subtle move "persuaded Piapot's band to return to their reserve."[28]

The Indian Department kept pressing the Mounted Police to restrict the movement of aboriginals, using the excuse that roving bands of Indians could not be at home working the land on their reserves as part of their transition to farming. Hayter Reed wrote to Commissioner Irvine that "it is desirable that steps be taken with a view of preventing such a body of Indians roaming the country, as the same not only tends to alarm settlers but emboldens the young bucks to commit acts of depredation which they would not otherwise be guilty of and as you are well aware the policy of the government is to keep all Indians on their reserves as much as possible, more especially at this season of the year when time is so essential to putting in their crops."[29]

Lieutenant Governor Dewdney made a trip to the Battleford area to see the situation there for himself and somehow concluded that there was nothing to worry about since "Indian matters were on the whole satisfactory and instead of finding the Indians malcontent I never saw them more contented, taken as a whole." Any trouble he did detect he attributed to the unsettling influence of Big Bear, noting that "the new arrivals from the south last Fall, distributed as they were among all the bands in the north kept up a constant agitation among the Indians during the winter, and runners were dispatched from one part of the Territories to the other with the object of bringing about large gatherings and making demands on us which they knew they could not get while scattered on their several reserves."[30] Dewdney had now become acutely aware that the deliberate policy of starving the Indians into submission was not only failing to bring them into line but appeared to be strengthening their determination to act together. At the same time, there was concern that overtures to Crowfoot, made by Little Pine, might reduce the long-standing enmity between the Cree and the Blackfoot, creating an even stronger alliance.

When Big Bear arrived in the Battleford area prior to the Thirst Dance, he met with Lieutenant Governor Dewdney and elected to take a reserve near his friend Poundmaker outside Battleford. Both Dewdney and Indian Agent Rae agreed with this move. Rae said, "My own idea is that Big Bear might just as well be allowed to settle near Poundmaker . . . I feel sure that if proper power is placed in my hands and supplies given me so that I can deal more liberally with these bands, there will be no more trouble, but I do not think that Big Bear or any others are going to submit to be starved out, and there is no doubt that these men are particularly hard up." Rae, who on this occasion was more perceptive than usual, concluded "if on the other hand, the Department are bound to stick to their present orders, then preparations should be made to fight them as it will sooner or later come to this if more liberal treatment is not given."[31]

As soon as the proposal for Big Bear to have a reserve near Poundmaker's reached Ottawa, it was vetoed by Vankoughnet. Big Bear admitted to Dewdney that he had invited all the Indians to meet him and wanted them to ask for a large reserve, but he failed to get them to agree and they were all pulling different ways. He said he had no bad intentions in calling the meeting. Some of the bands said bad talk had come to them from Battle River but they did not listen to it and would not allow anything wrong to take place.[32] With the increase in tension the *Edmonton Bulletin* suggested that ". . . all that is required is the occasion and a leader to land the North-West in the middle of a first-class Indian war."[33]

A Trying Time

The North-West Mounted Police continued to be concerned about the probability of trouble if no conciliatory steps were taken. In late June, Superintendent Crozier reported that "Just at present the Indians seem quiet though there is among them a great deal of discontent, and my opinion is, that in their present temper, an attempt to arrest one of them, or perform any duty not agreeable to them would lead to trouble again, for they seem to have made up their minds to resist any interference with them, even to the length of going to war."[34] The interference and the trouble were not far off.

- 4 -
The Craig Incident

In June 1884, more than 2,000 Indians assembled at the Lucky Man and Little Pine Reserves for the Thirst Dance sponsored by Big Bear. While assembled there, a number of the Indians under Big Bear and Poundmaker went into Battleford to perform a Hunger Dance. They did this occasionally since the local merchants and townspeople enjoyed the performances and rewarded the dancers by donating food supplies. Inspector Antrobus rode up on his horse during the dance to watch. Big Bear's sons, Imasees and Okemow Peeaysis ran up to him and suddenly opened umbrellas.[1] The movement caused Antrobus' horse to shy and his white helmet fell off and rolled away, amusing the crowd and annoying the Inspector.

In an attempt to prevent the Thirst Dance, Indian Agent Rae and Inspector Antrobus went to the camp to order the visiting Indians to return to their reserves. A confrontation took place between Rae, Antrobus and Big Bear which ended with Rae fining the Indians six days rations for leaving their reserve without permission. In a move which could be considered anything from unwise to downright stupid, Antrobus threatened to arrest all the assembled Indians if they did not immediately go home. While Antrobus probably acted out of irritation, he should have realized that it was unwise to make a threat he could not carry out. Probably more amused than intimidated, the Indians simply ignored his order so Rae and Antrobus returned to Battleford. The Indians had now successfully defied the Mounted Police.

Concerned about the activity at the Thirst Dance camp, Superintendent Crozier at Battleford sent a small Mounted Police detachment under Corporal Ralph Sleigh to maintain surveillance on the proceedings.[2] The Indian Agent, John Rae accompanied the policemen in a rare appearance in the same location as Indians. He once again ordered Big Bear and all the visiting Indians to return to their home reserves. When the Indians again ignored him, he retreated to Battleford after

35

spitefully ordering that rations be cut off, hoping to starve out the visitors. Big Bear and the other visitors stayed where they were and built two weirs across the river to catch fish for food. The police detachment tactfully withdrew a short distance but maintained their surveillance.

On June 18, two members of Big Bear's band "The Clothing" and "The-Man-Who-Speaks-Our-Language" (Kahweechatwaymat), sons of Lucky Man, went to see John Craig, the Farm Instructor, to obtain food. They had been receiving rations because they were ill but Craig, who spoke little if any Cree, decided that The-Man-Who-Speaks-Our-Language no longer qualified and would not issue rations to him. This decision led to a shoving match which ended when The-Man-Who-Speaks-Our-Language seized an axe handle and stuck Craig on the hand, arm and shoulder.

Although Father Louis Cochin, who was in the camp, reported that Craig's elbow was stained with blood, Robert Jefferson, the Farm Instructor on Poundmaker's Reserve was of the opinion that "Craig's arm was not injured but his feelings were, so he took his case to the police."[3] Craig complained to Corporal Sleigh that "the insult called for immediate arrest." Craig and Sleigh then went to the Indian camp where the Thirst Dance had started but, faced with hundreds of Indians involved in the ceremony, Sleigh sought the assistance of the chiefs. Neither Big Bear nor Little Pine, knowing how touchy the situation was, would aid in an arrest while the Thirst Dance was in progress, so Sleigh went to Superintendent Crozier in Battleford to report what had occurred, telling him he "considered it better not to attempt the arrest with the small number of men he had."[4]

Superintendent Crozier left Battleford for the Thirst Dance site at Little Pine's Reserve on the morning of June 18 accompanied by Inspector Antrobus, Surgeon Robert Miller, Sergeant Frederick Bagley and twenty-five men. The Indian Agent John Rae, his courage renewed, accompanied the force. Wisely leaving the

Superintendent Lief N.F. Crozier

PAM N-12374

main force at some distance from the Indian camp, Crozier went forward with Rae and two men in an attempt to identify and apprehend the accused. The Indians told him he would not be able to make an arrest without trouble. The two men involved in the altercation with Craig had joined the other young men in the Thirst Dance. Because he had struck back at the highly despised Farm Instructor, The-Man-Who-Speaks-Our-Language was enjoying enormous prestige among the excited dancers. He made it clear he was unwilling to surrender to the Mounted Police and he had the support of many of the young men present.

There are differing reports on the conduct of the search for The-Man-Who-Speaks-Our-Language who, being heavily painted for the Thirst Dance, could not be readily recognized. John Turner records that ". . . the little party pushed through to the circle of dancers who showed no concern at the intrusion,"[5] while Stone child and Waiter believe that the interruption was an insult to the sacred ceremony that was in progress.[6] Superintendent Crozier asked Corporal Sleigh to try to identify the wanted man but he was unable to do so. Croziers did not take Craig into the medicine lodge since he "knew the Indians would be greatly incensed against him."[7] When the police withdrew they were greeted with jeers by a large number of Indians who then followed them as they went to see the chiefs.

Superintendent Crozier sought the cooperation of Big Bear and Poundmaker, both of whom reiterated that it was not their responsibility to make arrests and advised Crozier that it would not be wise to attempt it at this time. Father Cochin also spoke to the chiefs but said they "had not listened to anything."[8] In an attempt to cooperate as much as they reasonably could, the chiefs undertook to assist in the matter when the Thirst Dance was finished. Big Bear promised to bring the whole camp to the old agency house on Poundmaker's Reserve. Crozier, while not pleased with this option, saw no reasonable alternative since he was badly outnumbered. He later reported that the Chiefs, including Big Bear, were doing or seemed to be doing everything they could to have the man surrender quietly, although they kept insisting that they did not consider their influence was sufficient to induce the young warriors to agree to this course and if any attempt was made to arrest the suspect forcibly they felt certain bloodshed would follow.[9]

After his discussion with the chiefs, Superintendent Crozier sent to Battleford for additional reinforcements "as the Indians were in a bad temper, very numerous, and were displaying, so the interpreter said, a signal that they were at war." He then moved his men back to the agency buildings on the Poundmaker Reserve and ordered all government supplies and cattle on the Little Pine and Lucky Man Reserves to be transferred there. The Mounted Police took four ox teams, with both Craig and Robert Jefferson pressed into service as drivers and started to make the move along a trail which ran straight through the Thirst Dance Camp. They made a detour around the medicine lodge site in an attempt to avoid a confrontation but were met by more than 200 Indians who made a mock attack and surrounded the policemen shouting and firing their rifles. Crozier reported "they did not fire at us, at least their bullets went into the air and over our heads."[10] While fording Cut Knife Creek, the four wagons were mired and had to be unloaded, extricated from the creek, then reloaded, with all the work being done in a highly charged atmosphere.

When the party arrived at the old agency house on Poundmaker's Reserve about 11:00 p.m., the men were immediately put to work building bastions at each end of the house and generally strengthening the defences. Inside the building, loopholes were cut in the walls which were strengthened by piling sacks of flour and bacon against them and some rifle pits were dug outside the building. On June 19, an additional 60 policemen under Sergeant Major Michael Kirk arrived from Battleford about 4:00 p.m. and immediately joined in the work on the defences.[11] The situation was so tense that "a large number of alarmed farmers and settlers flocked into Battleford for protection."[12]

39

A Trying Time

On June 20, the whole Indian camp arrived as promised but stopped on top of a hill about a quarter of a mile from the fortified buildings. The Indians, about half mounted and half on foot, had stripped down to breechclouts and their women were heading for the bush, an ominous sign. Superintendent Crozier deployed ten of his men in the newly built bastions and formed the remainder into two groups, one mounted and one on foot. Accompanied by his interpreter, Louis Laronde, and Craig, Crozier then moved forward to talk to the Indians. He had previously refrained from taking Craig to parley in order not to unduly annoy the Indians. Now, as the police advanced, the Indians became highly excited and threatening. Speaking to the chiefs, Crozier demanded that The Clothing and The-Man-Who-Speaks-Our-Language be turned over to the police but the chiefs cautioned that the young men were in a highly excited state and would not listen to them.

Superintendent Crozier had his dismounted men under Inspector Antrobus line up close to the Indians. The mounted men were directly behind the men on foot. Craig could not see The-Man-Who-Speaks-Our-Language who was hidden in the crowd. Crozier shouted, "Bring us the prisoner or I shall arrest you all if we have to fight for it." Fortunately, no one called his bluff and Lucky Man brought The-Man-Who-Speaks-Our-Language forward. When Crozier went to arrest him, the accused man stepped aside and said "Don't touch me," to which Crozier responded, "I shall not touch you if you come with me."[13] Crozier then managed to seize the prisoner, assisted by Constable Warren Kerr who grabbed him by his long braids.[14] The prisoner's arms were seized by Constable John Guthrie and the Interpreter, Louis Laronde, and he was rushed into the Mounted Police ranks. [15]

When the policemen had the prisoner surrounded, Inspector Antrobus ordered the dismounted men to form fours and they started back toward the fortified buildings, with highly irate Indians milling all around them. One constable recalled seeing Poundmaker running along beside the police, wielding his pummakin, a large club with three knife blades embedded in it. The constable realized ". . . he meant

40

business. I thought this is where it starts."[16] When Poundmaker threatened Antrobus, with whom he had previously quarreled, he was immediately covered by Winchesters, including that of Constable Frederick Prior who "stuck his carbine in the chief's face and he lowered his three-bladed club."[17]

The police party was all mixed up with the Indians as they struggled back toward the agent's house, backing up most of the way with their rifles leveled and occasionally prodding their prisoner. Constable William McQuarrie related that one Indian "put his heels to his pony and made the pony run, then he reached over and hit me a nice crack in the face with his whip."[18] The highly agitated mob managed to separate one of the policemen from his comrades and quickly took his tunic, Winchester and pistol. The Indians also overpowered the interpreter, Louis Laronde, and held him for a time until William McKay of the Hudson's Bay Company interceded and had him freed. Robert Jefferson recalled, "It would be impossible to describe the excitement that prevailed during all this time - it was not more than half an hour from start to finish, but it seemed ages - the tension; the shouts of incitement of the young bloods to finish us off without delay; the cautioning of older heads, to let the white men begin the fight - the racing to-and-fro - and the piercing war whoops - all combined to make an indelible impression on the memory. Events were on a hair trigger for a while - yet nothing happened."[19]

The small force retreated to the makeshift fort at Jefferson's house where they were completely surrounded by angry Indians. William McKay suggested to Crozier that they distribute some of the flour and bacon which lined the walls of their improvised fort. The appearance of the food changed the mood of the hungry crowd and defused the tense situation. The second wanted man, The Clothing, was arrested without any difficulty when he came to take some of the rations. McKay recovered the Winchester from Poundmaker, Laronde returned safely and one of Big Bear's sons, Twin Wolverine, later came to Battleford and turned in the revolver commandeered in the scuffle.

41

Superintendent Crozier returned to Battleford with the prisoners. He left a small detachment of nine men, under Sergeant Frederick Bagley to keep an eye on things on the reserves.[20] This detachment stayed at Cut Knife Hill until Big Bear left for Fort Pitt in September.

With the situation still very tense, Crozier sent a message to Irvine informing him that he had ". . . taken prisoners by force from Poundmaker's Camp. Tried for three days to take them gently but could not."[21] Crozier conducted a preliminary examination then adjourned the case to provide time for the accused to call witnesses. When the case came up again, he ordered The Clothing released and The-Man-Who-Speaks-Our-Language held over for the District Court. He noted that from the evidence he believed Craig was also at fault but cautioned that individuals should not take the law into their own hands and must not resist the authority of the Police. Unfortunately, Craig was not charged, since this would have demonstrated fairness and impartiality. The-Man-Who-Speaks-Our-Language entered a guilty plea and received a one week sentence. On his release he joined Big Bear's band at Fort Pitt and was involved in the Frog Lake Massacre. His final contact with the Police came less than a year later when he was mortally wounded at the Battle of Frenchman Butte.

In his report on this incident, Crozier said he was confident about the immediate outcome of any trouble since he had his supplies and ammunition well protected, but he was anxious to avoid a collision since the first shot "would be the excuse for an Indian outbreak with all its attendant horrors."[22] He was also concerned that the Indians in camp who were well disposed toward the Mounted Police would join their people against the whites once firing commenced and the problem would spread. He ended his report with an ominous warning: "Everything is now seemingly quiet, the Indians are peaceably disposed, but I have not confidence in their remaining so, when we have again to execute upon them some process of law, unless the policy of the Indian Department toward them is in some

42

measure amended."[23] In a report a short time later, Crozier observed that "what took place the other day with the Indians at Poundmaker's should I think serve as a warning as to how they may act in the future for I unhesitatingly state that never since the occupation of the country by the Police was there anything like such a determination shown by any Indians anywhere in the Territories as there was by these to resist the authority of the government and we should congratulate ourselves that the affair terminated as it did."[24] The Mounted Police could certainly see the need for a change in policy if disaster was to be averted. Unfortunately those in Ottawa did not appear to have the same clarity of vision.

This was the end of an incident which could easily have been avoided if Craig just used a little common sense. Had either the Indians or Mounted Police reacted to the others' provocation, the situation could easily have become a tragedy. It was significant since it showed that relations between the Indians and the Mounted Police were becoming increasingly strained. Fortunately, Big Bear, Poundmaker and the other chiefs did not seem to be interested in becoming involved in a war at this time, but only wished to influence the government to improve conditions. They somehow managed to exercise control over the younger men, although their ability to restrain them was being rapidly eroded. One of the constables involved remarked that "If there was a cool officer and a brave man it was Superintendent Crozier that day."[25]

In an assessment made at the time of the incident, Superintendent Crozier informed Commissioner Irvine that the Indians were undoubtedly sympathetic to the Métis, who were constantly advising them and creating discontent in the process. He believed it would not be difficult to incite the Indians to resist the authority of the government and recommended that the Mounted Police be increased to at least one thousand men in order to prevent serious trouble. If this was not done, he was "strongly of the opinion that we shall have the Manitoba difficulties of 1870 re-enacted with the addition of the Indian population as allies to the halfbreeds."[26]

A list of the members of the North-West Mounted Police present at the Craig Incident can be found at Appendix "A."

- 5 -
Riel Returns

The delegation of Gabriel Dumont and James Isbister, sent to the United States by the local people around Batoche to see Louis Riel, reached St. Pierre Mission in Montana on June 4 and persuaded Riel to come back to Canada with them. On the day following his arrival on the South Branch, the whole of the Métis community came to the Church of St. Anthony de Padua, where Riel urged them to be patient and make use of any constituent means available to them. He strongly suggested they continue to submit petitions. The North-West Mounted Police kept a close watch on events on the South Branch and Superintendent Crozier reported Louis Riel's arrival with his family at Duck Lake, ". . . brought in by the half breeds. They brought him in, it is said, as their leader agitating their rights."[1] Crozier informed Commissioner Irvine ". . . I have already reported that I believe the Indians sympathize with the halfbreeds, nor could anything else be expected, being close blood relations and speaking the same language."[2]

Reports were passed on to Ottawa and Sir John A. Macdonald recognized there was a problem and offered the opinion that there were "certain uneasy elements" in the west - "The Farmer's Union Agitators, the French Halfbreeds, advised by Riel and the Indian element headed by such loafers as Big Bear, Piapot etc. The last, the Indian element is not to be dreaded unless there is a white or halfbreed rising. If this should ever happen, the Indians would be apt to join any insurgent body. . . ."[3] The *Saskatchewan Herald* noted "that Riel came in on the invitation of his friends to be their leader is freely admitted, but no other declaration has lately been made as to just what they want. It is a suspicious circumstance, however, that immediately following his arrival in the country threats of armed rebellion should be indulged in, and that stories of the cooperation of the Indians should be put into circulation, as they are now."[4]

45

Louis Riel   PAM N-5737

Riel Returns

Sir John A. Macdonald attributed much of the trouble to land speculators. He told the Governor General, Lord Lansdowne, that "The land sharks that abound in the N.W. urge on the half breeds to demand, in addition, scrip to the same amount as granted to them in Manitoba. The scrip is sold for a song to the sharks and spent in whiskey, and this we desire above all things to avoid."[5]

Since the government was encouraging settlers to come to the west, they were not anxious to have reports circulating about Indian unrest and they denied there was any starvation or other problems. When Assistant Indian Commissioner, Hayter Reed, downplayed the situation in an interview, Indian Agent John Rae was apparently incensed by what he read in the press. He wrote to Dewdney saying, "I see from the papers that Mr. Reed seems to laugh at any idea of danger here and says he has been in the same position many times. This is perfect nonsense. I have been dealing with Indians for the past 14 years and never saw the Indians mean business before. The thing has to be looked at seriously and precautions taken ere it is too late."[6]

By midsummer, while politicians and officials in Ottawa continued to disregard signs of trouble, the local concern about Riel's activities grew much stronger. The *Saskatchewan Herald* stated that Riel had "shown his hand at Prince Albert and has already gone as far as he ought to be allowed to go." The editor suggested that rather than "sending a deputation to a far country to bring in an alien demagogue to set class against class and to mar the harmony between the races . . ." the Métis should have sent a representative to make their case in Ottawa. He expressed the hope that those "who sent for Riel will see what a grievous mistake they made and bid him return to his congenial elements in Montana, leaving them to put their trust in constitutional means to secure the redress of wrongs, if any, that they suffer from."[7] Given the government's failure to respond to repeated petitions this solemn sounding advice was taken as nothing more than rhetoric.

Following the Thirst Dance on Poundmaker's Reserve, Big Bear and Lucky Man met with seven chiefs and fourteen head men from the Duck Lake area to discuss a wide range of issues. At this meeting, Big Bear attempted to gain the chiefs' support for a united front in dealing with the Indian Department in order to bring pressure on the government and induce them to give in to Indian demands. The chiefs aired a number of grievances, including complaints about the Indian Agents and other officials. Sergeant William Brooks, who was keeping a watchful eye on events at Duck Lake, sent Superintendent Crozier a telegram on August 8 to report that Big Bear was still in Council with the other chiefs while Louis Riel held private meetings with a number of leading half-breeds.[8] Brooks also reported that Riel was at Batoche's house and held meetings with people as they came from church. Some of the people in Prince Albert who signed the petition for Louis Riel to return, told Brooks they did so thinking "it would draw the attention of the government to the place."[9]

The Sub-Indian Agent, John Ansdell Macrae, invited the chiefs to move the Council from Beardy's Reserve to Fort Carlton where he promised to provide them with rations. His reported purpose was to "bring the Council to Carlton, where the malign influences that were said to be at work would have a lesser chance of manifestation."[10] It also made it much easier to keep the chiefs under surveillance and know what was discussed. At the conclusion of the Duck Lake Council, the chiefs issued a statement expressing pleasure that their young men had not succumbed to violence despite the pressures to do so caused by the government's failure to keep its promises. They warned they would only wait until the following summer to have the promises met or they would take matters into their own hands. Hayter Reed pointed out to Dewdney that unless the government was able to prevent it, there would be another Council of chiefs the next year "where some course of action antagonistic to the government is to be decided upon."[11] It is interesting that the Indian Department was concentrating on means of preventing

48

the bands gathering rather than dealing with the reasons they wanted to gather together.

Sergeant Brooks stationed Constable Joseph MacDermot at the South Branch to keep an eye on events.[12] While he considered him "a good man," he noted that "he is pretty well known as a policeman."[13] This is not surprising since it would be rather difficult for an Irishman in a scarlet tunic to remain *incognito* for long at Duck Lake or Batoche. MacDermot reported that at the end of the Duck Lake Council at Fort Carlton, two Indian chiefs, John Smith and James Smith of Prince Albert and Carrot River, met before going to see Louis Riel at Riel's invitation. They were not pleased with the *status quo* and said "Our grievances are not redressed. We will die fighting but will first try every possible way to open the eyes of the government as to the real state of affairs."[14]

When they met Louis Riel, the chiefs told him they no longer had "any faith in the government or its promises, and, now realized that we must have our grievances redressed or on the other hand, turn and face starvation and die - a robbed people but still human beings." Riel told the chiefs, "My friends, be careful, be patient, and with the help of God you will have your grievances redressed."[15] In August, Big Bear went to Prince Albert to meet Louis Riel. A newspaper report from Battleford said that Big Bear had been there on the way back "from his visit to the imported saviour of the country at Duck Lake. The old man does not seem to have been favourably impressed with the prospects held out to him."[16]

Lieutenant Governor Dewdney and officials of the Indian Department appear to have been less concerned about Louis Riel and the Métis than they were about the possibility that the Cree diplomatic initiative would work. If the initiative came about, the Department's policy of keeping the bands under control by separating and dividing them would be in disarray. Dewdney's response was to look for a way to replace uncooperative chiefs, arrest the leaders of the movement to unite the tribes and restrict the movements of Indians off their reservations. Faced with what appeared to be increasing aboriginal solidarity, Dewdney gave up his policy of trying to starve the Indians into submission. He got the Prime Minister's agreement to increase the strength of the Mounted Police and to introduce a rule that would prevent any Indian from being on a reserve other than his own without permission. Commissioner Irvine pointed out that a restriction of movement, such as the pass system, would be a breach of trust with the Indians since, during treaty negotiations, they were promised "they would be at liberty to travel about for legitimate hunting and trading purposes."[17]

Poundmaker, previously considered to be cooperative, now joined Big Bear on the government's list of troublemakers. Hayter Reed reported that Poundmaker "has become one of the worst, if not the worst, moving spirit in the country." He suggested to Dewdney that a pretext be found to arrest him and instructed Indian Agent Rae "to watch him carefully and endeavour to get some hold upon him whereby he can be made a prisoner and taken to Regina for I fear Rouleau is inclined too much to leniency where none should be shown . . ."[18] Poundmaker was warned that if he was uncooperative he would be deposed.

The ability of the bands to arrange large gatherings, such as that assembled for the Thirst Dance, alarmed government officials and they sought measures to prevent it happening again. Reed advised Dewdney that they "must endeavour to prevent large bodies of Indians coming together where they might be tempted to commit some cruel act - if they should come together we should be prepared to handle them with such a force of Police as would cause them to give in without an effort." He noted that "one thing should certainly be done and it is that the Mounted Police be debarred from rationing our Indians as Rae complains to me that many of his worst characters are refused by him only to go to the barracks to receive a belly full."[19] Superintendent Crozier pressed for a change in the policy of starving Indians into submission and warned that "Considering all that is at stake, it is poor, yes, false economy to cut down the expenditure so closely in connection with the feeding of the Indians that it would seem as if there was a wish to see upon how little a man can work and exist. . . . My firm conviction is if some such policy as I have outlined is not carried out, then there is only one other and that is to fight them."[20]

.   In the summer of 1884, Sergeant Brooks reported to Superintendent Crozier that on the South Branch there was very little talk of Riel. He said that he had "heard very few who are in any way well to do speak favourably of him. There is no doubt but what all the breeds swear by him and whatever he says is law with them. As near as I can learn he is advising them all very strongly to remain peaceable." [21] In September the Métis from the settlements around Batoche, along with some half-breeds and whites from Prince Albert, met at St. Laurent. A number of whites, including Jackson, Scott and Isbister were there. Sergeant Keenan reported that Louis Riel told him "the government through Bishop Grandin had offered him a seat in the Council or in the Dominion Senate."[22] A few weeks later he reported to Superintendent Crozier that "the crops here are almost a total failure and everything indicates that the Halfbreeds are going to be in very strained conditions before the end of the coming winter, which of course will make them more discontented and will probably drive them to an outbreak, and I believe that trouble is almost certain before the winter ends unless the government extends some aid to the Halfbreeds during the coming winter."[23]

Ottawa was being advised of the growing tension but chose to ignore the warnings. Roderick Macleod noted that "Irvine knew what was happening in his jurisdiction but he reported his belief that rebellion was imminent in 1884 with exactly the same emphasis that he used in reporting the amount of hay the force had in stock. The result was that no one paid much attention to anything he said."[24] There have probably been few developing insurrections where the authorities have been kept as well informed of what was going on. The North-West Mounted Police were operating in a surveillance and intelligence mode, the Indian Department was providing reports and assessments and the Hudson's Bay Company provided reports through its own channels. A lack of information was not a contributing factor in the period leading up to the rebellion. The failure to act effectively on the available information was the critical error.

Ottawa's response to the escalating tension was to increase the strength of the North-West Mounted Police in the area. The signs of trouble were sufficiently clear that Commissioner Irvine added an Inspector and 20 men to the Prince Albert detachment in August. Two months later he took 49 men to Fort Carlton and opened a detachment under Superintendent Sévère Gagnon in buildings rented from the Hudson's Bay Company which had moved most of its operation to Prince Albert.[25] When Inspector Joseph Howe appeared with so many men it "created considerable uneasiness amongst the people, the more so as some person circulated the report that their objective here was the arrest of Riel and his principal followers. The Halfbreeds were greatly excited and asserted that any attempt to take Riel would be resisted by armed force."[26]

Big Bear and Lucky Man arrived at Fort Pitt with their followers on October 1 and Inspector Dickens reported that he thought "that as long as they have enough to eat they will not give any serious trouble."[27] He confirmed his opinion that "unless the rations are stopped I do not anticipate trouble," but added that "should the Sub-Indian Agent receive orders to discontinue the issuing of rations the Indians might and would probably try to help themselves from the store in which case there might be a collision between them and ourselves."[28] Given this warning, the Indian Department promptly cut the rations. Shortly after the arrival of Big Bear's band Inspector Dickens checked the number and type of weapons they carried and found that about fifteen had Winchester rifles, but were short of ammunition, while another twenty had smoothbore muskets.[29]

Big Bear Trading At Fort Pitt   NAC C-014154

In October 1884, when Big Bear's and Little Poplar's bands were at Fort Pitt for treaty payments, they confronted Indian Agent Thomas Quinn and Farm Instructor John Delaney in an ominous preview of what was to come. Little Poplar told Quinn, "I have heard of you! I heard of you away over on the other side of the Missouri River. I started to come this way and the further I came the more I heard. You're the man the government sent up here to say No! to everything the Indians asked you."[30] Little Poplar asked Delaney, "Why doesn't the Big Chief Woman send agents who can do something? It is men like you that cause trouble between the Indians and the police like they had at Poundmaker's last summer!"[31] Little Poplar asked three times that an ox be killed to provide beef and three times Quinn said no. Little Poplar told the Indians, "Let him keep his peecoonta money!" and with yells of defiance the whole band swept out of the house, across the square and up the hill, firing their guns in the air as they went.[32]

That afternoon the Indians danced a war dance and Big Bear made a speech critical of both the government and the Hudson's Bay Company, then went up to Inspector Dickens, held out his hand and said, "You are a man whom Manitou made to be a chief. We like you: Your heart is good. As for that man" - he pointed at Quinn - "his heart is made of stone! He may go back to Frog Lake." Miserable Man told Quinn, "When I am hungry this winter and ask for food, if you don't give it to me I will kill you."[33] To keep the peace, the Hudson's Bay Company slaughtered a steer.

When Lawrence Vankoughnet made a quick trip through the west, he told Big Bear to choose the location for his reserve by November 1884 or the provision of rations to the band would be stopped. After his return to Ottawa, Vankoughnet cut the budget, fired a number of Indian Department employees and reduced rations. He also further curtailed the limited discretionary powers of officials in the west and retained more control in his own office. Big Bear ignored Vankoughnet's deadline for selecting a reserve and was still at Fort Pitt in November, so the Indian Department cut off rations to his band.

In December 1884, Superintendent Gagnon reported that "the halfbreeds are pressing Riel to settle amongst them, and have given him, as a token of their gratitude for services rendered, a house well-furnished, and will further on 2nd January next present him with a purse." He noted that this tended to contradict rumours that some people lacked confidence in Riel because he appeared to be hot headed and was not in agreement with their priests.[34] There was still a great deal of support available to Riel. Gagnon related that when he sent some of his men from Fort Carlton to the South Branch to have some horses shod, the South Saskatchewan River was still full of floating ice and the men and horses could not cross. Somehow a report circulated on the other side of the river that the policemen were coming to arrest Riel, who was at the crossing, and "within an hour over one hundred men had collected to protect him."[35]

Everything had been deceptively quiet on the surface through the autumn months. The Métis and Settlers' Union sent a final petition to Ottawa on December 16, 1884. They asked Hudson's Bay Company Chief Factor Lawrence Clarke to plead their case. The only reaction by the government was to announce a committee to investigate their claims and the only action proposed was the enumeration of Métis on the South Branch.

1885 came in with everything remaining quiet on reserves across the west and at the Métis settlements on the South Branch. In January, Superintendent Gagnon at Fort Carlton reported "that nothing of importance had occurred in that district. They had, after New Years, a social meeting at which they presented their chief, Riel, with $60.00 as a token of their goodwill. The meeting was very orderly and loyal and no allusion was made to the actual troubles."[36] Gagnon also reported "that invitations to a large gathering in the Spring at Duck Lake were being circulated amongst the Indians and he was informed that an effort would be made to get the Qu'Appelle Valley Indians to attend."[37] Inspector Dickens at Fort Pitt reported ". . . all quiet. Big Bear's band has been freighting to Edmonton, drawing logs and cutting wood."[38] The Lieutenant Governor, reflecting the apparent quiet in the area, reported to Sir John A. Macdonald that he did not "anticipate much trouble unless through the Halfbreeds and if any of the Indians come out their leaders must be arrested." [39]

In January 1885, when some leading citizens asked Louis Riel to explain the Métis claims, a meeting was held at Truscott's Hall in Prince Albert chaired by Andrew Spence. Sergeant Alfred Stewart attended with four men. Riel spoke for two hours and was applauded but, as the applause died down, R.J. Deacon, an Englishman who had been in Winnipeg in 1870, jumped on a chair, pointed at Louis Riel and shouted "Look at him, there is blood on his hands." This was a reference to the murder of Thomas Scott at Fort Garry. The previously orderly meeting instantly became an uproar. Stewart knocked Deacon onto his back and while the Mounted Police prevented the audience from following, Riel and his followers scuttled out the back door and quickly left town.[40]

Louis Riel was apparently having financial difficulties at this time and needed food for his family. Inspector Howe reported that David Macdowall, Representative on the North-West Council for the District of Lorne, and Father Alexis André met with Riel to hear a proposal he wished placed before the government. "He first stated that he was poor and he did not know what would become of him, was afraid he would starve and starvation made men desperate, that he had great power over the Halfbreeds, and that he could influence them politically or otherwise as he saw fit." Riel said he would go back to Montana but he lacked the means and if the government gave him assistance and something to settle on his family, he would leave for Montana and stay there. He was also prepared to give up all connection with the Métis and would guarantee they would drop all claims against the government. (Macdowall was reported as thinking that $5,000 would suffice).[41] The Prime Minister, Sir John A. Macdonald, informed Lieutenant Governor Dewdney that the government had no money to give Riel and it would require a Parliamentary vote. He asked "How would it look to be obliged to confess we could not govern the country and were obliged to bribe a man to go away?"[42] In retrospect, the Parliamentary vote would have been the easiest course to follow.

Superintendent Gagnon reported that Louis Riel was receiving financial assistance from the Roman Catholic Mission at St. Laurent.[43] In February, a public meeting was held at the South Branch where it was announced that the government refused to recognize Riel as a British subject and there were rumours that he was soon going to leave the country.[44] A subsequent meeting was held on February 24 with the object of begging Riel to remain in Canada. Gagnon reported that it was evident from the meeting that Riel would now stay.[45] In the meantime, nothing had been heard from Ottawa about the Métis petitions and Father André wired Lieutenant Governor Dewdney that "Riel and his friends have been anxiously waiting for an answer to the request made by them to the government through Captain McDowall [sic] and myself."[46]

At Fort Garry in 1869-70, Louis Riel had the support of the Roman Catholic Church but in 1885 this support, which was initially there, quickly disappeared due to Riel's extreme views. When Riel broke with the Church, he alienated some of the Métis and disturbed others who, nevertheless, continued to follow him. In Fort Garry the Métis were a potent military force, but in the North-West Rebellion they had absolutely no chance of ultimate victory. Father André pressed the government to resolve the situation and Edgar Dewdney advised Sir John A. Macdonald "that the anxiety shown by Pere André for an understanding with Riel is that the Bishops and Priests feel that the Halfbreeds in St. Laurent Settlement have lost confidence in their priests."[47]

Sir John A. Macdonald and Edgar Dewdney considered arresting those regarded as trouble makers as a preemptive measure. They agreed "that such arrests should be made with great care that there is sufficient police force to enforce the arrest" and that such arrests would be made " . . . in clear cases where the incitement is to cause a sort of insurrection." Sir John A. Macdonald offered to communicate Dewdney's views "as to the expediency of long terms of punishment at certain seasons to the Stipendiary Magistrates and to invite their cooperation in the matter."[48]

Tension was rising and the inevitable outcome was quickly becoming evident. Superintendent Crozier, fully aware of the imminent danger, wired Lieutenant Governor Dewdney to "request that matters concerning the halfbreeds be settled without delay."[49] On March 4, Magistrate Hugh Richardson sent a message to Crozier to tell him that he had received information that Louis Riel addressed a meeting outside the Church at Batoche "in which he incited the halfbreeds to rebellion." He was reported to have said that "war was likely to occur between England and Russia and now was the time to strike when the eyes of Canadians were turned to Europe."[50] Frederick White advised Dewdney, "We must be prepared to put down any nonsense though I don't anticipate trouble."[51]

At a meeting held at St. Laurent on March 8, 1885, Louis Riel moved a motion for the formation of a provisional government and passage of a Bill of Rights. This was the same pattern that had been followed at Red River in 1870 and many of the Métis expected that the government reaction would be to open negotiations. When the provisional government was formed and a decision made to resort to arms, most of the remaining European settlers and English half-breeds withdrew their support. As one member of the Mounted Police later wrote, "Everything was approaching a crisis. Indeed we of the rank and file used to talk in quite a familiar way, in the barrack room, of the coming rebellion as a matter of course. We even had the date fixed."[52]

- 6 -
Duck Lake

By the end of 1884, there were 557 North-West Mounted Police members in the west, many of them with less than one year of service. Due to government cutbacks they were poorly paid, badly equipped and chronically short of horses and wagons. The fact that the organization functioned as effectively as it did was a tribute to the high quality and dedication of a few key individuals who provided the backbone of the force. Good steady men, often former noncommissioned officers in the Army, received rapid promotion, sometimes reaching the rank of corporal or sergeant in a matter of months where it now takes many years. The men themselves were a mixed lot. One former member describing his fellow constables said: "a third of the crowd were broken-down gentlemen, many with titles or a purser's name; a third were Canadian bucolics; the rest promiscuous desperadoes, old soldiers, cowboys, sailors and hell rake adventurers from all the ends of the earth."[1]

As tensions increased on the South Branch of the Saskatchewan, Superintendent Gagnon at Fort Carlton sent a message to Superintendent Crozier at Battleford advising, "halfbreeds excited, moving about more than usual. Preparing arms. Reported they propose preventing supplies coming in from 16th."[2] Crozier ordered Inspector William Morris at Battleford to send an additional 25 men and a 7-pounder gun from Fort Battleford to Fort Carlton.[3] He also passed on to Commissioner Irvine at Regina, the information given him by Gagnon, adding that Louis Riel would not allow people to leave their homes since he said they might be required. He expressed the belief that the immediate origin of the trouble was the letter Riel received stating that he was not recognized as a British subject.

Crozier reported he thought some whites were favourable to the movement.[4] Prophetically he had reported the previous year, in a reference to the whites who supported the return of Riel, that "no doubt there are those who would

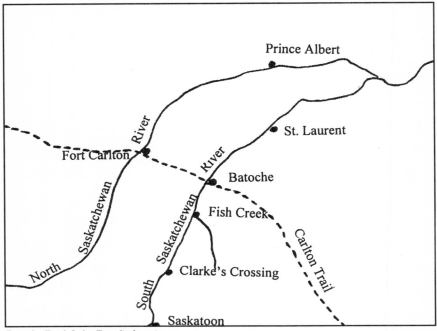

Batoche-Duck Lake-Fort Carlton Area

like to see a large body of troops sent, but then their private interests might be served thereby if that matters." He added that he believed "such people in an underhanded way encouraged agitation like the present but even if by sending troops we are playing into the hands of such people it will have to be done or the consequences taken."[5] Lieutenant Governor Dewdney, as a precautionary measure, took steps to prevent the sale of fixed ammunition in northeast Saskatchewan.[6]

A couple of days later, Superintendent Crozier sent Commissioner Irvine another urgent telegram telling him, "Halfbreed rebellion liable to break out at any moment. Troops must be largely reinforced. If halfbreeds rise, Indians will join them." In forwarding this intelligence to Ottawa, Irvine added a recommendation that "at least 100 men be sent at once."[7] On March 15, he informed Ottawa that Lieutenant Governor Dewdney thought he should go north with the men immediately since "roads and rivers will soon break up."[8] Ottawa agreed and ordered Irvine to start north as soon as possible with all available men. To find the necessary numbers, Irvine transferred 25 men and 20 horses from Calgary by rail to augment those in Regina. Just as they were ready to go, Crozier advised that "present movements and preparations have quieted matters. No cause for alarm now."[9] At this point, in what may well have been the year's most inaccurate report, Peter Ballendine reported to Dewdney, "I must say that I never left any band of Indians this winter more satisfied than those round Frog Lake. I only hope they will continue to be so."[10]

This quiet time was short lived. The Métis had asked the Chief Factor of the Hudson's Bay Company at Prince Albert, Lawrence Clarke, to make representations on their behalf in Ottawa with regard to their request for an issue of scrip similar to that given to Manitoba half-breeds and other matters. In some ways Clarke was an odd choice as an emissary for the Métis. A decade earlier, in 1875, Commissioner George French complained to the Minister of Justice that "the mischievous and alarming reports offered concerning the Force last summer were circulated mainly by Hudson's Bay Company officers and notably by . . . Mr. Clarke. . . ."[11] A few months later, Clarke wrote to Lieutenant Governor Alexander Morris at Fort Garry, reporting that the Métis "assumed to themselves the right to enact laws, rules and regulations for government of the colony and surrounding country of a most tyrannical nature." He asked for a protective force at Fort Carlton.[12]

As a result of this plea, a fifty-man detachment of Mounted Police made a hasty, eight-day trip from Swan River Barracks, only to find the trouble was greatly exaggerated and Commissioner French reported that "as I expected, there is no reason for alarm with reference to the affair of Gabriel Dumont."[13] The Minister of Justice decided that "there does not appear to have been the slightest foundation for the alarm expressed by Mr. Clarke. . . ."[14] It is interesting that the only person charged in this affair was Gabriel Dumont, and the Mounted Police officer involved was Lief Crozier.

A full decade later, in May 1884, Clarke wrote a letter to Sir John A. Macdonald informing him that European and Métis radicals were holding secret meetings which were a serious threat to national security. The wording was remarkably similar to that in his letter to Morris. In addition, on May 11, 1884, he sent a telegram to Lieutenant Governor Dewdney informing him that the Métis had held a series of secret meetings "to pass resolutions complaining of their treatment by the government . . . ." He advised that two men had been "appointed to interview Riel, asking him to assist them if he could not come to advise them what to do."[15]

Clarke went to Ottawa in February 1885 and, on his way back, stopped in Regina to see Lieutenant Governor Dewdney before starting north. On March 18, 1885, while travelling from Qu'Appelle to Fort Carlton, he met several Métis who were curious about the government's response to their petitions. Clarke allegedly informed them that their petitions would be answered by bullets, and added that on his way north he passed a camp of 500 policemen coming to arrest Riel. His highly excited listeners galloped off to St. Laurent to report this news. When Louis Riel heard of Clarke's remarks, he is said to have become very excited and called on his followers to take up arms. Whether Clarke's comments were attributable to a misguided sense of humour, sheer stupidity or a wilful attempt to fuel Métis discontent, is hard to tell. What is obvious is that his action escalated the simmering discontent into overt lawless acts and insurrection.

Clarke's action is often cited by proponents of an unproven conspiracy theory which links some of the white settlers with an alleged attempt by the Macdonald government to provoke a rebellion in order to discredit the Métis and provide an excuse for the government to fund the completion of the Canadian Pacific Railway. There are some who argue that Lawrence Clarke was an *agent provocateur* who stirred up trouble and, finally, triggered the rebellion. While there is some indication that he may have been involved in land speculation and otherwise pursuing his own agenda, there is no clear evidence linking the government to Clarke's actions. When concern about his activities appeared in the press, his superiors in the Hudson's Bay Company suggested it would be better for him "not to act publicly but leave responsibility on Government."[16]

In the first overt acts of the rebellion, a meeting was held at the South Branch to launch a "provisional government" and Riel's followers seized general stores on both sides of the river, including the Stobart, Eden & Co. trading post at Duck Lake. Guards were assigned to cover the trails to and from Prince Albert, Fort Carlton and the south, to intercept supplies and prevent entry of the Mounted Police. Louis Riel said, "Our people have repeatedly sought redress from the Government of Canada, and every appeal has been answered by an increase in the police force. But what is the police force? Nothing but a myth, and before one month it will be wiped out of existence."[17] Events had now crossed the line from peaceful protest to armed insurrection. When Louis Riel sought the cooperation of the English half-breeds, he asked them not to remain neutral but "For the love of God help us to save the Saskatchewan." They replied that while they continued to sympathize with the Métis cause, they did not approve of armed insurrection or inciting the Indians to rise.[18] Now, just as his actions reached a critical point, some of Riel's support was weakening.

On the evening of March 18, in an atmosphere of heightened tension, Superintendent Crozier wired Commissioner Irvine to tell him "Rumours tonight Indians being tampered with. Large force should be sent without delay that arrests may be made if necessary to prevent further and continuous trouble from Riel and his followers. Crozier also asked Irvine to "send as many men as possible. Mass meeting of halfbreeds tonight. Report of immediate trouble - must stamp this out."[19]

Commissioner A.G. Irvine   NAC PA-042139

Duck Lake

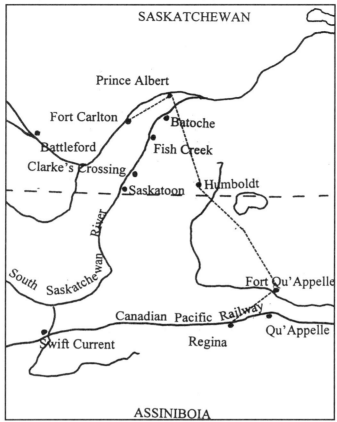

SASKATCHEWAN

Prince Albert

Fort Carlton

Batoche

Battleford

Fish Creek

Clarke's Crossing

Saskatoon

Humboldt

South Saskatchewan River

Fort Qu'Appelle

Canadian Pacific Railway

Qu'Appelle

Swift Current

Regina

ASSINIBOIA

Commissioner Irvine's Route To Prince Albert And Fort Carlton

Commissioner Irvine was not at Regina to receive messages. He left at 6:00 a.m. with Inspectors Frederick Drayner, Gilbert Sanders and Montague White-Fraser, 89 men and 66 horses, travelling in a long line of sleighs, several of them loaded with forage and provisions which would be unobtainable on the trail. The chronic shortage of horses in the Mounted Police was so acute that when Irvine's force departed there were no horses left at the Mounted Police barracks in Regina and some had to be borrowed from the Indian Department.[20] The column halted at Piapot's Reserve for dinner and later stopped for the night at the Muskowpeetung

Reserve in the Qu'Appelle Valley. It has been claimed that Irvine's movement was intended to intimidate the Indians, who were disturbed by the activity since they did not know what was going on. If Piapot wanted to know what was happening, he could simply have asked Irvine over a cup of tea since ". . . a halt was made at Piapot's Reserve for dinner, to which Piapot was invited and of which he partook sumptuously."[21]

One of Irvine's men, Constable Roger Pocock, described how, on March 21, they made camp on the Salt Plains in a thaw that saw everyone soaking wet. When Reveille sounded at 3:30 the next morning, the temperature was -25°F. Pocock could not find his moccasins which he had been told to wear on the march, and struggled into his frozen boots. Once on the trail, he was unable to continue running alongside the sleigh and had to ride. On reaching Humboldt that evening, his feet were found to be frozen. To add to his discomfort, he became snow blind the next day, along with 22 other members of the force. The hospital noncommissioned officer treated the snow blind men with tea leaves and, when they had to move, had them form a line with each man putting his hand on the shoulder of the man in front of him.[22]

An Englishman, named Gordon, travelled overland from Fort Carlton on snowshoes to intercept Commissioner Irvine and his men as they struggled across the Salt Plains. He warned the Commissioner that the rebels at Batoche had prepared an ambush near the Church of St. Antoine, where the ground was bare and movement difficult for the sleighs. The woods on both sides of the trail were lined with rifle pitts.[23] With at least 23 of his 89 men suffering from snow blindness, Irvine would have been at a serious disadvantage had the column had to fight its way across the South Saskatchewan River. He also had concerns about the security of Prince Albert and decided to avoid the Batoche area. Irvine sent a message to Frederick White informing him that he intended to bypass Batoche and go to Fort Carlton via Prince Albert. Hayter Reed, the Assistant Indian

66

North West Mounted Police On The March   Usask Lib Spec Coll Pam LXII-37

Commissioner, joined the column at Humboldt and was appointed Brigade Major of Irvine's force.

On March 23, Commissioner Irvine found his first evidence of the insurrection at the Hoodoo stage station which had already been raided by Riel's men. The food and forage had been taken and the stage drivers and horses captured. When the Mounted Police resumed their journey, they caught up with a load of oats that had been commandeered by the rebels who ordered the driver to take it to Batoche. Irvine promptly repossessed the grain and used it to feed the police horses. This same day in Ottawa, the Minister of Militia and Defence, Adolphe Caron, ordered Major General Frederick Middleton, Commander of the Canadian Militia, to go west. The mobilization of militia units started.

On March 24, the column moved stealthily around Batoche on the east side, with the men holding loaded weapons and forbidden to speak aloud. Constable Pocock sat on a sleigh box for seven hours of this march "luxurious with six ounces of brandy inside" and his feet in a bucket of ice and snow.[24] Commissioner Irvine's force avoided the rebels, crossed the river at Agnew's Ferry and arrived in Prince Albert on the evening of March 24. Pocock considered the march from Regina to Prince Albert a major accomplishment. He noted that "we watched the colonel's sorrel top go roan with worry, but what with his iron discipline, splendid horsemanship, and a perfect service of scouts we made the 300-mile march over snowbound plains and through hostile country at an average of 42 miles a day."[25] The press were not confident of Irvine's ability to reach Prince Albert, and the *Globe* of March 25, 1885 noted that "Present appearances indicate that Col. Irvine will find considerable difficulty in crossing the South Saskatchewan with his force if he finds himself watched by a force of five times that number who hold the opposite bank. The banks of the Saskatchewan at what is familiarly known as Gabriel Dumond's [sic] crossing, are extremely high and precipitous."[26]

Meanwhile, at Fort Carlton, Superintendent Crozier sent "Gentleman Joe" McKay to Prince Albert with a request for volunteers to augment his force. McKay was a scout whose nickname came from his courteous manner and immaculate dress. Crozier also sent a message to Commissioner Irvine to inform him that the rebels "seized stores at South Branch and made Mr. Lash, Indian Agent, prisoner, have committed other acts - gathering for an attack on Fort Carlton. . . . "[27] John Lash, the Indian Agent at Fort Carlton, went with his interpreter, William Tompkins, to investigate rumours that there was "tampering" with One Arrow's band.[28] His outward trip to the reserve was uneventful and, after warning One Arrow not to join Riel and to stay on his reserve, he began his return trip to Fort Carlton via Batoche and Duck Lake. Around Batoche he was taken prisoner by armed Métis. In addition, the rebels were reported to have captured a merchant, Henry Walters, two telegraph technicians, Jack McKeen and Peter Tompkins, brother of the Indian Department interpreter, who had been sent out to repair the cut telegraph line, and Hillyard Mitchell of Duck Lake. The report about Mitchell was incorrect.

Superintendent Crozier, who estimated the rebel strength at between two hundred and four hundred men and increasing rapidly, had the impression that many of the Indian bands would rise. He advised Irvine that the rebel plan was "to seize any troops coming into the country at the South Branch, then march on Carlton, then on Prince Albert."[29] The Métis Council prepared an ultimatum to be presented to the Mounted Police, calling on them to surrender. The surrender would include all government properties at Fort Carlton and Battleford. The Métis promised that the Mounted Police would be set free on giving their word to keep the peace, while any who chose to leave would be given teams and provisions to get to Qu'Appelle. If they failed to accept these conditions, the Métis said they would attack them the next day and start a war of extermination.[30]

Louis Riel sent a message asking to meet with Superintendent Crozier in order to negotiate. Crozier agreed to meet him at a place halfway between Carlton and Duck Lake and said he would go without an escort and promised that Riel would "have a chance of saying whatever he wished and further that, upon that occasion I would not arrest him."[31] Riel replied that he would not meet Crozier personally but would send emissaries, so Crozier, instead of going himself, sent Captain Harold S. Moore, a Prince Albert Volunteer, and Thomas McKay as his representatives. It turned out that Riel's emissaries, Charles Nolin and Maxime Lepine, were not there to negotiate but only to deliver an ultimatum that Fort Carlton be surrendered. In response, Crozier's representatives delivered his message "that the gravest offences had been committed against the law, and that the leaders and instigators of the rebellion would have to be delivered up to the authorities to be dealt with in accordance with the law."[32] The following day, March 24, the Métis Council or Exovedate decided to send pairs of messengers, a

Métis and an Indian on each team, to surrounding reserves with messages designed to stir up the Indians. One band, Big Cap's Sioux, started to move toward Prince Albert, probably influenced by Alexis LeBombarde, who had been one of the witnesses to the Cypress Hills Massacre, but changed their minds when they heard that Irvine's column was in the area.

In response to Superintendent Crozier's request for volunteers, delivered by Thomas McKay, Prince Albert raised about seventy civilian volunteers to support the garrison at Fort Carlton. This came about despite suggestions that the Mounted Police should abandon it and base the available men in Prince Albert. By this time, the authorities in Ottawa realized the gravity of the situation in the North-West and were starting to take action. Frederick White sent a message informing Irvine that "Major General Commanding Militia proceeds forthwith to Red River. On his arrival, in military operations when acting with Militia, take orders from him."[33]

Following the hard journey from Regina a number of Irvine's horses had to be shod, "several rifles were found to be out of working order . . . some of the ammunition was bad and the defence of Prince Albert had to be organized."[34] The Commissioner decided to spend March 25 looking after these matters, having been assured by Thomas McKay that all was quiet at Fort Carlton. This apparently insignificant decision may well have altered the course of history since, had Irvine arrived at Fort Carlton that day, the clash at Duck Lake would likely never have taken place. Meanwhile, at Fort Carlton, a small number of people arrived from Duck Lake, including the storekeeper, Hillyard Mitchell, who had hidden badly needed ammunition, supplies and oats from his store.

On the evening of March 25, to keep abreast of any activity around Batoche, Crozier sent Prince Albert Deputy Sheriff, Harold Ross, a former member of the Mounted Police, and surveyor John Astley on a reconnaissance.[35] They were told that Duck Lake had been quiet all day and the rebels had made no move toward the village. Unknown to them, Gabriel Dumont and a large number of rebels had come to Duck Lake. Shortly after midnight, two Métis scouts posted along the trail near Beardy's Reserve, hurried back to Dumont and his companions to tell them that two men had gone down the trail in the dark. The Métis galloped in pursuit of Ross and Astley and took them prisoner. The Métis were ready to return to Batoche when Phillippe Garnot is reported to have learned from the prisoners, that the Police would be coming to Duck Lake that day to remove supplies. The rebels therefore remained at Beardy's to watch the road from Fort Carlton.[36]

Superintendent Crozier was short of supplies, given the influx of men and horses, so Hillyard Mitchell, the storekeeper, told him that there was a large supply at Duck Lake. On March 26, about 4:00 a.m., Crozier sent Sergeant Alfred Stewart and seventeen constables in eight sleighs "accompanied by and under the direction of Mr. Thomas McKay of Prince Albert, to Hillyard Mitchell's store at Duck Lake to recover the ammunition, supplies and oats concealed there."[37] About three miles from Duck Lake, two of the police scouts, Constable Edward Waite and Constable Robert Jamieson returned to say that there were a large number of Métis on the road.[38] Four Mounted Police scouts came riding back pursued by a number of half-breeds and Indians. McKay rode back to the sleighs and told the men to load their rifles and get ready, then went to meet the large group of armed and mounted rebels. The first Métis to reach Thomas McKay was his friend, Patrice Fleury, who advised him that Duck Lake was strongly held by the rebels who would not give it up without a fight. McKay agreed to take the Police back to Fort Carlton but at that point Gabriel Dumont and the other Métis rode up and confronted him.

In an overbearing and excited manner, the rebels demanded the immediate surrender of the party or they would fire. McKay refused and told them in Cree that two could play at that game. Gabriel Dumont and others kept prodding McKay in the ribs with loaded and cocked guns, while declaring they would blow his brains out. Two of the rebels jumped into a sleigh belonging to the Police party and tried to take possession of the team but McKay told the driver to hold on. The Indians kept jeering at the small party and calling out, "if you are men, now come on." The party turned back to Fort Carlton and McKay told the rebels not to follow as he would not be responsible for what his men might do. During the parley, Dumont fired a rifle between McKay and a teamster.[39] A messenger, Constable John Retallack, was sent to tell Crozier what happened, so that by the time the patrol returned to Fort Carlton, a large body of troops had each been issued 60 rounds of ball ammunition and was ready to go to Duck Lake.[40]

The historian Norman Black, who spoke to Sergeant Stewart afterward, says that when Stewart and his men returned to Fort Carlton, Crozier "had quite properly given up the idea of making any onslaught upon the rioters at Duck Lake." Unfortunately, some of the civilians present challenged Crozier "to teach the rebels a lesson if he were not afraid of them."[41] Lawrence Clarke, the Hudson's Bay Company Chief Factor at Prince Albert who was present, is alleged to have goaded Crozier, asking him, "Are we to be turned back by a parcel of half-breeds? Now is the time, Crozier, to show if you have sand in you."[42] One of the volunteers, heard by Sergeant Stewart, told Crozier that if he returned to Fort Carlton "he would brand him a coward." Crozier then replied, "Very well, if you want to go to Duck Lake, I'll take you."[43] On the way Crozier, "who with all his bravery unites a great deal of prudence, again wished to return" but Clarke induced him to continue.[44] In later years, Captain Roger Pocock, the constable who had his right foot frozen on the march to Prince Albert, said "things happened quickly" when somebody called Crozier a coward and "the hot Irish gentleman broke loose from discipline, threw his career to the winds, sounded 'Boots and Saddle,' paraded 60 police and marched."[45]

Superintendent Crozier had been told that the main body of rebels was at Batoche, on the south side of the river. Thus he "was led to believe that the party north of Duck Lake was but a detachment from the main body engaged in a marauding expedition, and I considered that, with the hundred men I had with me

I would be able to overcome their resistance, if any, and get the stores in spite of them."[46] Superintendent Gagnon informed Commissioner Irvine, who was on his way from Prince Albert, that "Superintendent Crozier with one hundred men started out at 10:00 a.m. on Duck Lake road to help one of our sergeants and small party in difficulty at Mitchell's store. I have seventy men and can hold post against odds. Do not expect Crozier to push on further than Duck Lake. Everything quiet here."[47] Irvine received this message when he was about nine miles away from Fort Carlton.

Some of the Mounted Police in Crozier's party were in sleighs and some mounted and, as they moved along, the 7-pounder's wheels tended to sink in the snow, slowing the column. When they were a short distance from Duck Lake, the advance scouts encountered the rebels who pursued them as they galloped back to warn Superintendent Crozier. The force moved up cautiously to where the rebels occupied the same position at which Sergeant Stewart's men had run into them. The Mounted Police stopped and Crozier sent the interpreter, Gentleman Joe McKay, to see what the rebels wanted. As McKay advanced, the rebels began to move out on both flanks in an encircling movement. Crozier put his sleighs at right angles to the trail and the Prince Albert volunteers spread out to the right. The 7-pounder gun was positioned in the centre and the unhitched horses were moved to the rear.

There are almost as many versions of what happened next as there were participants in the clash at Duck Lake. The Métis and Indians say the Mounted Police fired the first shot and this is corroborated by Joseph McKay who admitted being the one who fired. At the rebellion trials, Corporal Hugh Davidson testified that the rebels fired first. Sergeant William Smart said the rebels fired on him as he rode back to the main body and hit his saddle but no shots were fired by the Mounted Police until ordered. Constable Ernest Todd said the rebels fired on the advance guard. William C. Ramsay, a Prince Albert Volunteer, identified a rebel, Le Framboise, as the one who fired first.[48]

As Joseph McKay recalls events, he went forward with Superintendent Crozier and Sergeant Brooks to speak to two men who came out of a hollow with a white flag.[49] One of the men was an elderly, partially blind Indian from Beardy's Reserve by the name of Asee-wee-yin, who started what McKay described as an incoherent conversation in Cree.[50] Crozier sent Brooks back to tell the Police and volunteers to be ready for trouble. McKay couldn't make any headway in the attempt to parley and Crozier believed it was a ruse by the Métis to gain time while they surrounded his force. When Crozier turned to go back to his men, Assee-wee-yin allegedly attempted to seize him but he broke away, leaving McKay behind grappling with the Indian, while covered by Isadore Dumont, the second rebel. As they continued to grapple, Assee-wee-yin grabbed McKay's revolver and said, "You have too many guns, grandson. Give me this."[51] At this point Crozier gave the order to commence firing and McKay drew his pistol and shot Isadore Dumont and mortally wounded Asee-wee-yin.

The fighting that broke out was quite intense for about half an hour. The Mounted Police were in a vulnerable position with the Métis firing on them from good cover. Although the sleighs afforded some protection to the Police, the Prince Albert volunteers, spread out along the fence line, had little cover. As soon as the firing started, Inspector Howe ordered the 7-pounder gun into "Action Front," but firing did not commence and a number of rebels in front disappeared. Asked why they had not fired, the gun crew told Superintendent Crozier that he had been in the line of fire. He is said to have responded, "Well, I am only one man, you should have fired anyway."[52] Because the gun had been positioned too far forward in the line of march, it was now within musket range of the concealed Métis and came under heavy small arms fire. The gun had fired two rounds of shrapnel and two rounds of case when the Number 3 on the gun crew, Constable George Garrett, was shot through the lungs and put out of action.[53] His place was taken by a spare man, Constable Louis Fontaine.[54] In the heat and excitement of the battle, Fontaine

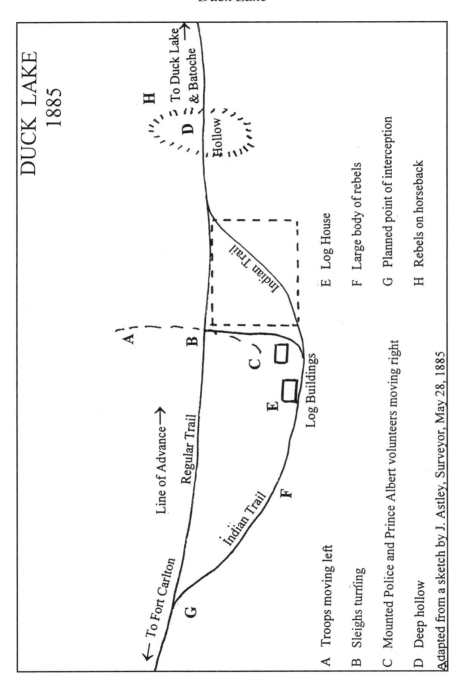

DUCK LAKE
1885

Line of Advance →

Regular Trail

To Fort Carlton ←

Indian Trail

G

F

A

B

C

E

Log Buildings

Indian Trail

H

D

Hollow

To Duck Lake → & Batoche

A Troops moving left

B Sleighs turfing

C Mounted Police and Prince Albert volunteers moving right

D Deep hollow

E Log House

F Large body of rebels

G Planned point of interception

H Rebels on horseback

Adapted from a sketch by J. Astley, Surveyor, May 28, 1885

dropped a case shot into the barrel before the charge, rendering the muzzle loading gun useless until the charge and projectile could be ejected and reloaded properly. By the time Inspector Howe had Sergeant Smart raise the trail and roll the charge and shot out, the rebels were too close for effective use of the gun. Constable Thomas Gibson, driver of the ammunition sleigh was just getting out of his seat when he was shot through the heart and died instantly.[55] This was not a memorable day for gunners.

Casualties mounted quickly, especially for the more exposed volunteers who had nine killed and five wounded out of a total of 43 members. Sergeant Stewart "time and again rallied and encouraged the men under a galling fire."[56] The Mounted Police suffered three killed and five wounded out of 53 members present. Constable George Arnold "received four bullet wounds, one in the groin, one through the chest, one through the neck and a scalp wound. He bravely continued firing after receiving his first wound and when he went down said, 'Tell the boys I died game.'"[57] The North-West Mounted Police wounded included the officer commanding, Superintendent Lief Crozier, who received a cut on the cheek from a stray bullet and Inspector Joseph Howe, who was wounded in the leg. Constable Sydney Gordon was shot through both legs, while Corporal Thomas Gilchrist, who had his leg shattered, asked "the boys to take him home and not let the black devils get his hair."[58] One of the lucky ones was Constable Andrew McMillan who was thought to be seriously wounded, but turned out to have been hit by a spent bullet which knocked him unconscious and gave him a large bruise.[59] He didn't even get on the list of wounded. Equally fortunate was Surgeon Robert Miller, whose life was saved when his case of instruments stopped a bullet.[60]

Realizing he was in a trap and up against a superior number of rebels, Superintendent Crozier ordered a withdrawal and extricated his men, sleighs and the 7-pounder gun. John Astley, the Surveyor who had been captured by the rebels, later reported that had the force gone as far as the hollow before halting, the men

Fighting At Duck Lake   NAC C-033058

in the log buildings would have moved onto the trail behind them. If this did not work, there was another plan. Mounted rebels moving westward on the Indian trail were to cut off the Mounted Police if they tried to retreat. These rebels were slow to obey the order to move and stopped to take a few pot shots. Due to the rapid withdrawal made by Crozier, they arrived at the main trail too late to trap the Police.[61]

Just as the last sleighs were leaving, a shot passed close to Prince Albert volunteer Hugh Nelson, who involuntarily ducked. Sergeant Major Frederick Dann told him, "No use ducking lad, it was past before you heard it."[62] Five Mounted Police horses were killed or wounded and two sleighs and a jumper had to be abandoned. As the Police made their withdrawal, the Métis who wanted to follow them were stopped by Louis Riel who shouted, "For the love of God kill no more of them."[63]   The very deep snow with a hard crust made movement difficult, but the badly mauled force was soon clear and travelling through the lightly falling snow, on the trail back to Fort Carlton.

A list of the members of the North-West Mounted Police and the Special Constables of the Prince Albert volunteers present at the engagement at Duck Lake can be found at Appendix "B."

- 7 -
Retreat From Fort Carlton

Just after Superintendent Crozier's force withdrew to Fort Carlton, they were joined by Commissioner Irvine and the force from Prince Albert. As soon as he obtained details, Irvine sent a message to inform Sir John A. Macdonald what had happened.[1] The Mounted Police member killed at Duck Lake, Constable Thomas Gibson, and those who subsequently died of wounds, Constables George Arnold and George Garrett, were buried in a single grave near Fort Carlton on the afternoon of March 27. Two years later, in 1887, Sergeant William Parker and three constables disinterred the three bodies which were re-buried in the cemetery at Prince Albert.[2]

Commissioner Irvine reported that "on learning the intent and demeanour of the rebels, as well as being advised of the number of Indians who had joined them, I deemed it expedient to abandon Fort Carlton." He admitted that he was influenced in his decision by the volunteers being at Fort Carlton when both he and the volunteers believed they should have been in Prince Albert protecting their homes. He also had to consider "the untenable position of the Fort and the inutility of holding it as a means of protecting the settlers of the country."[3] Fort Carlton was built on flat land by the river and was overlooked by vantage points which offered an enemy clear fields of fire on the trails and the river approaches. Irvine was also concerned that if Prince Albert was left undefended, the rebels would make a raid on it.[4]

Commissioner Irvine held a Council of War with his officers and Lawrence Clarke, representing the Hudson's Bay Company, the owners of Fort Carlton. Captain Charles F. Young, a Prince Albert volunteer at Fort Carlton and a former Sub-Inspector in the North-West Mounted Police, who was one of those at the conference, recalled that Irvine "pointed out to us, that we now really knew what

Fort Carlton From The Hill   NAC PA-117931

the intentions of the rebels were, that they were in greater numbers than ourselves and that owing to their initial advantage at Duck Lake they were apt to have an increase in numbers." He also thought "though we might hold Carlton, he did not see any advantage to be gained by doing so, that he had left orders at Prince Albert to collect supplies and that the women and children were all there and but few arms there to enable the people there to protect themselves."[5]

Justus Willson, a sergeant in the Prince Albert volunteers, who was in the engagement at Duck Lake and later became a general in the Canadian Army, recalled that in the discussion with his officers, Commissioner Irvine gave three possible courses of action and sought their advice, while retaining his right to make the final decision. The first option was to resume the offensive with the increased force in the hope that they could bring the rebellion to a quick end. The second option was to remain at Fort Carlton, strengthen the defences and hold off any attack. The third course open to them was to remove the maximum possible quantity of supplies, destroy what could not be taken away, then abandon Fort Carlton and take up a strong position in Prince Albert. Superintendent Crozier and Inspector Sanders both wanted to secure Fort Carlton then take the offensive to end the revolt and restore the authority of the Police, but Irvine decided to return to Prince Albert, partly at the urging of his volunteers who wanted to protect their homes and families, and partly because he realized Fort Carlton was largely indefensible.[6]

Commissioner Irvine planned to have the Mounted Police load all the provisions they could carry and destroy what could not be taken. The original plan was to cut holes in the ice and dump the supplies in the river. When this did not work, the Mounted Police destroyed the surplus flour by ripping open the sacks, spilling it on the ground and pouring coal oil on it or contaminating it with manure. Hayter Reed took some of the food that was to be destroyed and gave it to a Farm Instructor to issue to the Indians saying it was "better for the loyal Indians to get them than the rebels to benefit from them."[7] Lawrence Clarke, always looking out for the interests of the Hudson's Bay Company, later informed his superior that he estimated the loss in stores to be $27,000 and "Irvine ordered destruction taking responsibility of saving goods off our hands."[8]

At first Irvine's officers decided, unanimously, that the buildings should be destroyed but someone suggested that setting fire to the fort might attract the rebels, so the idea was left in abeyance. Events took the decision out of their hands at about 2:00 a.m. when a fire started as loading was underway. Apparently, hay being used to fill mattresses for the wounded was ignited by coming in contact with a stovepipe in the quarters of Sergeant Major Frederick Dann. The fire was in a room above the main gate which was the only exit, so additional openings were hastily made in the temporary cordwood stockade that surrounded the fort.

A Trying Time

The burning fort was like a beacon in the dark, so a strong guard was posted while the horses were hitched up and the fort evacuated. As the long train of teams moved out in the flickering light of the fire, a strong line of skirmishers was pushed forward to cover the highly vulnerable string of sleighs. The trail leading out of Fort Carlton passed through a dense thicket of woods, climbing from the fort to the summit of the nearby hill on a steep single cart track about a mile in length. This trail then crossed the prairie until it reached a feature called "The Firs," a very hilly four-mile long forest of spruce and jack pine. On the night of the retreat from Fort Carlton, travelling was especially difficult because of the depth of the snow and the thickness of the crust which restricted travel to a single track. Some of the sleighs were so heavily laden that part of the loads had to be jettisoned on the way up the steep slope and the horses were used up by the time they reached Prince Albert.

It took four hours for the last sleigh to clear the hill on the trail out of Fort Carlton and to set off for Prince Albert. Commissioner Irvine stayed and saw the last sleigh away, then moved up the hill to the head of the line and joined the skirmishers in the advance guard while the rear party, under Sergeant James Pringle, covered the tail of the column.[9] For the few mounted policemen in the column who had taken part in the march west of 1874, there must have been a feeling of *deja vu* as they watched grossly overloaded wagons straining across the countryside. Everyone in the column was apprehensive: "We knew that the Rebels were not at any rate farther off than Duck Lake and that if they attacked us in our retreat encumbered as we were with our loaded teams and wounded men and families of the neighbouring settlers who had taken refuge in the Fort and were coming with us to Prince Albert, the results could only be disastrous."[10] Gabriel Dumont is said to have told Louis Riel he knew a place where the Mounted Police column would have to pass through a narrow gap in a thick grove of trees, putting it in a perfect position to be ambushed. Riel would not allow the attack. A few years later

Fort Carlton After Being Burned   NAC C-18705

Dumont complained the rebels could have inflicted many casualties but Riel would not agree to the ambush. The sleighs reached Prince Albert safely about four o'clock in the afternoon.

The buildings and supplies at Fort Carlton were not totally destroyed and the day after the Police left, six or seven rebels were seen loading supplies. Harold Ross, the ex-mounted policeman, who was taken to Fort Carlton with some other prisoners on March 30, said that there were 50 rebels there moving everything that could be taken to Batoche. About a week after the evacuation, armed men came from the South Branch and lived in the buildings that survived the fire, but they eventually burned these buildings and returned to Batoche.[11]

In his report on the Duck Lake incident, Commissioner Irvine said, "I cannot but consider it a matter of regret that with the knowledge that both myself and command were within a few miles of and en route to Fort Carlton, Superintendent Crozier should have marched out as he did, particularly in the face of what transpired earlier in the day. I am led to the belief that this officer's better judgement was overruled by the impetuosity displayed by both Police and

83

Volunteers. However, once this action had been taken much confidence, power and prestige were established throughout the rebel ranks, and thus Riel found his hands materially strengthened."[12]

Louis Riel was more upbeat. Immediately after the engagement at Duck Lake, he sent messengers to all the Indian reserves telling them: "We have the pleasure to let you know that on the 26th of last month, God has given us a victory over the Mounted Police. Thirty Half-breeds and some five or six Cree Indians, have met one hundred and twenty policemen and volunteers. Thanks to God, we have defeated them. Yourselves, Dear relatives, be courageous. Do what you can. If it is not done, take the stores, the provisions and munitions. And without delay, come this way, as many as it is possible. Send us news."[13] Riel's figures are challenged by other witnesses. Two of the prisoners, John Astley, the surveyor and John Lash, the Indian Agent, say they counted the armed men who left Batoche just prior to the clash and estimate the number at more than 300.[14]

Duck Lake was the beginning of the end for Superintendent Crozier's career in the Mounted Police. Although he was not yet aware of it, his promotion to Assistant Commissioner was already promulgated, but he would now be accused of errors in judgement, lack of common sense, and impetuosity. When things go wrong, somebody has to take the blame and Crozier was the obvious recipient in this case. In his defence it must be remembered that the estimates he had of rebel strength were inaccurate and he was also, to some extent, the victim of the idea that a display of moral force would allow the Mounted Police to overcome any odds. Bold and intrepid action worked in the early days when small numbers of policemen went into Indian camps and arrested prisoners in front of hundreds of angry warriors, so the Mounted Police were surrounded with an aura of invincibility. Crozier was goaded into attempting to overcome resistance at any cost but was unsuccessful so, unfortunately, at Duck Lake, moral superiority no longer worked and the shocked Mounted Police retired to Prince Albert and went into a defensive position, watching to see how events would unfold and waiting for assistance from the east.

As the tragic events unfolded at Duck Lake, General Frederick Middleton was travelling from Ottawa to Winnipeg, his first visit to the west. By the time he arrived at Winnipeg, on March 22, mobilization was well underway and 120 men of the 90th Battalion from Winnipeg had already left for Qu'Appelle, the closest point to Batoche on the Canadian Pacific Railway. Middleton continued from Winnipeg to Qu'Appelle with the rest of the 90th, while additional units from Eastern Canada, mostly infantry, followed. Lord Melgund, Military Secretary to the Governor General, Lord Lansdowne, was appointed Chief of Staff to General Middleton and departed for the west shortly behind him. He wired Lansdowne from Portage la Prairie, telling him that he heard the Duck Lake Indians were retreating and noting that ". . . it is desirable to raise all the mounted men possible" and that he thought "infantry will not be of much use."[15]

Word of the Duck Lake debacle spread quickly throughout the west, causing widespread alarm among the settlers. More than anything else, those in small communities and on isolated farms or ranches feared an Indian uprising. There were no troops in the Northwest Territories and the relatively small number of Mounted Police members was sharply reduced in order to provide the men required for Commissioner Irvine's force.

Because of the widespread unrest and the activity of Riel's emissaries, there was concern that some Indians in the south might rise and that help for Riel would arrive from across the border. This placed a heavy responsibility on the reduced number of Mounted Police members who remained in the small detachments south of the area in which the engagements of the North-West Rebellion were fought. Initially the settlers throughout the plains were understandably alarmed as wild rumours circulated and they daily expected a mass Indian uprising. Those within reach of towns like Calgary, Edmonton, Fort

Macleod, Battleford or Prince Albert flocked into town to seek protection in numbers or from the North-West Mounted Police. In most communities some kind of home guard or militia was formed, usually led by former military or Mounted Police officers.

The citizens of Calgary were worried due to their proximity to the tribes of the Blackfoot Nation who had reputations as the most warlike bands on the plains. There was a series of town hall meetings, some chaired by General Thomas Bland Strange prior to his appointment to command the Alberta Field Force. A home guard was organized for the town and a troop of scout cavalry to watch the outlying districts. Major George Hatton, a former militia officer, organized a cavalry corps, the Alberta Mounted Rifles, which was later incorporated into the Alberta Field Force.[16] As things got organized, the defence of Calgary became the responsibility of Major James Walker, an ex-Superintendent of the North-West Mounted Police.

At Fort Macleod, Superintendent John Cotton, commander of the North-West Mounted Police post, prepared for the defence of the community and surrounding area by adding bastions to the stockade and taking precautionary defensive measures. "Provisions were secured and stored in the Fort, twenty horses saddled night and day - not that anyone intended to attempt escape, for there were no cowards but for emergencies and the use of couriers."[17] Fort Macleod had no telegraph or rail connections so Cotton established couriers at 12 mile intervals to relay messages to and from Calgary. At the same time, work started on a rail line and telegraph from Medicine Hat to Fort Macleod. An auxiliary unit was organized and equipped by Major John Stewart, a former militia officer, under the authority of the Militia Department. This unit, known as the Rocky Mountain Rangers, operated in conjunction with the Mounted Police to patrol between Fort Macleod and Medicine Hat, as well as to protect working parties on the railway construction between Dunmore and Lethbridge and the telegraph line between Dunmore and Fort Macleod.

There was a considerable amount of concern about what the Blackfoot would do since there were rumours of Cree messengers taking tobacco to the tribes and inviting them to join in the uprising. It was known that Louis Riel had tried to influence them to join him when they were camping in close proximity in Montana during the last great buffalo hunts. As soon as the rebellion started, attention was given to ensuring that the tribes of the Blackfoot Confederacy remained neutral. Cecil Denny, a former Inspector in the North-West Mounted Police, had been the Indian Agent for Treaty Seven. Following a hasty visit through the area by Lawrence Vankoughnet in 1884, Denny's staff was cut in an absurd move to save money. Denny promptly resigned in protest. When the rebellion started, he was asked to take charge of the Indians in Treaty Seven but declined to do so unless he was given full control and there was no interference from Ottawa. Denny's conditions were agreed to and he promptly doubled the rations for the Blackfoot, Bloods and Peigans. Throughout the period of tension, he visited the bands frequently and found they remained peaceful without outside intervention.

A factor in the government's favour was the traditional enmity between the Cree and the Blackfoot. When Indian Agent William B. Pocklington and Superintendent Cotton visited the Blood Reserve on April 7, the chief, Red Crow, told them the Bloods were willing to fight the Crees.[18] The idea of using Indians was given serious consideration in Ottawa and Sir John A. Macdonald asked whether some Blackfoot under white control could be trusted.[19] The chiefs quickly realized that the rebels had placed them in a position to drive a hard bargain with the government. The tribes of the Blackfoot Confederacy had their rations doubled and the Indian Agents and others dealing with them appear to have suddenly become more conciliatory. Cotton remained suspicious of their motives, even when the chiefs assured him of their loyalty.

A Trying Time

At Regina, Superintendent R. Burton Deane hired five Sioux in the Moose Jaw region to work as scouts under an ex-police interpreter, Jules Quesnel, who was taken on as a Special Constable. These scouts kept Deane informed of what was happening in Indian camps in the area. Inspector A.R. Macdonell, who had served there in previous years, returned to Wood Mountain with four men to supervise a number of half-breed scouts working under the direction of Jean Louis Légaré of Willow Bunch. They patrolled a long stretch from Moose Mountain to south-west of Old Wives' Lake. Later, as more men became available, twenty mounted men were sent from Regina to form an inner line of outposts to react to any intelligence received from the half-breed scouts.

When settlers and their families from Red Deer came into Calgary to report that their houses and stores had been raided by Indians, they were issued weapons and sent home with an escort of 15 scouts under Lieutenant John Corryell.[20] Closer to Edmonton, at Battle River Crossing, there were two Methodist missions, a Roman Catholic mission, a Hudson's Bay Company post, an I.G. Baker post and a free trader. Of the four Indian bands in the area, Bobtail's band was ready and willing to join the rebels, while those of Samson, Ermineskin and Muddy Bull were not. When the government staff fled to Edmonton and the Hudson's Bay Company post was abandoned, the chiefs could no longer control the young men in the bands and the trading post was pillaged. The trader said the Indians told him that Edmonton had been captured and there would be no goods left for them there and if they did not take his goods they would get nothing.[21]

The two Protestant missionaries, Reverend John Nelson and Reverend D.B. Glass, decided to take their families to Calgary. They were at the Nelson home loading up for the trip when the Indians arrived. The Indians trashed the house and took the horses but left the families unharmed.[22] Father Constantine Scollen, the Roman Catholic missionary, was able to exert some influence on the Indians who had done the looting and much of what was taken was returned, albeit the worse for

88

wear. He sent a message to the Mounted Police in Calgary saying that he "managed to crush the thing in the bud."[23]

When word of the uprising reached Fort Saskatchewan, Inspector Arthur Griesbach, who was the first man to join the North West Mounted Police in 1873, sent men out to warn the local settlers to move their families into the fort for protection. The stockade was repaired and the shrubbery cut to give clear fields of fire and view for 300 yards.[24] The citizens of Edmonton asked Griesbach to abandon Fort Saskatchewan and come into Edmonton with his men. He would not do this but agreed to help them organize their defences. He reported that the decision not to move his men to Edmonton resulted in his receiving "a large amount of abuse for not complying with their wishes."[25] Griesbach organized and armed a home guard, under Captain William Stiff and Lieutenant William Ibbotson based on the Hudson's Bay Company's Fort Edmonton. He had the fort's old brass 4-pounder guns refurbished and remounted. Due to a shortage of case shot, a homemade variety was produced by making tins to fit the bore of the guns and filling them with shot.

The settlers in the west filled the void when large numbers of Mounted Police were withdrawn from detachments and sent to the Saskatchewan. Eventually, there were home guards at such diverse places as Carrot River, Qu'Appelle, Battleford, Sturgeon River, Calgary, Edmonton, Pincher Creek, High River and Medicine Hat. In addition, there were troops along the Canadian Pacific Railway from Winnipeg to the Rockies for security. Most of these areas remained secure, but along the North Saskatchewan River trouble was brewing.

- 8 -
Frog Lake and Fort Pitt

The small settlement of Frog Lake, located approximately 35 miles north west of Fort Pitt and 140 miles from Battleford, had a native population of about 520 Wood Cree and Plains Cree in the area at the beginning of 1885. Frog Lake was the site of an Indian Agency, a Roman Catholic Church, a Hudson's Bay Company trading post and another store operated by George Dill. A grist mill was under construction about two miles away. The Frog Lake Mounted Police detachment was established on December 12, 1884, when the Indian Department asked for the men and agreed to provide accommodation.[1] This co-location with the Indian Department made it difficult for the Indians to see the Police as fair and impartial when any dispute or difference of opinion arose between them and the Farm Instructors or Indian Agents.

Following the Thirst Dance at Poundmaker's Reserve in 1884, Big Bear and his band moved to Fort Pitt and finally to Frog Lake when they were promised rations to get them through the winter. They might have remained there quietly despite the militant attitude of the war chief, Wandering Spirit, and Big Bear's son, Imasees, had the promise of providing rations been kept and had a less aggressive Indian Agent been in charge. The Indian Agent, Thomas Quinn, was left in Frog Lake despite, or perhaps because of, the knowledge that he was detested by the Indians. Although he was married to Owl Sitting, the niece of Lone Man of Big Bear's band, Quinn was hated by the Cree who referred to his as "Dog Agent." Quinn enjoyed exercising control over the starving Indians, keeping them subservient and dependent on him for food. In order to keep eating, they had to conceal their resentment, which grew deeper and stronger as they saw their children starve. To make matters worse there was a long-standing animosity between Quinn and the war chief, Wandering Spirit, so that "no opportunity had been lost by either to give vent to a mutual, though suppressed antipathy existing between them."[2]

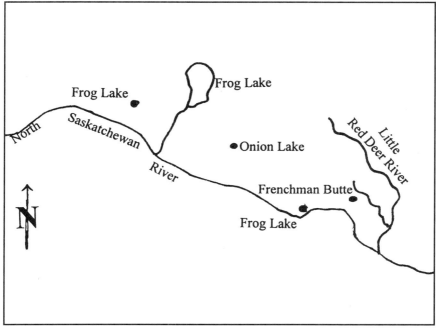

Frog Lake - Fort Pitt Area

Thomas Quinn was not the only object of Indian animosity. John Delaney, the Farm Instructor at Frog Lake, was equally detested by the Cree. He was alleged to have stolen the wife of an Indian, Sand Fly, then had the man jailed for theft when he protested. He also got into an altercation with Sand Fly's brother, Dancing Bull, and had him jailed, allegedly for the rather odd offence of witnessing the killing of a government ox. Sand Fly escaped from jail and was back in Frog Lake at the time of the massacre. There was a complaint about Delaney's behaviour which led to an investigation by the Mounted Police. Inspector Antrobus considered that Delaney had managed the arrests "in order to accomplish his designs," but Hayter Reed decided that this was not borne out by anything he could glean and Delaney remained in his position.[3]

91

A Trying Time

On March 31 when Inspector Dickens received news of the clash at Duck Lake, he sent Constable William Anderson to Frog Lake with a message to the Indian Agent, Thomas Quinn.[4] Anderson rode the 35 miles in just more than three hours in bad weather and darkness. The message he carried suggested that the whites at Frog Lake could come to Fort Pitt or, alternatively, Dickens and his men would come to Frog Lake, should the white residents decide to stay there. Quinn responded that the Indians were friendly and he did not foresee any trouble. He had apparently given some thought to the white people leaving but changed his mind, supposedly influenced by Father Felix Fafard who believed the whites should stay to show confidence in the Indians. Later that day, the whites met at the home of John Delaney and decided that the greatest potential source of danger was a clash between the Mounted Police detachment and the Indians. When Quinn told Corporal Sleigh to return to Fort Pitt with his detachment, Sleigh refused to leave and abandon the white women. Quinn then ordered him to go and gave him a letter to Inspector Dickens in which he explained that "the presence of a few policemen only served to irritate the Indians who had no animosity to the Indian Department officials, but only disliked the police."[5] Although this explanation is ludicrous given the intense animosity of the Indians toward both Quinn and Delaney, the police detachment departed in the early hours of April 1, taking with them the arms and ammunition from the Hudson's Bay Company post.

Thomas Quinn called a meeting of Big Bear's band at the Frog Lake Agency where he informed them of what had happened at Duck Lake and told them that 12 policemen had been killed. He asked them to send a message to Big Bear who was out hunting. The following day, when Big Bear returned, he came with his whole band to Quinn's house where the agent repeated the news about Duck Lake. Offering advice which unfortunately went unheeded, Wandering Spirit told Quinn that the best way to avoid trouble was for him and the other whites to go to Fort Pitt and leave someone else in charge of distributing rations until the Métis

92

agitation was resolved. Big Bear's son, Imasees, suggested that his father be provided sufficient rations for a feast since his hunting trip had been unsuccessful. Being totally insensitive to the seriousness of the situation in which he found himself, Quinn refused the request and when it was repeated he lost his temper.[6]

On the night of April 1, Imasees, Wandering Spirit and several of the young warriors hatched a plot, and the following morning the whites were rounded up by the Indians who had become completely frustrated by their treatment at Quinn's hands. Having lost faith in Big Bear's nonaggressive tactics, they decided to take the white people prisoner and help themselves to much-needed food and supplies. In the early hours of April 2, Choquapocase and Little Bad Man, two Plains Cree, entered the house of Thomas Quinn and took him prisoner. At the Hudson's Bay Company house, William Cameron had breakfast with Father Fafard, the local priest, Father Felix Marchand, the missionary visiting from Onion Lake, and Henry Quinn, nephew of the Indian Agent. Shortly afterward, Henry Quinn, warned by a friendly Métis, slipped away on foot to head for Fort Pitt. The Indians then ordered all the white men to Thomas Quinn's office, along with the interpreter, John Pritchard. Quinn, now sensing the full extent of the danger, called for an ox to be slaughtered in order to buy time. It was too little too late.

At the Hudson's Bay Company post several young Indians were busily helping themselves to anything they wanted. Fortunately, there was little ammunition because William Cameron and Constable Clarence Loasby had loaded most of it and sent it to Fort Pitt with Corporal Sleigh. At 10:00, the white people went to mass, followed by a number of Indians. While the service was in progress, Wandering Spirit entered and knelt on the floor with his Winchester in his hand, occasionally leveling it at the priest. The service was cut short. After leaving the church, the whites were ordered to assemble at the Mounted Police and Indian Department buildings. When the Indians started looting the stores, homes and church, they came across large supplies of liquid pain killers which contained a high percentage of alcohol as well as a number of casks of communion wine, which they consumed.

The long-standing feud between Wandering Spirit and Thomas Quinn now escalated into a fatal confrontation, triggered by Quinn's arrogance and ignorance. When Wandering Spirit told Thomas Quinn to move to a new camp on the shore of Frog Lake, Quinn refused, saying he would not take orders. Wandering Spirit warned him twice and when the warnings went unheeded, he shot him. This started a blood bath as the Indians escorting the other whites to government buildings gave vent to suppressed rage which had built up over a number of years. Several of the bodies were then mutilated or burned.[7]

Charles Jouin, a Métis, who was wounded in the first volley, was shot at close range by Miserable Man. When Big Bear heard the shots, he ran out shouting "Stop! Stop!" Father Marchand was shot trying to reach his friend Father Fafard. George Dill, the storekeeper and William Gilchrist ran, but were ridden down and killed. John Williscroft, the Farm Instructor, and John Delaney were also shot. The only white male survivor was William Bleasdell Cameron who was taken by Yellow Bear and sent quietly away from the scene with a group of women. Because he had befriended the Indians, Wandering Spirit agreed that Cameron need not die. The bodies of Father Fafard, Father Marchand, John Gowanlock and John Delaney were thrown into the cellar of the Church and the dirt walls were pushed in on them. Quinn and Gouin were buried in the cellar of John Pritchard's house.[8] The others were left where they fell.

Two Métis, John Pritchard and Louis Goulet, were taken prisoner, as were Mrs. Therese Gowanlock and Mrs. Therese Delaney. The two white women were in serious danger but John Pritchard sold all his possessions to trade for them with his captors and was thus able to protect the women. Big Bear visited the women and apologized for what had happened, telling them "there were many bad men in his camp over whom he had no control."[9] Shortly after the killings, the Hudson's

Frog Lake And Fort Pitt

Bay Company supervisor, James Simpson, returned from Fort Pitt and was also taken prisoner. Big Bear immediately visited him to assure him that the murders were not his doing When Simpson admonished him, saying he never thought he would live to see such a thing, Big Bear told him, "It is not my work. They have tried for a long time to take away my good names and they have done it at last."[10]

Following the clash at Duck Lake and the massacre at Frog Lake, there were isolated incidents of local looting. On April 26, the Beaver Lake band, under pressure to join Wandering Spirit and the Frog Lake Cree, raided two abandoned trading posts. The Island Lake and Waterhen bands looted the Hudson's Bay Company depot at Green Lake.[11] On April 11 at Bear's Hills, south of Edmonton, some young warriors raided the Hudson's Bay Company post and some empty homes at Battle River Crossing.[12] The Frog Lake Cree went forty miles north to Cold Lake and seized the Hudson's Bay Company post and captured Henry Halpin of the Hudson's Bay Company and John Fitzpatrick of the Indian Department and brought them to Frog Lake. Since Fitzpatrick was an American and Riel expected to have help from the United States, the Métis did not harm him.

Whatever hope Big Bear may have had of gaining concessions for his people by mounting a successful diplomatic crusade was now gone. The fact that Wandering Spirit, Imasees, Lucky Man and the "Warriors Lodge" had taken control of the band made no difference in people's perceptions. Big Bear was considered the leader and he would take the blame. All the Indians in the area were dragged into the rebellion, although many may not have wanted any part of it. These murders implicated the Cree in the Métis rebellion and there was now no turning back for them. As the news spread, this event would do more than almost any other single event to harden the attitude of the people in Canada against Big Bear and his band.

Big Bear had now lost much of his power and influence and could only attempt to minimize the damage. When the young men erected a warrior lodge, Big

95

Bear lost most of his authority and Wandering Spirit, as war chief, became the primary leader. Big Bear could counsel restraint and exert some influence but in the final analysis he lacked any real authority and control was now in the hands of Wandering Spirit, Little Poplar, and Big Bear's son, Imasees. Later, at his trial, Big Bear said: "You think I encouraged my people to take part in the trouble. I did not. I advised them against it. I felt sorry when they killed those men at Frog Lake, but the truth is when the news of the fight at Duck Lake reached us my band ignored my authority and despised me because I did not side with the half-breeds. I did not so much as take a white man's horse. I always believed that by being the friend of the white man, I and my people would be helped by those of them who had wealth. I always thought it paid to do all the good I could. Now my heart is on the ground."[13]

Thirty-five miles away, in Fort Pitt, Inspector Dickens was, at this point, totally unaware of the events at Frog Lake. Fort Pitt was not a fort in any military sense of the word. It was essentially a group of buildings in the form of a hollow square on a flat area on the north bank of the North Saskatchewan River. There were no palisades, no bastions and no cannon. The whole area was surrounded by hills which afforded excellent fields of fire to an attacking enemy. In any protracted fight, the so-called fort would be virtually indefensible and could be put out of action very quickly. Even Chief Factor William McLean's young daughter was not impressed, noting "We could not have withstood a siege even for a few days, since the fort was built on a flat with the hills around us, and though there were lots of provisions in the store, we had no water in the fort, but had to get it from the river - a distance of about four hundred yards. It seems strange for a Hudson's Bay fort that no well had been dug within its walls."[14]

The North-West Mounted Police detachment, consisting of an Inspector and 22 men, was largely tied down in the fort due to a chronic shortage of horses.

North West Mounted Police At Fort Pitt   HBCA N-13504

In addition to the policemen, there were twenty-eight civilians, mostly traders and their families. Some time previously, Chief Factor William McLean of the Hudson's Bay Company had spoken to Inspector Dickens and Thomas Quinn about the Indian's hostile attitude and advised that government employees and other whites be brought into Fort Pitt. Dickens said this fell within the jurisdiction of the Indian Agent and he did not wish to interfere.[15]

On March 23, 1885, Inspector Dickens heard that the Indians in the Fort Carlton area were in arms but official word did not come until a week later when Indian Agent Rae wrote giving full details of the events at Duck Lake. There was concern that Big Bear's Indians would head for Battleford, but Quinn assured Dickens that he could keep them from leaving Frog Lake "by feeding them well and treating them kindly."[16] Despite his assurances, he then refused to feed them and treated them anything but kindly.

The policemen at Fort Pitt prepared for an attack as best they could, filling the gaps between buildings "with carts, wagons and timber."[17] The windows in the buildings were barricaded by sacks of flour and loopholes cut in the walls. Some small outbuildings that could provide shelter and cover for attacking Indians were pulled down and the material from them used in the barricades between the buildings.[18]   Since they had few horses, the Hudson's Bay Company carpenters started work on a scow in which anyone evacuated could float down the river if necessary.

In a letter to Inspector Dickens, sent with Corporal Sleigh, Thomas Quinn had repeated that things were quiet at Frog Lake and he had no fear of a disturbance, but he asked Dickens to check on Mrs. George Mann, wife of the Farm Instructor at Onion Lake, to see if she wanted to leave.   Dickens sent Sergeant John Martin to Onion Lake on April 1 and while he was there the Indians came up to the house firing their weapons and yelling.[19]   When they told Martin they had heard 2,000 soldiers were on the way, coming to kill them, he assured them that if they remained quiet they would come to no harm.[20]

On April 2, Constable Frederick Roby went from Fort Pitt to Onion Lake for a load of lumber.[21]   On his return, he reported to Inspector Dickens that there were vague rumours of "troubles"   That afternoon friendly Indians came and told the Mann family what had happened at Frog Lake and warned them to flee.   They showed the Manns a back way to escape and the family barely got away when they heard shouts and gunfire behind them as their house was looted.[22] The following morning at 1:00 a.m., George Mann and family arrived at Fort Pitt and confirmed the news of the Frog Lake massacre.   A few hours later, about 5:00 a.m., Chief Cut Arm from the Onion Lake Reserve arrived on the high ridge behind Fort Pitt and signed that he wanted someone to come out to see him.   When Inspector Dickens decided it was unsafe for him or any of his men to go, William McLean went with his interpreter.   The Indians had brought Reverend and Mrs. Charles Quinney from Frog Lake.   Chief Cut Arm told McLean that the stories from Frog Lake were true that no Hudson's Bay Company men had been killed and that the two white women, Mrs. Gowanlock and Mrs. Delaney, were alive and prisoners of Big Bear.

Frog Lake And Fort Pitt

Later in the day, Harry Quinn, who escaped from Frog Lake just in time, arrived at Fort Pitt and was subsequently sent on to Battleford with a letter to Inspector Morris telling him what had happened and asking for 50 men. Morris' reply, which was never received at Fort Pitt, since the courier was intercepted and his dispatch taken away, said "I am wholly powerless and can render you no assistance whatever as we are surrounded by Indians and need all the men we have to cope with them here. . . . Please make no delay in coming to Battleford."[23] On his return to Fort Pitt, Quinn was sworn in as a Special Constable. Following this, all was quiet for several days although those in the fort spent their time in constant fear and apprehension.

On April 13, Inspector Dickens sent out a three-man patrol in an attempt to establish the whereabouts of the Indian bands. Chief Factor William McLean later recalled that he "remonstrated" with Dickens, since the men were not familiar with the country and did not understand Indian tactics. He warned Dickens that the men, their horses and their weapons were almost certain to be captured by the Indians.[24] Dickens insisted and around eleven in the morning, three mounted scouts, Constable David Cowan, Constable Clarence Loasby and Special Constable Harry Quinn, went out.[25] The three scouts reached Frog Lake Village where they saw burned out buildings but no activity.

Not long after the scouts left, about 250 Crees arrived on the high ground above Fort Pitt and, as the occupants of the Fort watched, some of the Indians rode slowly down from the hill and opened fire on the cattle grazing outside the fort. The Indians then butchered the animals and carried the meat back up the hill for their feast.[26] An old Indian came to the fort and asked for tea, tobacco, a blanket and some kettles, all of which were provided.[27] The people in the Fort were told, by a man named Dufresne, that the Indians had brought coal oil with them from Frog Lake to burn Fort Pitt, that Edmonton had fallen, and the Métis were on the way to assist the Indians.[28] Despite this disturbing news and the fact that the position was virtually indefensible, Dickens resolved to defend the fort until help arrived. There was a critical shortage of ammunition, with the policemen having about forty rounds each, a few of the civilians eighteen and the rest were armed with muzzle loaders from the Hudson's Bay Company stores.[29]

In the evening, some Indians approached the Fort, stopped some 300 yards away and sent a messenger to ask Chief Factor McLean to come talk to them. Some of the Head Men told him the chiefs wished to see him in the morning at which time they would tell him what they had come for and what they intended to do.[30] They assured him that there would be no attack on the Fort that night. McLean returned the next day and was told that Big Bear and the other chiefs were in Council at the top of the hill and to go up to them. When McLean met with them, the chiefs reiterated their long list of grievances and, when McLean tried to persuade them to return to the reserves Chief Cut Arm told him "Your words are mighty, but we did not consult you in time, and now we cannot act on your good advice as we are pledged to Louis Riel to carry on what he got us to commence."[31] The chiefs added "that the time had now arrived when they were going to kill all the red coats and clean all the white people out of the country." As McLean continued his attempt to dissuade them, Wandering Spirit walked up to him, loading cartridges into his rifle, put a hand on his shoulder and said, "That will do, you have said enough, we do not want to hear anything about the government and if you want to live to do so I will tell you don't be stubborn, that is the reason why I shot the agent." [32]

While McLean was talking to the chiefs, the three man patrol sent to Frog Lake the previous day was on its way back to Fort Pitt, unaware that the Indians were already there. As they approached the fort, they came across the trail of many hoof prints but were undecided about what they meant. When they discovered that the Indians lay between them and the fort, eighteen-year-old Constable Cowan, described by Sam Steele as "a fiery, hot-headed lad," who was in charge of the patrol, decided to ride through them.[33] Harry Quinn did not agree but Cowan jeered and called him scared and then rode on.[34] Loasby followed Cowan while Quinn turned back into the woods and escaped.

As Constables Cowan and Loasby galloped through the Indian camp, there was great excitement. As Louis Goulet described the scene: "It was just past noon, the tea kettles and pots were starting to sing, when somebody shouted: 'Look out it's the Mounted Police coming at us from the rear!' Ah!, cré diable, you should have seen the excitement then!"[35] The Indians rushed to cut off the two policemen, while firing at them at the same time. Constable Cowan was right in the line of fire and, as the shots rang out, his horse reared and threw him. When one of the Indians, Lewison Mongrain, approached Cowan, who was lying on the ground, the young policeman raised his head and said, "Don't shoot me brother."[36] Mongrain was reported to have shot him twice in the head and taken his equipment, but Cameron and Goulet say that Mongrain left Cowan who was then shot from the woods by somebody else. Later, when Louis Goulet went to where a crowd of Indians was gathered around Cowan's body, he found they had opened the chest and torn out his heart. One of the Indians said to him, "Take a look at this. An Indian can eat the heart of a white man, but a white man can't eat an Indian's."[37] The remains of the mutilated heart were impaled on a stick near the body.

The second scout, Constable Loasby, was hit by a bullet from behind and a little to the left while riding at high speed and pursued by Lone Man. A second bullet was fired at close range by an Indian galloping at the off quarters of Loasby's horse, which was also hit by a bullet from the same Winchester. The Indian who fired, presumably Lone Man, and his horse collided with Loasby and his wounded mount and the two men and their horses were all thrown to the ground.[38] As Loasby rose and tried to run, Lone Man knelt and shot him in the back, then rolled him over and stripped him of his cartridge belt and weapons. When Amelia McLean saw an Indian approach Loasby with a drawn knife, she was the first person to shoot from a loophole to give Loasby covering fire. To everyone's surprise, Loasby got to his feet, spurting blood, and staggered to the barricade where he was rescued by a Hudson's Bay Company clerk named Stanley Simpson who jumped over the barricade, got him to his feet and dragged him into the Fort. The Police in the fort fired at Lone Man but did not hit him. The third man on the patrol, Special Constable Harry Quinn, who veered off from the Indian camp, rode down the bank of the North Saskatchewan River and hid among the poplars along the river bank.

Chief Factor McLean who was talking to the Indians when the Mounted Police patrol appeared, jumped up to return to the fort. Wandering Spirit, who had gone in pursuit of the policemen, returned with his smoking Winchester and made it clear to McLean that he and his interpreter, Francois Dufresne, were prisoners. He made McLean hold up his hands and swear that he would not leave the Indians.[39] When McLean witnessed the death of Cowan and the wounding of Loasby, he realized that he and the other occupants of the fort were in a very dangerous position. Wandering Spirit assured him that if he promised not to escape, he and his family would be spared and cared for. He explained that the young warriors wanted to attack the Mounted Police but McLean's family was in the way so he should send his wife a note and ask her to come out of the fort. On consideration, McLean realized that the fort could not be held and that it would be better for his family to surrender voluntarily.

McLean asked that the Police to be allowed to go free, since the Indians would then have the supplies from the fort and the civilians as hostages, but Wandering Spirit said they would kill them before sundown. Big Bear intervened and the Indians eventually agreed to allow the Police to go, on the condition that they surrendered their arms. McLean then "explained to them that the soldiers of the Queen were supposed to die with their arms rather than give them up without a struggle, and that I felt sure there would be no use asking them to give up their rifles, but as for their horses and other things they might not care so much."[40] Given that the Police were woefully short of horses this was not a great sacrifice.

Big Bear told William McLean to have his family and the other civilians come out of the fort and to tell the Mounted Police to evacuate immediately since he could not restrain his young men any longer.[41] McLean sent a note to his wife to tell her of Big Bear's demands and warn her that the Indians would burn the buildings. Two of McLean's daughters, Amelia 18 and Kitty 14, came out to see him and assured him all was well inside the Fort. He told them of the terms set by the Indians and his plan that the Mounted Police should leave by the barge that had been built in the Fort, thus frustrating any plan Wandering Spirit might have to pursue them if they left on foot. He told his wife that she should be the last to leave, thus ensuring that the policemen would get away. The two girls went back with the message and the Mounted Police immediately began tarring the seams of the newly constructed scow in an attempt to make it waterproof. McLean subsequently received a note from his wife in which she said she had shown Inspector Dickens the note about her going out with the family to join him but that "he was so confused and excited that he did not know what to suggest, nor how to act."[42] McLean also told his wife to advise Dickens to take the furs that were stored in the fort because, being baled, they could be piled up around the sides of the boat as some protection from small arms fire.

The Indians sent a messenger under a flag of a truce with a letter dictated to John Pritchard by Big Bear. The letter said the Police should get out of Fort Pitt as soon as possible. They were advised to try to get away before afternoon since the "young men are wild and hard to keep in hand."[43] Inspector Dickens, who had resolved to defend the fort, now decided that with nobody left to protect he would abandon it since more than 20 policemen becoming martyrs would not accomplish anything. When all was ready, the men boarded the scow, which was laden with provisions, arms and ammunition, and moved downstream and across the river, out of the way of the Indians. Mrs. McLean waited while they embarked and did not leave Fort Pitt until the scow "disappeared among the drifting ice round the first bend of the river."[44]

Those who remained watched the crossing with apprehension. Elizabeth McLean recalled that "the river was a raging torrent with huge slabs of ice piling up. It was a miracle they ever got across safely. It seemed to us the scow might be upset any minute."[45] The leaking scow was piloted through the ice with great skill by Constable Richard Routledge and, with much hard baling, came to a halt on the south bank about a mile downstream from Fort Pitt.[46] After a miserable night with a heavy snowfall, the policemen resumed the perilous 100 mile journey down the ice filled North Saskatchewan River to Battleford. For six days, they made their way through the ice jams, in extremely cold weather, with everyone suffering greatly, especially the wounded man, Constable Loasby. Eventually, after several narrow escapes, they reached Battleford safely and joined the garrison there, possibly feeling a little like they had come out of the frying pan into the fire.

The *Kingston Daily News* later stated that Factor McLean's "timidity embarrassed the police, and proved fatal to the liberty of more than twenty-five whites, man, women and children."[47] Inspector Dickens, in the same vein, reported that "The surrender of the civilians was entirely owing to the pusillanimity of Mr. Maclean [sic] of the Hudson's Bay Company."[48] When McLean heard what was in the Police report, he responded in a surprisingly mild way, saying that "the endeavour to place the responsibility for the downfall of Fort Pitt upon him was, to say the least of it . . . both inconsiderate and unkind."[49] General Middleton supported McLean, saying ". . . I am of the opinion that Mr. McLean is not responsible for the fall of Fort Pitt, and that his line of conduct in the matter showed considerable strength of mind, and great confidence in his personal influence over the Indians, which the result shows he was fully justified in having."[50]

North West Mounted Police Band Plays For Fort Pitt Survivors   PAM N-12395

The abandonment of Fort Pitt ultimately made good sense but it did nothing to enhance the reputation of Inspector Dickens, who had never been highly regarded by his superiors. Instead of being looked on as one who had extricated his men from a no-win situation, he was seen as an officer who abandoned his post, and the women and children in it, to the Indians. It is interesting that, despite the threats that were made, the Cree did not organize an attack on the Mounted Police who were highly vulnerable in the scow on the river.

As soon as the Mounted Police were out of the fort, the Indians came in and looted everything in sight. Special Constable Harry Quinn who, after his narrow escape, had hidden in some poplars, crept down to the fort during the night. At dawn he carefully approached the fort and called out for Sergeant John Martin. To his surprise his call was answered by Wandering Spirit. When he tried to escape again, Quinn was quickly captured. Fortunately, his life was spared. The prisoners were assigned to the custody of certain tribe members. William McLean reported that he found himself ". . . with my family and servants consigned to the care of one of the leading men of Chief Big Bear, a Plain Cree, known as 'Little Poplar,' who, though a very active and turbulent agitator, proved himself a very indifferent caterer."[51]

The Cree continued to loot the buildings at Fort Pitt then, when they were done, moved back to Frog Lake in a straggling column which stretched for miles with scouts in front and a rearguard to gather up anyone who lagged. The trail was rough, with snow, water and mud, and the prisoners had to walk. By this time, the Indians had twenty-seven whites and a much larger number of Métis as prisoners and hostages. The messengers sent by Louis Riel to bring the Cree to his aid, kept up the pressure on them to move east and join Poundmaker, then take Battleford and move on to join Riel. McLean got the Wood Cree to resist this in the council and the Indians decided to send couriers to determine what the situation was at Battleford.[52] These couriers were present when the battle started at Cut Knife Hill but did not stay to see the end. They reported that soldiers and Police were fighting Poundmaker's band and they thought the soldiers would win.[53]

Big Bear, whose influence was greatly diminished, went through the camp and told the people "You have heard the report brought to you by the couriers that were sent to bring news from Poundmaker. It is an alarming one for you, what are you going to do about it? You were in a hurry to commence trouble and now you have it. The soldiers of the Queen have come to fight you and very shortly you will likely have to show how you can fight them."[54] The Cree first remained in the Frog Lake area for some time, uncertain what to do, then returned to Fort Pitt and camped on Pipestone Creek. They took more supplies of flour and bacon out of the buildings at Fort Pitt then set fire to those used by the Mounted Police. The fire spread and most of the buildings burned to the ground.

A list of the North-West Mounted Police members in the Frog Lake Detachment in 1885 can be found at Appendix "C." A list of the members of the North-West Mounted Police in the Fort Pitt Detachment in 1885 can be found at Appendix "D."

- 9 -
Battleford

Battleford, the largest settlement between Prince Albert and Edmonton, was the home of a large concentration of Mounted Police and the Indian Department Agency for a large surrounding area. The town, situated at the junction of the Battle and North Saskatchewan rivers, consisted of what was called the Old Town, the New Town and the North-West Mounted Police Barracks or Fort Battleford, all separated by the rivers. At freeze-up in the fall and break up in the spring these rivers became virtually impassable. In 1885, the Mounted Police detachment of 43 men was commanded by Inspector William S. Morris, a New Brunswicker, who had been appointed to the force the previous year at the age of 36. He was not popular with the local residents, had little experience with Indians and settlers and did not seem comfortable dealing with them.

The residents in the Battleford area had never been happy about the large numbers of armed Indians who roamed the plains near their homes. Their concerns grew more acute when the government moved additional Indians, including Big Bear's and Piapot's bands, from the south. As the settlers' apprehension grew along the Saskatchewan, the tension also increased. On March 11, in response to the heightened tension, Inspector Joseph Howe took 25 men and a 7-pounder gun to Fort Carlton. Surgeon Robert Miller and 20 more men followed five days later but, due to a shortage of horses, had to hire civilian transport.[1]

The departure of so many men to reinforce Fort Carlton created concern for the citizens of Battleford who felt they were inadequately protected so, on March 20, some 42 civilians enrolled in the Home Guard. By this time, personnel problems in the North-West Mounted Police had become so acute that the Commissioner authorized the return of deserters to duty.[2] Men who would have been invalided or dismissed were now retained for the duration of the emergency. A constable who was found medically unfit on March 15, 1885, shortly before the

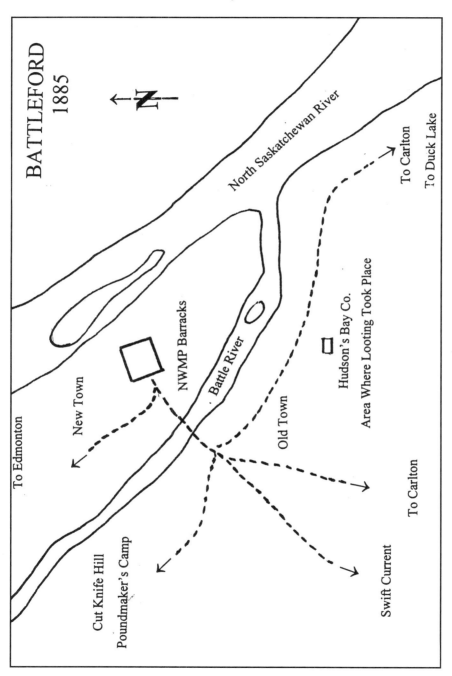

clash at Duck Lake, because he could not ride and was shortsighted, was retained until the insurrection was over. On August 22, 1885, following the rebellion, Assistant Surgeon J. Widmer Rolph confirmed him as unfit, noting that "He has never shot but once at a target in over four years as he could not see it clearly enough to distinguish a bull's eye from an outer."[3]

On March 27, when a messenger arrived with details of the fighting at Duck Lake, panic set in around Battleford. The Mounted Police barracks was fortified by erecting two bastions at opposite ends of the stockade and removing any nearby buildings that would provide cover for an enemy and restrict fields of fire. As at Fort Pitt, the barracks had no well and water had to be drawn from the Battle River where water parties were vulnerable to small arms fire from concealed positions, so the Police brought all available barrels in the area into the barracks and filled them with water. The local residents, including large numbers of women and children, moved into the barracks for protection and to their chagrin were immediately placed under strict military discipline by Inspector Morris.

Peter Ballendine went to Poundmaker's Reserve to inform the bands located there about the events at Duck Lake. Seeing this as an opportunity to get extra rations for affirming his loyalty, Poundmaker decided to go to Battleford and in order that officials would be aware of his plans, sent a message to say he was coming into town to see the Indian Agent.[4] When the settlers heard the Indians were on the move, there was widespread panic and those who were not already there fled to the Mounted Police barracks in Battleford, abandoning their farms, homes, horses, food, weapons and ammunition.

In this high state of excitement, Inspector Morris received a request from Commissioner Irvine to provide reinforcements for Fort Carlton. He immediately responded, saying "I have forty-three men and fifteen horses. I am sending forthwith twenty-five policemen and twenty-five volunteers to Carlton."[5] The citizens of Battleford were very unhappy at the prospect of being left, as they saw

110

Inspector William S. Morris   NAC PA-042149

it, practically undefended. The civilian volunteers did not materialize. Sergeant Frederick Bagley left immediately with 25 men, ammunition and stores. When he was about 6 miles from Fort Carlton, he could see the abandoned fort burning. A messenger arrived with a note from Irvine directing him to return to Battleford.

On the way back the party was engulfed in a raging snow storm a short distance from Battleford and when they reached the North Saskatchewan River they found that following a recent thaw and the new wet snow, the river ice was covered with three feet of running water. By attaching long ropes and pulling the sleighs across by hand, they managed to get everything across the river. The men and horses, spaced at a safe distance from each other, waded across and all returned to the barracks safely.[6]

On March 28, Indian Agent John Rae went to the Stoney Reserve where he was assured by the Farm Instructor, James Payne, that the Stoneys would not give trouble and would, in fact, side with the whites if trouble came. Judge Charles Rouleau, not relishing the thought of a visit from the Indians, left with his family and that of James Rae, who would have been very happy had he been able to join them on the trip himself. When he departed, Judge Rouleau assured the editor of the *Saskatchewan Herald* that "his only object in going away was to hasten troops to our relief." The editor commented that "if their progress is the result of what he calls haste we would like to know what he calls leisure."[7]

On their way into Battleford, some of the 200 armed Indians from Little Pine's band broke into the Finlayson brothers' farm house and removed everything they could carry as well as breaking into two houses in the old town at Battleford.[8] In his inimitable style, P.G. Laurie reported in the *Saskatchewan Herald* that "these 'peaceable and well-disposed Indians' raided the houses of Daniel Finlayson, John D. Finlayson, Thomas Macfarlane, J.M. Macfarlane, burning some of them, driving off a hundred head of choice cattle and half as many horses; and this done they were ready for a 'friendly' talk with the agent."[9]

Battleford

Early on the morning of March 30, the Indians who had assembled at Poundmaker's Reserve arrived in Battleford and went to Indian Agent Rae's office on the south bank of the Battle River where the houses and stores had been deserted. They were met by William McKay of the Hudson's Bay Company and Peter Ballendine. Poundmaker said they had come to ask for supplies and insisted on speaking to Rae who was not about to endanger himself by leaving the fort. "During a heated talk Poundmaker expressed surprise that the agent would not meet them."[10] He wanted to send a message to Rae, who was hunkering down inside the fort and unlikely to move. Ballendine sent a note but added a postscript of his own that indicated that the Indians were "armed to the teeth . . . pretty hostile . . . and . . . I won't advise you to come over."[11] Rae, who needed no encouragement to stay in the fort and avoid Indians, sent a message to Lieutenant Governor Dewdney in Regina saying "Indians 300 strong in possession of Indian School and mean war."[12]

Meanwhile, inside the fortified barracks, Inspector Morris telegraphed Frederick White to tell him that "the Indians are now camped within a mile of the barracks." He reported that "their program was to burn the village and attack the barracks last night." He estimated the number of Indians at "about six hundred all told" and added "it is said the Riel party are on the way to join Poundmaker which they can easily do now the Commissioner has gone to Prince Albert." Morris ended his message by saying, "It is urgent that we should have reinforcements at once. Any delay will prove most disastrous."[13] The Indians milling around the abandoned buildings were fed by Arthur Dobbs, the cook at the Indian School, and provided with food from the Hudson's Bay Company store by William McKay.[14]

Since this part of town was deserted, the Indians soon began to help themselves to items from abandoned homes and stores, despite efforts by some of their leaders to bring them under control. After a time, realizing there would be repercussions to what they had done, the Indians left to go back to the reserve. Dewdney telegraphed Frederick White to tell him, "Indians at Battleford gone with

Looting Of Old Town Of Battleford   NAC C-007523

booty to Poundmaker's Reserve, taking horses and cattle. . . ."[15] Inspector Morris, in the barracks, does not seem to have been as well informed since he telegraphed that he was "well fortified have 200 determined men. May be attacked tonight but do not think so. Indians extremely wild."[16] After the abortive attempt to meet with the Indian Agent, the Cree returned to their reserve, leaving the only activity around Battleford to some Stoneys and Métis. Had the Cree been so inclined, they could easily have laid siege to the Mounted Police barracks, cut off access to the water supply in the river and, at a minimum, made life even more miserable for the demoralized townspeople huddled in the fort.

Since the telegraph lines were down from time to time, it was necessary to use couriers to carry messages between Battleford, Fort Pitt, Prince Albert and Swift Current. A curious aspect of the rebellion was that Métis working as couriers for the Militia or North-West Mounted Police often travelled in relative safety. Most of them had relatives or friends with the rebels and would not be killed, although

114

they were usually robbed and sent on their way or, in the worst cases, held prisoner. Mounted policemen were at much greater risk. All couriers were instructed to destroy the messages they had with them if they were in imminent danger of being captured.

Judge Rouleau's party that fled from Battleford stopped for the night at James Payne's house on the Stoney Reserve south of town. The Rouleau family had an old nurse who was very nervous. She woke the family early in the morning and once they were up they decided to be on their way.[17] They continued on to Swift Current. Later in the morning, a Stoney Indian named Itka or Crooked Legs came to the Payne home, looking for food. Payne and Itka had a long-standing enmity. Some time previously, Payne's wife, who was a daughter of Chief Grizzly Bear's Head, had treated her niece, who was Itka's daughter, for tuberculosis. The girl had a habit of walking into Payne's house without knocking, which annoyed Payne and he threw her out the door. She then had a hemorrhage and died. Up to this time her father, Itka, had buried his resentment but it was now payback time with a vengeance. Itka and Payne soon became involved in a short argument and Itka was evicted. He then returned and shot and killed Payne, a killing more of revenge than rebellion.

Early on the morning of March 31, Chief Red Pheasant and his brother, Baptiste, woke their Farm Instructor, George Applegarth, to warn him of danger. Applegarth gathered his family and the school teacher, George Cunningham, and left. A little time later, five Assiniboine Indians, Way-wah-nitch, Itengeska, Shinacap, Keonkask and Niantanach, came upon a rancher, Barney Tremont, greasing his wagon for a trip into town. Tremont was said to be notorious among the Indians for having once turned a half-frozen boy away from his house during a blizzard. Without any warning, Way-wah-nitch shot Tremont through the back of the head, clubbed him, and trashed his house before moving on. The Indians then went to Prongua where they looted and burned the homes of some ex-members of the Mounted Police who had taken up farming - Harry Nash, Anthony Prongua, George Gopsill, Joseph Price, a '74 Original, and a civilian, Harry Phipps.[18] The residents had started for Battleford but were caught on the road by the Indians who demanded that the Gopsill family and Thomas Hodson, who accompanied them, give up their horses and any personal property they had with them. When Hodson gave the Indians a horse, the party was allowed to go on with the team and their wagon, which the Indians emptied. One Indian even tried to tear a shawl from the Gopsill child. Joseph Price, with his wife and children, who were driving behind the Gopsills, was not so lucky. He and his family were ousted from their wagon and left, without transport, ten miles from town. Nez Perce Jack, who had tried to grab the Gopsill child's shawl, now unsuccessfully tried to take Mrs. Price's dress. Fortunately, George Gopsill saw what happened and brought the Prices into town on his wagon.[19]

In Battleford, looting was a problem. When the Cree first departed, parties were able to cross the river and bring back supplies which had been abandoned in the hasty rush to seek the protection of the fort. Once the Métis moved in to systematically loot whatever had been left in the town, parties attempting to cross the river were fired on, as were some of those sent out to draw water. When four men seen robbing a store were fired on by the 7-pounder gun at the fort, the home guard crossed the river and recovered the wagons and their contents for the fort. The following day, when several Indians and Métis were seen removing loot from stores in South Battleford, the gun again came into use and the thieves fled, abandoning a horse and buckboard, which were also retrieved.

When two Métis, Joseph Nolin and Joseph Vandal, were caught looting the Hudson's Bay Company store, Inspector Morris sent Sergeant Major Kirk and 12 men to raid the Métis camp at the junction of the Battle and North Saskatchewan Rivers. A number of occupants were rounded up and taken to the fort. At about this time, a man named Bremner arrived from Bresaylor Settlement and asked for an escort to go there to bring the people in safely. When questioned, his responses were considered contradictory and he was incarcerated in the guard room. The people in Bresaylor were subsequently rounded up by the rebels and taken to Poundmaker's camp.

Burning and looting increased as the Indians plundered and torched the farm of Robert Wyld and Frederick Bourke.[20] In Battleford, rebels with fifty carts were systematically emptying buildings while abandoned houses on the south bank of the river were looted by Stoney Indians who had a clash with the local home guard. The Mahaffy and Clinkskill general store and the Indian School stables were burned.

The telegraph line from Battleford was working well some of the time and Inspector Morris poured out an impressive flood of situation reports and appeals for help. There was some strange message traffic passing through the system, such as when Morris reported that a courier met 300 mounted Indians about 25 miles from Battleford and "not knowing the country he was not sure in which direction they were moving."[21] Using couriers who do not know the country and the points of the compass seems a curious practice. He also once reported "I am totally in the dark as to the movements of Indians; I have not seen one the whole day."[22]

On April 9, Morris sent a telegram reporting that "Poundmaker's program was to attack us three days ago. Running of river interfered. Indians line river and keep up steady fire on our watermen. . . . Forty Stonies have gone up to join Big Bear. No word of Herchmer yet."[23] On April 11, he sent another message to Ottawa warning that "Poundmaker's program is to take Pitt, consolidate force and take Battleford. One hundred men pushed on with despatch would reach here in time and frustrate their plans. Nearly four hundred women and children expect this and must be saved."[24] There was no indication of the source of the intelligence about Poundmaker's plans being passed on by Inspector Morris, but it might have been from half-breed couriers who were usually the only people outside the fort, other than Mounted Police patrols.

By mid April there was concern that nothing had been heard from Fort Pitt since the massacre. Josie Alexander, the courier sent to Fort Pitt, was robbed of his weapon, horse and dispatches so Morris had difficulty getting another man to go. Due to the large number of Métis in the barracks, he noted that he feared "the enemy within more than I do those without at this fort."[25] When this caught the eye of those in Ottawa, Commissioner Irvine was later ordered to obtain from Morris, confidential reports on the individuals "of whose loyalty there were the gravest suspicions."[26]

On April 19, John Pambrun and James Bird returned from Fort Pitt with news of the fall of the fort and said that no whites had been seen. There was a report that two men had been killed and the rest escaped by boat. On April 21, Constables John Hynes and Charles Allen, with guide Josie Alexander, returned from a patrol to report that the Mounted Police from Frog Lake and Fort Pitt who escaped in a scow down the ice choked North Saskatchewan River, were about 45 miles upstream.[27] The next day the men arrived at Battleford to an honour guard and a band playing. The *Battleford Post Journal* said the reasons for Inspector Dickens having abandoned Fort Pitt were that the Mounted Police were outnumbered 12 to one, and due to "McLean and his family and all the civilians in the Fort going into Big Bear's camp for safety, preferring to trust 'Big Bear' rather than the Police."[28] On his arrival in Battleford, Dickens, being senior, should have assumed command but Inspector Morris appears for some reason to have been reluctant to relinquish the reins.

While impatiently waiting for the arrival of Otter's Column, which had not yet even started from Swift Current, Inspector Morris fired off a series of messages appealing for help and emphasizing the danger to the occupants of the fort. On April 13, he warned, "do not assume danger is less imminent as it may explode at

Superintendent William Herchmer   NAC PA-042142

any minute."[29] The next day he noted, "there is a general uneasiness on the part of the women in barracks."[30] Under pressure from residents as well as their relatives in Eastern Canada, Adolphe Caron wired General Middleton that it was "most important Battleford should be relieved. Men, women and children all crowded into the barracks. Stoney Indians have risen, they are in great danger."[31] On April 11, Middleton reluctantly changed his plans and told Colonel William Dillon Otter, "I want you to get to Battleford as soon as possible if steamers are ready at Swift Current within two days and can transport you."[32]

The following day he sent a message instructing Otter to "go by land to Battleford. I have directed transport and supplies to be got to you as soon as possible. . . ."[33] Having been ordered by the Minister to get troops to Battleford, Middleton did his best to make it look as if he had done so out of the goodness of his heart. He explained the diversion of Otter's Column by saying that he "continued however, to receive such heart rending appeals from Superintendent [sic] Morris at Battleford, I telegraphed that day, . . . to Lieutenant Colonel Otter at Swift Current to leave at once for Battleford with all the troops he had."[34]

Almost two weeks previously, General Middleton had instructed Superintendent Herchmer, who had come from Calgary, to take 50 Mounted Police and a 7-pounder gun from Regina to Swift Current and then to Battleford. They left Regina quite certain they would be unable to cross the river due to the ice breaking up.[35] The following day it was reported that the force had gone through to Medicine Hat instead of stopping at Swift Current and now planned to go down the river on a steamer.[36] When Herchmer and his men arrived at Medicine Hat, the Indians who had been reported to be threatening the town, had all disappeared. The men were put to work for two days getting vessels in the water and then told to return to Swift Current.[37]

Meanwhile, back in Battleford, the Indians, still defiant, burned down the Hudson's Bay Company buildings in South Battleford. Despite the presence of

Otter's Column Approaches The South Saskatchewan River   PAM N-12393

Indians in the area, teams were sent out to bring in supplies from the South side. On April 14, seven teams were sent to "Prince's" to get five loads of hay and two loads of oats.[38] Growing apprehensive, Morris sent a message asking, "Are we going to have assistance?   When and how?   We can't hold place."   Caron responded by saying, "Tell your officer at Battleford, that five hundred men are now far advanced to Battleford."[39]

On April 12, a number of Mounted Police under Superintendent Percy Neale left Swift Current for Saskatchewan Landing to prepare for the crossing of Otter's Column.   The crossing was held by a small Mounted Police detachment under Corporal John Richards based on Tim's Store. The Mounted Police started crossing on April 15 but were slowed by cold, wet weather. By April 18, the whole of Otter's column, consisting of 745 men and 450 horses, had been moved across the river with the help of the steamer *Northcote* and marched north from Saskatchewan Landing for Battleford.

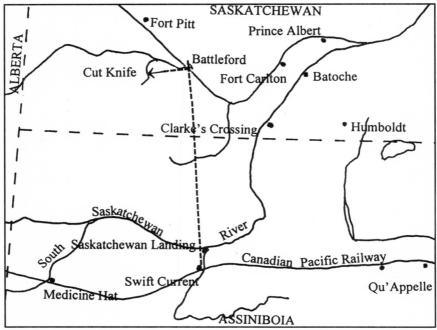

The Route Of Otter's Column To Battleford

The routine on the march was to start at 5:30 a.m., take a two-hour rest at noon, then continue to march until 5:00 p.m. The Mounted Police and civilian scouts formed the advance guard on the march, riding about a mile ahead and to the side "beating every coulee or clump of poplar where an enemy might be ambushed, thus absolutely preventing the possibility of anything like a surprise"[40] At night the wagons were formed into a square with the horses inside and the tents outside, and the Mounted Police providing the outer piquet. For three days the column, which stretched out on the march for four miles, pushed northward keeping a close watch for Indians. The terrain was rough and there was a need for the troops to undertake minor engineering tasks at places such as Eagle Hills Creek where three wagon loads of lumber were used to build a bridge to facilitate the crossing.

122

Battleford

On April 22, the scouts encountered Indians. Constable Charlie Ross came upon a small band dressing a calf they had killed. When he approached to speak to them, they waited until he was about 200 yards away then fired in his direction. Ross had fallen from his horse the evening before and, unknown to him, the barrel of his rifle was plugged with mud so, when he returned their fire, "the barrel on his rifle burst, rendering it useless, and the Indians galloped off."[41] When the column reached Payne's farm, an unsuccessful search was made for his body. A large stock of food was found and the column took over a considerable quantity of flour and bacon.

Meanwhile, at Battleford, mounted patrols, made up of one civilian and one mounted policeman, were routinely sent out around the barracks during the evenings. On April 22, a patrol consisting of Frank Smart and Constable Tom White had gone about three miles on patrol when they found some cattle, which they started to round up.[42] When White heard shots, he looked back and saw Smart fall out of his saddle. The shots came from the edge of a nearby coulee and Smart was killed by the first shot, while Constable White, who had two shots fired at him, fortunately escaped unharmed.[43] He rode straight back to the fort to give the alarm and Sergeant Major Michael Kirk immediately took out a strong patrol to recover the body.

On April 23, as people in Battleford came back from the funeral of Frank Smart, they saw Constable Ross riding down the hill toward the Battle River. He told them the troops were about 18 miles out and would camp for the night outside the town. That evening, the main body of Otter's Column arrived on the outskirts of Battleford and bivouacked for the night about three miles away. As a parting gesture, the Indians set fire to the house of Judge Rouleau. Superintendent Herchmer sent scouts out and about an hour later the sound of firing came from the direction of town. Apparently, when the scouts saw some mounted Indians riding

The Relief Of Battleford   PAM N-12394

away and called upon them to halt, they just kept going, so the scouts fired at them but did not score any hits.[44]

Superintendent Herchmer, finding there was some reluctance by Inspector Morris to hand over command to Inspector Dickens, or some reluctance by Dickens to accept it, immediately ordered Dickens to assume command of the North-West Mounted Police detachment at Battleford. Morris told Captain Hamlyn Todd that his duties had been so demanding that he had been unable to undress for the past twenty-eight days. Herchmer transferred Sergeant George Fraser, Corporal William McCounsell, Corporal Ralph Sleigh and 28 constables, along with 18 Mounted Police horses and two privately owned horses to his Mounted Police contingent outside the barracks with Otter's Column. This left the Battleford barracks with four horses, all of them unfit for duty.[45]

Battleford

Colonel Otter was being pressed by Commissioner Joseph Wrigley of the Hudson's Bay Company to rescue the company's employees from Frog Lake and Fort Pitt who were being held captive by Big Bear's band. Beside being in the wrong place and having no authority to do anything, Otter had very little sympathy for the captives. Otter's copy of Wrigley's telegram appealing for help was annotated, "It is positively ascertained that McLean joined the Indians of his own free will - every arrangement made for his escape."[46] There was considerable pressure from the residents of Battleford to punish the Indians for the killing and looting that had occurred. Colonel Otter, who was anxious to see action, was more sympathetic to their cause.

A list of the North-West Mounted Police members in Otter's Column can be found at Appendix "E." A list of the North-West Mounted Police members in Battleford in March 1885 can be found at Appendix "F."

- 10 -
Cut Knife Hill

When the majority of the Cree withdrew from Battleford in early April, they returned to their reserve and camped along a creek near Cut Knife Hill. En route, they were joined on the trail by the Assiniboines who had killed Payne and Tremont so, by association, they were identified with those atrocities. Once back on their reserves, the Indians waited to see what would happen next, probably expecting some chastisement for their transgressions in looting at Battleford. Under this threat, the Rattlers Society took control of the band, built a Soldier's Lodge and confined everyone to camp. Riel sent a messenger to bring the Indians to Batoche but, under the circumstances, the Métis representatives had a letter drafted on April 29 asking that they be given help from Batoche instead. It was allegedly signed by Poundmaker and other chiefs. Given Louis Riel's preoccupation with matters at Batoche, it was a vain hope.

Back at Battleford, Colonel Otter, having relieved the town, decided to punish the Indians. His motivation may have been to redress the burning of buildings and the murders in the Battleford area, to get his troops into action against what he perceived as an incompetent enemy or, perhaps, to enhance his personal career by being the architect of a victory at a time when they were practically nonexistent. Whatever his motivation, he now moved forward with plans for a punitive expedition disguised as a reconnaissance. Otter had no mandate to go beyond Battleford and he began searching for some means of getting what could be construed as approval for his venture.

Otter telegraphed Lieutenant Governor Dewdney that he "would propose taking part of my force at once to punish Poundmaker."[1] Dewdney replied, "Think you cannot act too energetically or Indians will gather in large numbers. Herchmer knows country to Poundmaker's Reserve. Sand Hills most dangerous country to march through. Be sure to secure good reliable scouts." Otter's copy of this message is annotated, "Have sent scouts to find Poundmaker's whereabouts - am ready then to move out."[2] Middleton, meanwhile, telegraphed Otter to " . . . remain at Battleford until you ascertain more about Poundmaker's force and the kind of country he is in."[3] To find out just where the Indians were, Otter sent out a North-West Mounted Police patrol under Sergeant Frederick Bagley, with Constables John Storer, John Hynes and William Potter.[4]

The Mounted Police scouts sent out by Colonel Otter found the Indians camped on the east side of Cut Knife Creek. Otter made up a column with representation from all the units under his command for the reconnaissance in force to Poundmaker's camp. At this time, a serious error in judgement occurred when Otter was somehow convinced that the trail to Cut Knife Hill was too soft for the heavy 9-pounder gun to get through and "B" Battery substituted the North-West Mounted Police 7-pounder mountain guns and a Gatling Gun. Considering the type of terrain over which General Strange's column was successfully taking a 9-pounder gun, this decision is difficult to understand. The 7-pounders had first been acquired by the North-West Mounted Police in 1876 for use in Fort Walsh and the original narrow mountain gun carriages and limbers were replaced locally by a pattern more adapted to the prairies. By 1878, Commissioner Irvine had described the carriages as "virtually unserviceable" and said they would be replaced when the necessary skilled labour was available.[5] Unfortunately, this had not been done.

When Colonel Otter was all set to go, he sent another message to General Middleton asking "Am I to attack? Please give me definite instructions."[6] Asking Middleton for definite instructions was about the same as asking the Pope to get married. Middleton seems to have been unwilling or incapable of issuing clear and definite orders. He told Otter that "fighting these men entails heavy responsibility. Six men judiciously placed would shoot down half your force. Had better for present content yourself with holding Battleford and patrolling about the country."[7]

Otter had what he wanted, since he could construe his proposed foray as "patrolling about the country."

On May 1, Otter sent a message saying "Poundmaker hesitating between peace and war - am going today to try and settle matters with him."[8]   General Middleton, now finding Otter's messages just as confusing as Otter found his, telegraphed him "Don't understand your telegram about Poundmaker. Hope you have not gone with small force. He must be punished not treated with. You had better confine yourself to reconnoitering for the present."[9]   By the time this message was received, Otter and his column had moved out and were on the way to Cut Knife Hill. Otter was complying with orders at least to the extent that he had not gone forth with a small force. Middleton complained that "Otter has . . . gone off contrary to the spirit of my orders to attack Poundmaker and I am rather uneasy. He and all his forces are untried in actual fighting."[10]

On the afternoon of May 1, Otter left Battleford with 325 men, including seventy-five from the Mounted Police. His scouts had reported on April 28 that the Indians were concentrated in large numbers on Little Pine's Reservation. Colonel Otter was under the same serious misconception as General Middleton, that the sight of his force would strike terror in the Indians causing them to flee or surrender. He also appears to have believed he could take the Indian camp by surprise. On the trail, the Mounted Police scouts were employed in their usual role, fanning out in an arc ahead of the infantry who were being carried in 48 wagons, and checking for concealed rebel ambushes in the sloughs and ravines. As darkness fell the column halted about halfway to Poundmaker's Reserve to get what rest they could in the chilly night and wait for the moon to rise and light their way.

When the moon rose, the column moved off again as far as the Indian campsite previously found by the police scouts, only to discover there were no Indians there. There was a clear trail showing the direction the Indians had taken, but for some reason it was assumed they had moved several miles, whereas, in

Poundmaker   PAM N-16095

reality, they had only gone a couple of miles to a better defensive position. The Mounted Police arrived first and the rest of the troops followed, so that by 4:45 a.m. the whole force was there. Not having found the enemy, Otter decided to move across Cut Knife Creek, climb the hill, then give the troops breakfast and allow the horses to rest before going further.

The troops had to ford Cut Knife Creek before climbing the hill and the failure to find the Indians in the expected location seems to have disorganized them. The scouts moved carefully across the creek, after checking the copses and ravines for ambushes, followed by the Mounted Police and the artillery, then started up the hill. As soon as they were on the far side of the creek and moving up the slope, they realized the Indian village was in sight ahead of them. The troops following the Mounted Police and artillery were disorganized and spread out, having relaxed a bit at the thought of a pause for breakfast. One of the soldiers recalled that as they walked up the hill he was "feeling tired out, having had no sleep and a great deal of jolting in the wagons during the night."[11] At about the same time, the scouts saw the first mounted Indians deploying toward them, so they dismounted, took cover and started to fire at them. Superintendent Herchmer, seeing the scouts dismount and take up firing positions, ordered the Mounted Police to dismount and had their horses taken to the rear. Constable Alfred Rumball recalled that after they crossed the creek, "every bush, every stone, every tree seemed to belch forth flame, and bullets whistled through the air like hail . . . "[12] The advance had now lost its momentum.

The artillery, who were close behind, took up positions among the Police and, except for the actual gun crews, acted as a protective force for the guns. The 7-pounders were unlimbered and opened fire at the Indian tepees about 1,500 yards away, causing the occupants to flee to Cut Knife Hill. The guns caused damage to the Indian camp and the Gatling chopped down small trees and willows, but most of the bullets went over the heads of the rebels. The scouts, Mounted Police and

Battle Of Cut Knife Creek   PAM N-12346

artillerymen settled in to fire at the rebels with the 7-pounders making a great deal of noise but doing little real damage. The two sides exchanged fire at a distance, while the rest of the troops deployed. The rebels, using ravines on each side, outflanked the troops who were pinned down in a firefight with largely unseen enemies.

The 7-pounders, again located too far forward in the line of march, as they had been at Duck Lake, could not be used to full advantage. The two North-West Mounted Police guns, which were manned by "B" Battery of the School of Gunnery, did not fare well. The trail of one gun broke, putting it out of action. The trail of the other cracked and a field repair was done with a piece of oak which quickly worked loose, so that firing the gun was almost as dangerous to the crew as it was to those at whom it was aimed. Years later, the Indian took great delight

131

in telling of how the patched up second 7-pounder broke and was repaired with scrounged wood and rope. When it was fixed, and the gunners fired, there was a loud explosion, lots of smoke and the gun flew apart. The crew ran around picking up the pieces, including the barrel which rolled down the hill. The Indians enjoyed the spectacle, while taking occasional pot shots at the gun crew to make their task more difficult. This was not a textbook operation.

While the two sides exchanged shots from a distance, Fine Day, the War Chief, and a few followers used the available cover to get close enough to the 7-pounders to make a mad dash to capture them. This action forced Major Short, the artillery battery commander, to call for volunteers to repel the rebels. In this brief but brisk action, two Indians were killed. Corporal Ralph B. Sleigh, who had survived the Craig Incident at Poundmaker's Reserve the previous year, Frog Lake and Fort Pitt, was killed. Sergeant John Ward of the North-West Mounted Police was wounded, as was Lieutenant O.C.C. Pelletier of the Queen's Own and Sergeant J.T. Gaffney, a Gunner. The bullet which struck Sergeant Ward entered his left abdomen and was never found since the medical officer considered it too dangerous to explore for it.[13] While Major Short's men were falling back to the gun positions under covering fire from the rest of the troops, Corporal William Lowry of the North-West Mounted Police was hit and killed as he rose to fire.[14] Corporals Sleigh and Lowry, killed the same day, were at school together and then met again in the Mounted Police at Battleford. Constable Charlie Ross, the Mounted Police Scout, whose brother had been killed by Indians, was in the middle of the action. One report tells how, as "he was rushing down the ravine he came upon an Indian who seeing that he was discovered feigned death. But Ross's quick eye saw through the disguise. . . . As he ran past, he drew his revolver and like a flash a bullet sped into the redskin's brain."[15]

The Métis were armed with the latest Winchester repeating rifles but they were short of ammunition for them, having only an average of 30 rounds each, according to Father Louis Cochin. Most of the Indians had muskets or shotguns and were making their own ammunition out of the tin foil in tea packages from the Hudson's Bay Company store, which they wrapped around small stones to fit the bore of their weapons. This lack of ammunition saved many lives.[16]

By 6:00 a.m. fire had largely petered out from both sides and the combatants were at a stand-off. To the front, there were rebels in concealed positions while, on the right and left flanks, gullies running down to Cut Knife Creek provided cover for the rebels to move freely and snipe at the troops. By moving up and down these ravines, the rebels caused Otter to overestimate their numbers. The teamsters from the wagon train had forded the creek and formed their wagons in a square in a small depression half way up the hill. Surgeon Frederick Strange set his field hospital up inside the square where it was protected from snipers. To the rear of Otter's position, the heavily wooded banks of Cut Knife Creek offered concealment to the enemy. By 7:00 a.m. Colonel Otter grew concerned about fire from the rebels in the woods by the creek. He was unable to advance and had to keep a secure route open to the rear in case he decided to withdraw. He ordered the Battleford Rifles, who formed the rear guard, to clear the rebels and hold the positions. As soon as they were cleared, the rebels started to sneak back.

By noon, after about seven hours of fighting, Colonel Otter realized just how hopeless his position had become. He had become involved in a more serious conflict than anticipated and he now had to find a way out of it. Otters' immediate problem was to extricate his force with the fewest possible casualties. The 7-pounders and the Gatling Gun were moved to the rear. The horses were hitched to the wagons and the wounded evacuated to the old campsite. The force then fell back through the boggy ground by Cut Knife Creek and headed for Battleford, expecting to come under attack at any time. Two messengers, Constable John Storer and Constable Henry Ayre were sent ahead to warn Inspector Dickens of the imminent arrival of the casualties.[17]

A Trying Time

According to Robert Jefferson, several Indians mounted their horses and prepared to follow the retreating force but Poundmaker would not allow it saying, "they had beaten their enemy off; let that content them."[18] This raises a question about how much authority Poundmaker had since he must have had a tremendous amount of influence if he could stop the pursuit, when control of the band was supposedly in the hands of the war chief, Fine Day. In any case, no matter who was responsible, Otter's force was left to return to Battleford undisturbed.

With the Mounted Police acting as rearguard, the force that had gone to punish the Indians and had instead been punished themselves, arrived in Battleford at 10:00 p.m. that night. One participant summed the matter up by saying, "In the first place, it is hard to believe that Colonel Otter and Colonel Herchmer and their other Battleford informants could be such simpletons in their estimate of Poundmaker."[19] Years later, referring to the Craig incident, an opinion was expressed that "Superintendent Crozier did to Poundmaker a year earlier with 38 men what Colonel Otter couldn't do with 358 men at Cut Knife Hill."[20]

General Middleton was not pleased with the outcome of the battle at Cut Knife Hill. Colonel Otter argued that he had "acted for the best and would not have retired but for guns breaking down." and concluded that it would not be "wise to leave Battleford at present."[21] The guns also came to the attention of a Member of Parliament who noted that "anybody who has paid much attention to the detailed actions in the North-West knows that the bad quality of the guns in the hands of the Mounted Police on one occasion might have led to rather serious disaster."[22]

No matter what their previous intentions may have been, the Indians at Cut Knife Hill now knew they were unlikely to be able to resolve their problems amicably. This was just what Riel's messengers wanted. Some historians believe that, left alone, Poundmaker would have stayed quietly on his reserve.[23] Others believe he was already committed to join Riel. The McLean family, after their release, said that prior to the engagement at Cut Knife Hill, Big Bear was coming to

134

Capture Of Scout Lafontaine NAC C-006744

join with Poundmaker, then they would go together to Riel. When Big Bear was only 60 miles away, Poundmaker sent a message telling him that a big battle was in progress and requested assistance, which did not materialize since Big Bear had problems of his own. The *Saskatchewan Herald* in an editorial voiced the opinion that "had Colonel Otter's column not attacked Poundmaker it is now more than probable that the bands of Big Bear and Poundmaker would have reached Batoche before the General. It is not pleasant to think what might have been the result."[24]

In his official report, Colonel Otter cited Sergeant Major Thomas Wattam as one "whose brilliant example and dogged courage gave confidence and steadiness to those within sound of his voice."[25] Constable Charles Ross was commended as "always ready to lead a dash or take his place in the skirmish line, in fact, he seemed everywhere and at the proper time." Superintendent William Herchmer, he described as "a most valuable assistant . . . while the men of his command have time and again proved themselves as invaluable to my force."[26]

The Indians left Cut Knife Hill shortly after the battle and first moved about a mile and a half and made their camp in a steep coulee which would have been hard to attack. From here, they started to drift slowly southeast in the direction of Batoche. When Constable Ross and two of his scouts were south of the Battle River about 30 miles from Battleford and trying to establish the whereabouts of the Indians, they ran into a large group of rebels near Bresaylor. Ross and one of the scouts wheeled around and galloped for Battleford, escaping the rebels, while the other scout, Baptiste Lafontaine, dismounted or fell from his horse and tried to hide in a bush. He was captured but luckily for him he was taken by Métis who spared him. There were rumours at this time that some of the Indians had enough and Edgar Dewdney advised Sir John A. Macdonald that he "heard a few days ago . . . that Poundmaker wanted to come to terms but . . . the young men who ruled in the War Council would not hear of it and carried the day."[27]

Supplies for Battleford were being freighted in by wagon trains from Swift Current. These slow ox trains usually travelled without escorts, although the teamsters were each armed with a rifle. On May 14, 1885, a courier by the name of Kilgour came into Battleford where he reported the capture of a wagon train made up of twenty-one ox teams and ten horse teams with their loaded wagons and twenty-two teamsters. At a station on the trail the previous evening, Kilgour heard rumours of mounted Indians being spotted on the surrounding hills but the night passed without any trouble. The next day on his way into Battleford, he met some of the wagon drivers retreating hastily down the trail on horses taken from the wagons which had been captured by a party of Poundmaker's Indians.[28] One of the captured drivers, Neil Brodie, later reported that when the wagon train was surrounded by Indians about 12 miles south of Battleford, the drivers circled the wagons, unhitched the horses and oxen and prepared to defend themselves. Nine of the drivers took the opportunity to flee with the Indians and Métis firing after them. One of the teamsters, Frank Cox, negotiated with the Indians who said the drivers had to leave their wagons and would be escorted to a place near Battleford.

The drivers started for Battleford under an escort, but after a short distance were brought back by some of the band members who disagreed with the decision to free them. After a Council, it was agreed they would remain prisoners and be allowed to live, provided none of them attempted to escape.[29] Meanwhile, Kilgour, the courier, replaced his worn out pony with one of the teamsters' horses and headed into Battleford with the news. Although he attempted to avoid the Indians, he came close enough to see several of them in a coulee looting wagons, but managed to bypass them and hurried on to take the news to those in Battleford who were waiting for the supplies. Some of the freight included treats for the besieged residents and the Indians "feasted gloriously upon potted meats, preserved fruits, marmalade, jellies and held high carnival with fine brandies and luscious wines intended for the brave fellows shut up in Battleford. . . ."[30]

When the wagons were looted, the Indians and half-breeds estimated by one of the prisoners at about 800, with 300 well armed, moved off toward the southeast. Suddenly there was an alarm and the prisoners were forced to drive into a ravine while armed sharpshooters moved rapidly forward. When the scouts returned, they reported that they had killed a redcoat who was shot in the back. A prisoner reported that the policeman had been buried using soil from a nearby badger mound.[31] The party continued the move to the southeast for a time before stopping to wait for word from Riel who was fully occupied with events at Batoche.

The action reported by the prisoners occurred when a Police patrol of five men under Sergeant John Gordon, unaware of the close proximity of large bands of Indians and half-breeds, rode right into a rebel advance guard, numbering about thirty.[32] Both parties were surprised by the encounter but the Police patrol, hopelessly outnumbered, wheeled and withdrew under fire from the Indians. One man, Constable William Spencer was hit immediately but managed to ride straight back to Battleford, some ten miles away.[33] Another policeman, Constable Frank Elliot, was shot from his horse and ran to cover in a nearby bush.[34] The rest of the patrol fell back, returning fire until they were in the clear.

The following day, May 15, a strong patrol of twenty men under Sergeant Major Wattam returned to the area in an attempt to discover what happened to Constable Elliot. Eventually they found his body about three miles from the scene of the fight. The body was "wrapped in a waggon-sheet and covered with a few inches of sand. He had been shot twice, through the spine and head, and had received two heavy blows, one on the temple and another on the back of the head."[35] While the patrol was returning to Battleford with Elliot's body, they found themselves surrounded by Indians, but broke into a trot and managed to evade their followers without any further trouble. Obviously upset by the incident, someone noted in the Fort Battleford Post Journal that "This shows the folly of sending out small parties of four or five men and always following the same, or about the same, roads as we are ordered to do."[36] An Army officer in Battleford at the time commented that "this comes of our enforced inaction. The General has persistently refused to allow us to move against Poundmaker again and he being undisturbed has become bold once more."[37]

On May 20, some wagons appeared at Battleford with white flags on them. They carried the prisoners who had been held by Poundmaker's band, the priest and settlers from Bresaylor, the teamsters from the wagon train and the captured scout, Baptiste Lafontaine. They also brought a letter from Poundmaker asking about terms for surrender.

General Middleton left Colonel Otter and his force at Battleford, so they were not involved in the subsequent action at Batoche. Middleton seemed determined to relegate Otter's Column to minor roles, perhaps as a punishment for precipitating the engagement at Cut Knife Hill. On May 22, General Middleton left Prince Albert by steamer *en route* to Battleford to accept the surrender of Poundmaker and his followers.

A list of the North-West Mounted Police members who served under Superintendent Herchmer in Otter's Column can be found at Appendix "E." A list of the members of the North-West Mounted Police who were present at the engagement at Cut Knife Hill can be found at Appendix "G."

- 11 -
Fish Creek And Batoche

On his return from Fort Carlton following the debacle at Duck Lake, Commissioner Irvine set about organizing the defences of Prince Albert. This was a difficult settlement to defend since the community stretched for about five miles along the river. Irvine saw Prince Albert as the logical objective of any rebel attack and believed that any help from the east would come directly to Prince Albert as the first move in a campaign against Riel. Every able-bodied man in town was sworn in as part of the defence force, but not all the locals were fully cooperative. Amongst the residents, there were many who supported Riel, overtly or covertly, and others who just resented taking orders from the Mounted Police.

One disillusioned resident recalled that the internal divisions within the community were reflected in the organization of the defence force which consisted of four companies. The first two companies "were armed with rifles on account of their extreme loyalty and also their devotion to the powers that be." The third company was considered "equally loyal, but wanting in official reverence," so they were armed with shotguns. The fourth company "composed of farmers and citizens with grievances, consequently suspected of disloyalty and wholly devoid of veneration for their local rulers, were allowed to arm themselves with clubs or anything they could pick up."[1]

By this time, General Middleton was in Qu'Appelle where he formulated a simple campaign based on eliminating the rebels at Batoche, which he saw as the heart of the problem. His plan was to proceed north from Qu'Appelle with one column, while Colonel Otter advanced from Swift Current with a second column, hopefully using river steamers to get to Clarke's Crossing, where the two columns would rendezvous. The combined force would then move down both sides of the South Saskatchewan River.

140

Major General Sir Frederick Middleton   NAC PA-012197

A Trying Time

General Middleton moved quite quickly to assemble his largely untrained force and get it on the move. He marched his force to Fort Qu'Appelle and remained there long enough to organize the necessary transport and commissariat services since the sheer magnitude of the organization required to put this force in the field challenged the imagination. The fledgling Canadian Militia had no logistic services in place, no supply system of the type required and no transportation units. Two well-known Canadian institutions were called upon to, at least partially, fill the gap: the Hudson's Bay Company, which provided vast quantities of food and other supplies and the Canadian Pacific Railway, which moved large numbers of troops more rapidly than anyone thought possible. A Hudson's Bay Company officer reported that "the troops appear to have turned out promptly and present a creditable appearance but all military supply organization seems to be miserably defective."[2]

Commissioner Irvine was not in communication with anyone outside Prince Albert, so he was unaware of the massive mobilization taking place in eastern Canada. His first contact appears to have been a message from General Middleton saying that he would be leaving Qu'Appelle with 350 men on Monday, April 6 and would be in Humboldt by about Friday, April 10. He also informed Irvine that infantry would be coming via Swift Current. This was the start of a series of orders and counter orders which emanated from Middleton's headquarters, one after the other. Like the Grand Old Duke of York in the nursery rhyme who marched his men to the top of the hill then marched them down again, Middleton seemed unable to make a plan and stay with it.

Since many of Middleton's men had never fired a weapon, the time at Fort Qu'Appelle was used to give his men more range practice. Then, for possibly the only time in the campaign, General Middleton set off on schedule on April 6. Instructions were left for units arriving later to catch up with the column on the trail. Middleton was not overly concerned with numbers at this time since he did not

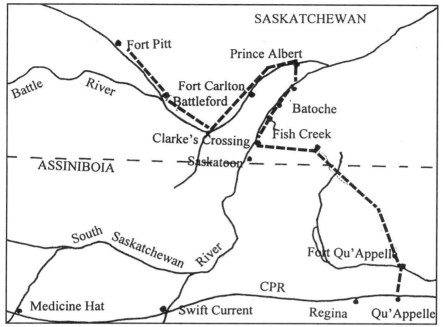

SASKATCHEWAN

Fort Pitt

Prince Albert

Battle River

Fort Carlton

Battleford

Batoche

Clarke's Crossing

Fish Creek

ASSINIBOIA

Saskatoon

South Saskatchewan River

Fort Qu'Appelle

CPR

Medicine Hat

Swift Current

Regina

Qu'Appelle

Middleton's Route To Fish Creek And Batoche

anticipate significant resistance and believed his troops would overawe the Métis and Indians, causing them to immediately disperse.

The inexperienced troops set off in good spirits, either riding in ox carts or marching. Despite Lord Melgund's observation about infantry being inappropriate, there were relatively few mounted troops. After leaving Fort Qu'Appelle, the weather was cold with wet snow and the men found marching increasingly difficult. The road out of Qu'Appelle along the river was steep and the snow had started to melt, so the inexperienced troops only travelled about 11 miles that day and got soaking wet in the process. That night the temperature fell sharply to -23°F, so in the morning the tent pegs had to be removed from the ground with axes.

After a halt in the Touchwood Hills to wait for rations and forage, the tired troops made a long, dreary march across the Salt Plains to Humboldt where they

143

received the first news of the Frog Lake Massacre. General Thomas Bland Strange and the Alberta Field Force in Calgary were immediately ordered to move via Edmonton to Fort Pitt. On April 13 General Middleton sent to Prince Albert two of his staff officers, David H. MacDowall, the Member of the Territorial Council for the District of Lorne, and Samuel L. Bedson, the Warden of Stony Mountain. They arrived on April 16, the same day Middleton moved his force to Clarke's Crossing. Commissioner Irvine later recalled that the message brought by MacDowall and Bedson informed him that Middleton intended to attack Batoche on April 18, although Middleton hedged his bet by saying it might be delayed until Sunday the 19th, and it was also possible it might happen earlier. The only clear instructions received from MacDowall and Bedson seem to have been that Irvine was not to attack Batoche but was to look out for escaping rebels, or "flying breeds" as they were called.

Irvine got the clear impression that the two staff officers "saw clearly the importance of the main body of the force under my command remaining at Prince Albert and it was understood they would inform Middleton accordingly."[3] General Middleton, on the other hand, says that Macdowall and Bedson carried orders directing Commissioner Irvine to march out with 150 men and cooperate on the west side of the river.[4] Colonel Gilbert Sanders, who was an Inspector with Irvine in Prince Albert, recalled in later years that as soon as the Mounted Police were placed under Middleton's command he wired Irvine that the Police were to stay in Prince Albert and do nothing more than protect the place and he would deal with the rebels. There was a general feeling that Middleton did not want anyone else dealing with Louis Riel and taking the credit from him.[5]

After a two-day halt at Humboldt, during which supplies caught up with them and additional units arrived, the column moved on to Clarke's Crossing, an important junction where many of the main trails in the area met. Here they established a base on the river. General Middleton hoped this base could be supplied by river steamers once the water level was high enough. Middleton's original intention had been for Colonel William Otter and his column to move to Clarke's Crossing by river steamer then move along the west side of the South Saskatchewan River in cooperation with Middleton's column on the east side. Middleton was now forced to send Otter's column to Battleford so it was not available. He did, however, stay with his original plan, dividing his own force in two to provide equal forces on each side of the river. Lateral movement was hampered by the river banks being blocked with large blocks of ice stuck in the mud. Middleton complained to Caron on April 14 that he "would like to attack Riel at once but I am sadly hampered by Irvine and Morris who both implore me to go to them at once. From all information I can get I believe neither of them are in actual danger but they both write about defenceless women and children. Between ourselves I believe they are both scared and unfit but I fear the chance of their being right. . . ."[6]

The next day, April 17, Macdowall and Bedson left Prince Albert to rejoin General Middleton. Bedson, always ready to follow his leader, told newspaper correspondents that "the forty-three miles of country between Batoche's and Prince Albert is clear of rebels."[7] When the two arrived back with General Middleton, Bedson reported in writing that "Irvine, after hearing Middleton's message, had said he thought it unwise to comply with the order about moving out of Prince Albert and that Irvine's staff officer and others agreed." He also said that Irvine had reported there were Teton Sioux in the area who could attack the town if he left it unprotected. Middleton was not impressed with talk about the Sioux, saying that they had been mentioned in the telegram from Irvine that he intercepted at Humboldt and he did "not think they ever did much damage to anyone! I now determined to leave the Prince Albert force out of my calculations in forming the plans for attacking Batoche."[8]

A Trying Time

There is, however, evidence of offensive activity by some of the Sioux. A resident outside Prince Albert later recalled that at the time of the trouble at Duck Lake they knew something was wrong from the behaviour of the Indians working with them on their farm. She said the Indians, who were Sioux, went to Duck Lake, painted for war, and were in the fighting there. The Indians came back after the fight bringing others with them. They were afraid they would be sent back to the United States because of their actions and went into hiding across the river until the rebellion was over.[9]

General Middleton frequently suggested that guides and couriers who reported problems with Indians were exaggerating. The deaths of Constable Frank Elliot and Frank Smart showed that some of the difficulties were real. Even when the enemy did not interfere, conditions were often very severe. The Mounted Police scout, George Harpur, described a trip from Battleford in April 1885 to take information and a request for help to Middleton on the South Branch. On the return trip, about 50 miles from Battleford, his half-breed guide's government horse, which was hobbled, fell into Raspberry Creek. When the guide refused to enter the water to rescue it, Harpur went in and released the horse but was thrown off his feet by the running ice and soaked to the skin. Due to the proximity of Indians they could not light a fire and had to spend the night, in sub-zero temperatures with snow and sleet and only a saddle blanket for cover. He rode into Battleford the next day with his clothes frozen stiff.[10]

Sunday, April 19, was the day General Middleton was supposed to attack Louis Riel. Irvine took about 200 policemen toward Batoche for a distance of about 12 miles to a place on "The Ridge," known as Scott's, after the owner, Thomas Scott, who was incarcerated in Prince Albert as a suspected rebel. Irvine pushed his scouts even closer. There was no sign of Middleton at Batoche and Irvine had no information on his location or intentions. While at Scott's, he received a letter from Lieutenant Colonel John Sproat and Lawrence Clarke in Prince Albert telling him that they had apprehended and interrogated two rebels, C.R. Swain and Frederick Fiddler.

When questioned, the captured rebels said that Riel had 800 men, 300 of them Indian and that of these, two hundred rebels under Albert Monkman were on the west side of the river opposite Batoche, while Louis Riel and the remainder were at Batoche. The prisoners told Clarke and Sproat that the Indians all had repeating rifles while the rest of the rebels had rifles and shotguns. Lawrence Clarke added a postscript to Irvine warning him that "Riel is on his guard and evidently will not wait for the General's attack." This note supposedly led Irvine to believe there could be an attack on Prince Albert, but it is difficult to see how the contents support that assumption.[11]

Irvine's official diary notes that "Having accomplished his purpose of thoroughly examining the country in front of us and ascertained the proximity of the rebel scouts from the tracks of rebel Indians in The Firs, and being anxious as to the security of Prince Albert in his absence, the Commissioner decided to return to Prince Albert and broke camp at once and commenced the return march shortly after 11:00 p.m." After his return to Prince Albert, Irvine learned, from his own scouts, that General Middleton was marching to Clarke's Crossing but on April 30 he found that Middleton intended to make the river crossing at Hudson's Bay ferry. Scows, built by Irvine's force, were positioned at this crossing and, having made all the necessary preparations, he sent a message to Middleton informing him that "Steamer left here Friday for Hudson's Bay ferry, South Branch. Four scows and four life boats are at the ferry in charge of two officers and thirty-one men."[12]

From a military point of view it is incredible that Middleton was allowed to march from Qu'Appelle to within a short distance of Batoche without encountering any offensive action on the part of the rebels. The Métis appear to have been fixated on defending Batoche with the possible exception of Gabriel Dumont's suggestion of an attack on the Mounted Police when they evacuated Fort Carlton.

147

Dumont had a reputation as a master tactician but there is little concrete evidence to back this up. In his assessment of the rebellion, Lord Melgund noted that "the Métis never showed themselves, but though good shots at short ranges, in other points they were contemptible. They never attacked a convoy, they never cut the wire behind us, and though Indians and 'Breeds' are born mounted infantry, who can shoot as well from their horses as on foot, they never harassed us on the march."[13]

General Middleton moved his force north from Clarke's Crossing on April 23 and camped for the night at McIntosh's Farm, just south of Tourond's Coulee or Fish Creek which was the outer perimeter of Métis territory. When word of Middleton's movement reached Batoche, Gabriel Dumont and Louis Riel set off with about 200 men. When they were near Fish Creek, a messenger came with a report that the Mounted Police from Prince Albert were approaching Batoche, so Riel immediately returned with 50 of the men.

The rebels were unable to find Middleton's camp in the dark and by the time it was located in the morning, Middleton was already preparing to move. The trail to Batoche led inland from the river then descended into a wide ravine and crossed Fish Creek. The constriction of the trail offered excellent opportunities for ambush and there were good fields of fire from the bushes and tree line. Gabriel Dumont deployed his men along the coulee then took some mounted men to hide in a poplar bluff from which they could attack the Militia from the rear after they passed. The Métis horsemen were not well concealed, so were seen by one of Boulton's Scouts who turned to gallop back to report. Dumont attempted to catch the scout but, when unable to do so, fired at him and the rest of the rebels immediately joined in. This alerted General Middleton's forces, who were advancing. As the Militia moved forward they were in the open so, as they approached the ravine, the troops came under heavy fire from well-concealed marksmen.

Fish Creek And Batoche

April 24 at Fish Creek, like March 22 at Duck Lake, was not a good day for gunners. The guns were deployed but quickly exhausted the supply of prepared ammunition, making it necessary for the gunners to fill the shells with powder and cut the fuses to the proper length. The screwdriver needed to open the powder barrels could not be found and they do not seem to have had a funnel, all of which tended to slow things down. Once these problems were solved, the gunners took out their frustration by destroying the farm buildings on the opposite side of the ravine. A number of rebels who were experiencing artillery fire for the first time, promptly deserted.

The intense small arms and artillery fire continued for some time, with heavy casualties to General Middleton's force - 11 dead and 40 wounded. The rebels lost at least four Métis and two Indians, as well as a very large number of horses. The force on the west bank, under Lieutenant Colonel Charles Montizambert, was ferried across the river with great difficulty but, by the time they arrived, Middleton decided not to commit them and both sides retired to lick their wounds. General Middleton's previous open contempt for the Métis had been tempered by his heavy casualties and he seemed in no hurry to test them again.

After resting, recuperating and evacuating his wounded, General Middleton was eventually ready to go again. On May 7, more than two weeks after he was stopped at Fish Creek, he started north again with nearly 900 men, artillery and a small party on the steamer *Northcote* who were to attack Batoche from the river. When Middleton made his first attack at Batoche on May 9, the ground troops met heavy fire from rifle pits and both sides settled down to two days of skirmishing. The *Northcote*, with a small detachment of Mounted Police among those aboard, immediately came to grief when the ferry cable across the South Saskatchewan River at Batoche, toppled the smoke stack and disabled the vessel, which then drifted downstream and came to rest on a sand bar.

A Trying Time

On May 12, General Middleton sent a small force to make a diversion and draw the attention of the rebels, allowing the main body to make an attack. Unfortunately the firing at the diversion, which was the signal to advance, was inaudible so there was no attack. When the infantry was unfairly rebuked for their failure to advance, they made an impromptu attack which seized the village in short order. Louis Riel, Gabriel Dumont and several leading Métis disappeared as the troops arrived.

The day after the capture of Batoche, Captain Ernest J. Chambers and Lieutenant Colonel Monitzambert spoke with some Métis and the Roman Catholic priests at St. Laurent Church. They asked why the Métis had taken no action against the Militia column during their long approach march, especially since their supply system was highly vulnerable. The Métis made it clear that they were afraid to venture too far from Batoche in case the Police from Prince Albert should attack their positions while they were gone. On the eve of the Fish Creek battle, some of the Métis and Indians wanted to make an assault on Middleton's base at McIntosh's, but others were reluctant to go beyond Fish Creek in case they had to return in a hurry to defend Batoche.[14] After the Rebellion, Father Alexis André related that Louis Riel told him the rebels had expected Irvine to leave Prince Albert to join General Middleton and said "in that case we have made up our mind to make a raid on Prince Albert, following the trail alongside of the southern branch of the Saskatchewan. . . ."[15]

As soon as Batoche was taken, the rebellion started to wind down. Four days after the fall of Batoche, Thomas Hourie and two Mounted Police scouts, Robert Armstrong and William Diehl, came across Louis Riel about 3 miles from General Middleton's headquarters. Riel was hesitant to surrender because he was uncertain about how he would be treated by the soldiers. He was escorted into camp and taken directly to General Middleton personally and anyone who asked was told that they had captured Riel's cook. Riel was quickly despatched to Regina

Capture Of Louis Riel   PAM N-14582

in the custody of Captain George Holmes Young, a Gunner, and turned over to the Mounted Police. A number of others, including Gabriel Dumont, Michel Dumas and Little Poplar fled to the United States.

When he had disposed of the prisoners and completed his preparations, General Middleton informed Commissioner Irvine that he would be in Prince Albert on the 15th although, in his usual way, he did not arrive until four days later, on the 19th. Since their scarlet uniforms were considered too conspicuous for the duties on which they were engaged, the regular members of the Mounted Police created an *ad hoc* field uniform from the items available in local clothing stores and all were provided with slouch hats.[16] On the occasion of the general's arrival the policemen had changed from their improvised field kit into scarlet uniforms, which had not been worn on operations. Middleton, in his official report, said that on his arrival at Prince Albert on May 20 the "Mounted Police looked smart and well and were a fine body of men." [17] The Mounted Police uniforms contrasted sharply with those of Middleton's travel and battle stained troops which were showing the wear and tear of the campaign. Middleton, highly annoyed, said to Commissioner Irvine, "Look at my men, Sir. Look at the colour of their uniforms."[18]

On May 22, General Middleton left Prince Albert by steamer for Battleford. En route, Robert Jefferson, the Farm Instructor from the Poundmaker Reserve, arrived in a canoe with a note from Poundmaker asking about terms of surrender. Middleton replied that he had defeated Riel and had not made terms with him and would not do so with Poundmaker. He instructed him to bring his chiefs to Battleford on May 26 to surrender. On the appointed day, he met Poundmaker and lectured him about his conduct, ignored his attempts at explanation and ordered his arrest, along with Lean Man, Yellow Mud Blanket, Breaking-Through-The-Ice and Wahwanitch.

General Middleton was pleased with events. The main engagements of the campaign had now been concluded, Riel and the Métis had been defeated and Poundmaker had surrendered. The only outstanding task was to capture Big Bear, release the white prisoners and bring those responsible for the Frog Lake Massacre to justice. While at Battleford, Middleton received news of the engagement between General Strange and Big Bear at Frenchman Butte and immediately moved his force to Fort Pitt to join in the pursuit of Big Bear, which up to this time had been carried out by the Alberta Field Force. The final chapter in the conflict was now to be written.

- 12 -
The Alberta Field Force

The third and most westerly column in General Middleton's force, the Alberta Field Force, was commanded by Major-General Thomas Bland Strange, a retired Royal Artillery officer who had commanded "B" Battery of the Canadian Artillery in Quebec before becoming a cattle rancher near Gleichen, in what is now Alberta. Strange had no ingrained bias against the Mounted Police and appreciated their special skills and ability. He welcomed them into his force. In direct contrast to Middleton, Strange, who spoke French, liked the militiamen from Quebec so Middleton happily sent Quebec units straight through to Calgary.

Inspector Sam Steele, who was in the Rockies maintaining order in the railway construction camps, was brought back to Calgary at the request of General Strange and appointed to command the cavalry element of the Alberta Field Force which Strange gave the title of Steele's Scouts.[1] The official strength of the subunit was three officers and 61 men, including the twenty-five men Steele brought with him from the mountains to Calgary as the nucleus of the new unit.[2] Other than the nucleus which was formed from the Mounted Police, the remainder was largely recruited locally by Steele from cowboys and horsemen. The civilian members had to provide their own horse, saddles and weapons. Steele now used many of his constables and former members to fill noncommissioned officers' positions in the scouts since he had a great respect and confidence in their ability. One of the Scouts, Ed Hayes, later commented that he could not "say much for the discipline of this cowboy troop, as we never saluted an officer from the time we left Calgary until we returned, but at the same time, we never forgot that Major Steele was our commanding officer."[3]

A second North-West Mounted Police element, consisting of 20 men under Inspector Aylesworth Bowen Perry, left Fort Macleod for Calgary on April 18 bringing a 9-pounder muzzle loading rifle and 150 rounds of gun ammunition with them. This was one of the two 9-pounders brought west in the original deployment of the Mounted Police in 1874 but, up until this time, never fired in anger. Because they held command positions in a mixed military and Mounted Police force, General Strange recommended that Steele and Perry be gazetted Majors in the Canadian Militia, much to the annoyance of General Middleton.

The Alberta Field Force assembled in Calgary. In addition to Quebec units, General Strange was given the Winnipeg Light Infantry under the command of Lieutenant Colonel W. Osborne Smith, who had been the temporary first Commissioner of the Mounted Police at Lower Fort Garry in 1873. By coincidence, there were also two future Commissioners of the Mounted Police in the Alberta Field Force at this time, Inspector A. Bowen Perry, the commander of the Mounted Police detachment from Fort Macleod and Lieutenant Cortland Starnes, with the 65th Regiment from Montreal, who would join the force after the North-West Rebellion. Another link to the Mounted Police was the Reverend John McDougall who was a scout with the Alberta Field Force. Over a decade previously, in 1874, he had been sent by Lieutenant Governor Morris to inform the Blackfoot Nation of the arrival on the plains of the Mounted Police. One of the Alberta Field Force scouts was Canon George McKay, the brother of Thomas McKay of Prince Albert, who had taken part in the engagement at Duck Lake and was now heading the scouts in Commissioner Irvine's force.

Preparations went on rapidly and by April 19 the first column, which included part of the 65th Mount Royal Rifles and Steele's Scouts, was ready to go. The second column, which included the Mounted Police detachment from Fort Macleod under Inspector Perry and the remainder of the 65th Regiment, would follow later. The Winnipeg Light Infantry was to remain in Calgary until the Alberta Mounted Rifles had sorted out logistics problems and were ready to move out. General Strange's force was immediately depleted by the need to protect his lines

Major General Thomas Bland Strange   NAC PA-138789

of communication and provide security to communities in the area. Subunits of the 65th Battalion were left at Fort Macleod, Edmonton and Fort Saskatchewan.

Inspector Steele wrote that when the first column under General Strange pulled out of Calgary on the morning of April 20, it was ". . . like a circus. The horses, with few exceptions, had seldom been ridden, and bucked whenever mounted, until two or three days had gentled them. This little performance interested the men from Montreal as they gazed at the gyrations of the cowpuncher soldiers and Mounted Police."[4] This must have reminded Steele of his days in charge of equitation in the fledgling first contingent of the Mounted Police, training at Lower Fort Garry in 1873. Interestingly, the horses used on that occasion, which had also seldom been ridden, were purchased for the Mounted Police by Lieutenant Colonel W. Osborne Smith, now commanding the Winnipeg Light Infantry. The scarlet tunics of the Mounted Police were far from ideal for scouts so, with the exception of Inspector Steele, the men exchanged them for canvas fatigue dress.

The march from Calgary to Edmonton was arduous, with difficult terrain and unprepared river crossings. The first of these was encountered almost immediately when the column had to wade through three feet of icy water while crossing the Bow River at Eau Claire Mills. The first day they camped only six miles out of Calgary and woke in the morning covered in snow. Heavy snow continued for two days along the trail making travel extremely difficult but no time was lost. Thick swamps, in which horses could find no footing, made it necessary for wagons to be dragged through the bog by soldiers of the 65th Battalion. Lieutenant John Corryell of Steele's Scouts had gone ahead to secure the important crossing of the Red Deer River and, due to the snowstorm, many of his men reached their destination snowblind. The Reverend John McDougall went on to Edmonton in advance to let the citizens know that General Strange and his force were coming. He also got the Hudson's Bay Company carpenters to start work on flat bottomed scows for the trip down the North Saskatchewan River. When the column reached

Route Of The Alberta Field Force

the Red Deer River which was swollen by rain, General Strange sent the infantry across to establish a bridgehead since the bush on the far bank was too dense for mounted scouts to work effectively. Despite the rising water, the column crossed safely, with the exception of a few carts which were washed downstream and later recovered.

From the Red Deer River to Edmonton, conditions were terrible with mud and bogs most of the way. A party had to be sent out in advance to undertake minor engineering tasks such as laying corduroy roads and building small bridges, in much the same way Inspector William Jarvis and "A" Troop had done on the march to Edmonton from the east in 1874. For the march from Calgary to Red Deer, across a prairie which offered no shelter, the column had to carry sufficient supplies of food, fuel and forage for at least two weeks, in addition to large quantities of

157

ammunition. This required 175 wagons and carts which formed a column stretching out 1½ to 2 miles on the march. General Strange later remarked "that it reached its destination in safety is, I believe, due to the precautions taken, and especially the careful scouting of Major Steele's force, as a handful of Indians could have easily stampeded horses not carefully guarded, and inflicted heavy loss on a force of 160 infantry trying to guard a convoy of such magnitude, marching through the swamps and forests north of Red Deer."[5]

At the Battle River, the column encountered large numbers of Indians for the first time. This was the home territory for a number of reserves, including those of Bobtail and Ermineskin who had written to Sir John A. Macdonald two years previously describing their plight and seeking help. Conditions had not improved, so, as word reached the reserve of the clash at Duck Lake, some of the young men in the bands looted the local Hudson's Bay Company post and missions. When General Strange met the chiefs, they quickly proclaimed their loyalty but Strange refused to shake hands with them, saying he would do so on his return if they had behaved. From the Battle River, the column moved on to the Saskatchewan River. The troops had to ferry across the wagons, supplies and men and arrived in Edmonton on May 1.

When Inspector Perry arrived at Calgary on April 21, he found General Strange had already gone on to Edmonton leaving him written orders to take charge of the second column which was to follow. On April 23, Perry and the second column left Calgary and marched 108 miles northward to the Red Deer River, through heavy rain and snow storms and over a track that was badly rutted from the passage of Strange's column moving ahead of them. When the first column reached the river a few days previously, it was rising from recent rains but they managed to get across. Twenty-four hours later, when Perry's troops arrived, they found it was impassable due to heavy rains which caused the river to rise until, at this point, it was 250 yards wide with a current running at five and a half miles per hour. The ferry that was normally in service here had been swept away by ice during the spring break up and the only craft available was a skiff which could carry six people. Some way had to be found to get the 9-pounder gun, ammunition and other heavy supplies across. Because of the problem of the fast current, Perry decided to build a new ferry if he could obtain the necessary material. In the meantime, he decided to attempt to raft the gun and ammunition across. An advance guard and a fatigue party crossed in the skiff while additional fatigue parties were sent downstream to recover any available parts from the old ferry and teams were sent to haul new lumber from a sawmill eight miles from the ford.

While this was going on, a raft capable of carrying six tons was built in two hours from some heavy squared timbers which were readily available at the crossing site. A 1200 foot long rope, improvised by joining the picketing ropes for the horses, was carried across the river and put around a tree, from which it could be paid out as the raft crossed. The raft was then loaded with the 9-pounder gun, ammunition and harness. Perry boarded the raft with the gun crew and Lieutenant J. Bedard Normandeau of the 65th Regiment and started toward the north bank. The rope which was being let out bound around the tree and broke, leaving the raft adrift in the swift current. Perry and Constable Herbert Diamond swam ashore with a rope and managed to attach it to a tree, but the raft was moving too fast to be stopped and this rope also broke.[6] The raft travelled another 3 miles downstream then, when it slowed in an eddy, was secured with a 2-inch rope. The men now faced a new challenge since the raft came to rest under a 30-foot high cut bank and the gun, carriage and ammunition all had to be manhandled to the top. A road about six miles in length was built around a swamp and through a heavy wooded area to bring the gun and ammunition back to the crossing point. Wagons then had to be ferried across and horses swum over so the ammunition could be hauled back.

Inspector Perry had been warned by General Strange that his column was under observation from Indian war parties. To secure his landing point on the north bank, Perry sent the 65th Regiment across to form a defensive perimeter. Since the only available transport was the six man skiff, the 65th worked all night in the darkness to move their men and equipment across the river. Meanwhile, the teams sent to the local sawmill for new lumber to build a ferry returned and said the owner refused to provide it. Perry sent Corporal Arthur Harper and an escort to convince the man that if he did not give it to them voluntarily they would take the lumber.[7] Realizing that discretion is the better part of valour, the mill owner then agreed. The next day, teams were sent for the material and when they got back to the crossing point in the late afternoon work started on building a ferry and continued all night until it was finished twenty-four hours later. A cable found on the north bank was then stretched across the river and secured. After a successful trial run the ferry was put into service and the force crossed. Leaving the Red Deer River, Superintendent Perry's column marched the remaining 105 miles into Edmonton, arriving there on May 5.

Due to the possibility that rebels might attempt to cut the column off, the Mounted Police were continuously employed on scouting and advance guard during the march. They quickly learned what every sled dog knows - it is better to be first in line - as they slogged along through the mud and snow churned up by the first column. A warm Chinook wind had melted the snow so the rivers were flooded and every possible low point had turned into a swamp into which mounted men and wagons seemed to be in danger of disappearing. When the Chinook finished, the temperature fell and snowstorms came. Coming last had some advantages since the troops benefitted from the work done by the pioneers in the first column.

The third column followed the same route. General Strange found out that the Indians at Battle River were not impressed by troops in dark uniforms who, they said, spoke like half-breeds. He issued an order that when the Winnipeg Light Infantry reached the reservation they were to march through it in scarlet tunics with fixed bayonets and the band playing. Whether this had the desired effect of dazzling the Indians is not known.   This last column reached the North Saskatchewan River and crossed by scow, arriving at Edmonton on May 10.

The arrival of the Alberta Field Force at Edmonton offered a chance for rest, training, equipment checks and other preparations before the trip downstream to Frog Lake and Fort Pitt. During this stay, the gun ammunition, which had come west with the Mounted Police in 1874, was tested and found to be good. An untrained six man detachment from the Winnipeg Light Infantry were attached to the gun crew and some training carried out. While this training was underway, units sent fatigue parties to assist the Hudson's Bay Company carpenters to complete the eight scows required for the trip. There were five infantry scows, a horse scow, a ferryboat scow with stores and wire to establish a ferry across the river, and a gun scow. The gun scow, which had a reinforced platform on which the 9-pounder could be lashed to absorb the recoil if the gun fired, was named Big Bear. It could be aimed, somewhat crudely, by pointing the scow's nose in the direction of a target. At Edmonton, Inspector Steele was reunited with his three brothers, Richard, Godfrey and James. Richard and Godfrey, who had been '73 Originals, and joined the North-West Mounted Police at its formation, now joined Steele's Scouts.

At this point, Lieutenant Colonel Osborne Smith, commanding the Winnipeg Light Infantry, raised a question about the safety of the scows that had been built, the ability of flour stacks to withstand bullets and the condition of the small arms ammunition provided. General Strange, obviously not impressed, reported that "the protest against the boats was met by ordering a board to assemble and take evidence of experienced H.B. Co. navigators and boat builders, the penetration of flour sacks was relegated to hostile bullets, and the objectors to the quality of ammunition advised to retain their fire for short range."[8] Inspector Steele commented that Strange was "given a great deal of unnecessary trouble which caused delay to the advance."[9] He may not have been completely unbiased since his view could well have been coloured by memories of the clash between Osborne Smith and Steele's friends Percy Neale and John McIllree at Fort Garry in 1873.[10]

Inspector Steele left Edmonton for Victoria (Pakan) with a mixed force of mounted rifles and infantry, followed by the main body of the Alberta Field Force. The force moved down the North Saskatchewan River toward Frog Lake and Fort Pitt hoping to find Big Bear's band and release the hostages. Perry's Mounted Police detachment was divided in two with Sergeant William Irwin and eleven men taking the land trail and the remainder, with the gun, going down the North Saskatchewan River on one of the scows built at Edmonton.[11] When the column reached Fort Saskatchewan, Steele met another old friend, Superintendent Arthur Griesbach, who had also been a '73 Original. Griesbach, Percy Neale, now with Otter's Column, and Sam Steele had been the first, second and third men to sign the attestation papers for the first contingent of the North-West Mounted Police at Lower Fort Garry in November 1873. At Fort Saskatchewan, the six gun horses that came from Edmonton by trail were also transferred to a scow. On the way down the river, this scow sank leaving the horses in the water. The animals were rescued and the scow refloated but the horses, adopting the old maxim of once bitten twice shy, swam across the river and went the rest of the way into Victoria by trail, arriving on May 16.

On the trail, the usual order of march was an advance guard of Mounted Police and Scouts riding about a quarter of a mile ahead of wagons carrying infantry and stores. These were followed by ammunition wagons and the remaining stores. A rear guard of Mounted Police and Scouts trailed the column. At times, the dense forest prevented mounted guards deploying on the flanks and crowded the column into a narrow track. At one point, a small stream became a considerable obstacle when the continuous passage of wagons cut up the clay bottom below the surface of the crossing. At first the wagons were pulled across by using double teams, then someone found that large numbers of men, termed "fifteen donkey power" by one of the participants, could do the job more quickly by pulling on a rope attached to the wagon tongue.[12]

After an uneventful trip the Alberta Field Force reached Victoria and stopped for five days. Here they made preparations for the next leg of the trip, organized a home guard and repaired the local Hudson's Bay Company fort. Since General Strange was not in communication with General Middleton at this time, he was unaware that Middleton had already captured Batoche and Louis Riel was a prisoner. At Victoria he sent two scouts, Sergeant George Borrodaile and Trooper William Scott of Steele's Scouts down the river in a canoe to try to establish communications.[13]

Steele's Scouts moved out again on May 18 and the rest of the force followed. From Victoria on, Steele's Scouts and the Winnipeg Light Infantry moved by land with the Mounted Police forming the advance guard while the 65th came down the river. For the next ten days, the men slogged along through heavy rain that turned the trail to mud. Those in the scows did not fare much better since their craft constantly leaked and the men had to bail continuously. Even with this hard bailing a horse barge sank twice.

The advance party of Steele's Scouts reached the ruins of the Frog Lake village on the afternoon of May 24, with the rest of the force arriving behind them. A strong odor from the ruins of the church led them to a terrible discovery. In the basement of the burned structure they found four headless bodies which had been mutilated. The four separated heads had been so badly burned they could not be identified.[14] The bodies of George Dill and William Gilchrist were found in the trees at the top of a hill, all terribly mutilated, while that of John Williscroft was lying in the bush where he was shot. Father Fafard, Father Marchand, John Gowanlock and John Delaney were in the church cellar, their bodies badly charred when the building burned. The bodies of Thomas Quinn and Charles Gouin were found in

163

the cellar of John Pritchard's house.[15] The men who removed the bodies had to improvise masks with "a sponge saturated with army rum."[16] Joseph Hicks said there had been doubts whether "some of the men . . . would fight the Indians when we got at them. But what a change of attitude the scene at Frog Lake made. It was then the other extreme."[17]

From Frog Lake, scouts under Captain James Oswald were sent out and returned at noon to report Indians in the vicinity of Fort Pitt. Steele's Scouts and the Winnipeg Light Infantry made a forced march to Fort Pitt which was a smoking ruin with one building left standing. Nearby the men found the badly mutilated and decomposing body of Constable David Cowan. He had been scalped and only a small forelock of his red hair remained. His face had several knife cuts and his legs were slashed and his heart was impaled on a stick. Constable Cowan was given a funeral with full military honours with the service read by Canon McKay. All that now remained was to capture the elusive Big Bear and his band and release the prisoners.

A list of the members of the North-West Mounted Police who served in Steele's Scouts in the Alberta Field Force in 1885 can be found at Appendix "H." A list of members of the North-West Mounted Police who served in the Alberta Field Force under Inspector Perry can be found at Appendix "J."

- 13 -
The Pursuit Of Big Bear

Having arrived at Fort Pitt General Strange was uncertain as to the exact location of Big Bear and his band and whether they had gone to join Poundmaker so scouts were sent in all directions. Inspector Perry, with 15 men and five scouts, was ferried across the Saskatchewan River to patrol toward the Battle River. For some unknown reason, Perry rushed on to Battleford, apparently leaving Strange in the dark as to his whereabouts and safety. Since Perry's patrol included most of the trained artillerymen, Strange was left short of people to man the 9-pounder. Sergeant O'Connor and the artillery drivers, Constable George Ward and Constable Charles Parker, stayed with the gun and the gun crew hastily trained from men of the Winnipeg Light Infantry, took over the task.[1]   Strange's son, Captain Harry Strange, who was acting as the general's Aide de Camp, proved to be a highly capable Gunner like his father.

Big Bear's Indians were not far away. Uncertain of what to do next, they sent Louis Goulet, who had recently been an interpreter for the Mounted Police, to see what the situation was in Batoche. They expected he would be gone for a week to ten days, and while they were waiting, they started a Thirst Dance a few miles from Fort Pitt. A huge lodge, 200 feet in circumference, was built for the ceremony and the Indians hoisted the Hudson's Bay Company flag which they adopted for ceremonial purposes. The flag was flown upside down and Kitty McLean happily explained to them that this was a bad omen. Very quickly thereafter word reached them about many soldiers and horses at Fort Pitt. Louis Goulet, the courier sent to Batoche, returned unexpectedly on the second day, reporting large numbers of soldiers at Battleford. The medicine lodge was quickly taken down, camp struck and the bands started to move. Wandering Spirit said they would fight the troops at Frenchman Butte, a knoll on the banks of Red Deer Creek.[2] A small party of Indians went toward Fort Pitt to steal horses from the approaching soldiers.[3]

165

A Trying Time

Leaving Fort Pitt, Inspector Steele and his scouts located well-used trails on the north shore with signs of Indians and some personal effects of the McLeans. The scouts followed the trail for the rest of the day in a 30-mile circle which led them right back to the river near Fort Pitt after darkness had fallen. Steele related that from the high ground he could see the campfires of the main body camped about three miles away. Since it was time to stop for the night, he took Sergeant Joseph Butlin and Corporal Thomas McLelland to look for a safe bivouac, but just as he found what he considered to be a suitable area, "an Indian, lying in the grass to my right front, sprang to his feet, fired two shots at us in rapid succession, and ran across my front towards a horse tied to a tree to the left."[4] McLelland, said to be the best pistol shot in Western Canada, shot the Indian who fired at them and the scouts instantly found themselves in the middle of a band of yelling warriors, all firing their weapons. This short but brisk fire fight ended when the warriors disappeared to the east, firing a few scattered shots in the dark as they moved off. They left behind a dead Indian, Meeminook, who was later scalped, allegedly by one of the teamsters with the force. These were the Indians on the horse stealing raid.

At daybreak, with Steele and his scouts out ahead of the force, General Strange pressed on with 300 men and the 9-pounder gun. Moving the heavy gun over unprepared trails required great skill on the part of the artillery drivers, Constables George Ward and Charles Parker, but even then accidents happened. When one of his horses sank in the muskeg, Ward was dragged and his leg was caught between the shaft and the horse, crushing his knee. Constable Parker extricated him. About nine miles out of Fort Pitt, the transport wagons were corralled and a base camp formed with the teamsters as guards. The fighting elements then resumed the advance and contact was made when the point men were pursued back to the main body by Indians who stopped at a safe distance when they saw Steele's men. After approximately 3 miles, Steele's Scouts found the Indians were assembling on a high knoll.

The Pursuit Of Big Bear

A small skirmish occurred when some Indians appeared in the 200-yard gap between the advance scouts and the main body. Then more Indians, both mounted and on foot, appeared on the bald summit of Frenchman Butte, taunting the troops while their mounted men rode in a circle as a signal to their camp. The 9-pounder fired some shrapnel over their heads dispersing the Indians who promptly disappeared. In later years, one of the Indians involved, Lone Man, told a former member of the Alberta Field Force that the first shell killed seven men and wounded several more.[5] Joseph Hicks, in Hatton's Scouts, said "not a man fired his rifle and that is what happened at Frenchman's Butte."[6] General Strange then took up the chase, advancing in the direction taken by the retreating Indians. When they reached the summit of Frenchman Butte, there were no Indians in sight and the advance continued to the east until nightfall when the wagons were again corralled in a tight defensive perimeter.

At dawn the next day, Strange pressed forward, preceded by Inspector Steele's dismounted Police and scouts, to a deep coulee about 2 miles from Frenchman Butte with the Little Red Deer River at the bottom. Since it was spring the river had overflowed and the banks at the bottom of the coulee were soft and marshy. The slopes on the side where the scouts arrived were wooded but the slope on the far side was bare at the bottom with trees at the very top. The Indian trail led across the stream and up a side coulee to the north. There was no movement or sign of life except for rifle pits and trenches, some of them dug by the prisoners, which could be seen through field glasses at the edge of the woods. The troops advanced on foot in skirmishing line with the Mounted Police on the left. As the men advanced into the valley, heavy fire came down on them from the Indians in the trenches above and was promptly returned. Many of the men who crossed the creek came under heavy fire from the willows and Constable Donald McRae was wounded in the thigh but "continued in action and was carried off the field against his will."[7]

A Trying Time

The field gun, under Captain Strange and Sergeant O'Connor and crewed by the Winnipeg Light Infantry, was in the action. William B. Cameron, one of the prisoners, recalled ". . . and what music in the ears of us captives was the earth-rocking roar of that nine-pounder field gun."[8] Another prisoner, Chief Factor McLean from Fort Pitt, reported that the Indians had decided, after a few shots, that the field gun could not be aimed. When a range order was overheard by a Cree who understood English, he told the others that the soldiers had the proper range and they were done for. The next shell wounded three Indians, and the following shell wounded another Indian and his horse. One of the wounded, Kahweechetwaymot, or The-Man-Who-Speaks-Our Language, who precipitated the Craig Incident in 1874, died that night. During the preliminary skirmishes and the actual engagement, the North-West Mounted Police 9-pounder fired twenty-two rounds of common and shrapnel shell at Frenchman Butte.[9] Wandering Spirit complained bitterly about "the unfair gun that spoke twice," referring to the sound of the propellant when the gun was fired and the explosive in the shell at the target.[10]

General Strange realized that an assault up the bare slopes on the far side of the creek would entail heavy casualties so he ordered Inspector Steele to mount his men and reconnoiter to the enemy's right. Wandering Spirit, seeing Steele's reconnaissance, paralleled the movement so the scouts reported the enemy in position behind the marshes along the stream for nearly 2 miles. Major George Hatton of the Alberta Mounted Rifles reported that the enemy had outflanked Strange's right and could open fire on the wagon corral, so Strange decided to withdraw, covered by the field gun. Once extricated from the fire fight the column retired an extra 6 miles in order to be free of the woods. This ended the Battle of Frenchman Butte. The Indians withdrew at about the same time and their retreat now became a rout, with baggage, carts and sundry other items abandoned in large quantities.[11]

Prisoners Of The Indians   NAC C-000595

A Trying Time

At this point, General Strange had not yet communicated with General Middleton. Meanwhile, Inspector Perry, who had been sent to patrol on the south bank had mistakenly taken his men to Battleford. General Strange later wrote "unfortunately, Captain Perry took it upon himself to ride into Battleford with his whole detachment, without sending any information and I neither saw nor heard anything of him for nine days."[12] In pouring rain, Perry and his men travelled all night and arrived at the Battle River at noon the next day. They continued east to a position within 18 miles of Battleford and had still seen no Indians. While they gave the horses a well-earned rest, an Indian, seen passing by, was pursued by Canon McKay and brought back to camp. He turned out to be a courier searching for Big Bear to give him a message from General Middleton that Riel and Poundmaker had surrendered. Perry, with his 15 men and five scouts, then continued on into Battleford.

When Inspector Perry briefed General Middleton on the situation in General Strange's column, the steamer *Northwest* was immediately loaded with supplies and steamed upstream from Battleford with a company of the 90th Rifles as well as Perry and his patrol. About 50 miles from Fort Pitt, they met a messenger in a canoe with despatches from Strange reporting the action at Frenchman Butte and requesting additional troops. Perry's patrol was put ashore to continue by land and the vessel returned to Battleford for reinforcements. When Middleton heard that Strange had attacked Big Bear on his own, he was angry and ordered the foot troops for the pursuit of Big Bear to leave on the steamers *Baroness, Northcote* and *Northwest* which were available. The mounted units were sent along the trail on the south side of the Saskatchewan River.

Almost as soon as General Middleton's force arrived at Fort Pitt, the prisoners who had been held by the Cree began to turn up. Major Clement Dale, on his way to meet Middleton, ran into the recently released William B. Cameron, Reverend Charles Quincey and Francois Dufresne, Jr. The following day Mrs.

170

Big Bear's Band Under Attack   PAM N-12475

Charles Quinney, Henry Halpin, Isadore Pambrun with this wife and family and Francois Dufresne, Sr. were found.

Meanwhile, Inspector Steele and about 70 mounted officers and men of the Mounted Police, Steele's Scouts and the Alberta Mounted Rifles were following the Indians. Assured that support from General Middleton's troops was not far behind him, Steele pursued the Cree with a minimum of supplies and ammunition. On June 2, ten miles out from the base camp, they found a note left by William McLean saying that all were well and the Indians were moving to the northeast. Twenty-five miles out, after resting and having a noon meal, Canon McKay, who was in the lead, came upon two Indians and fired at them. The Indians returned the fire and Scout Fisk was hit in the arm. As the Indians retreated, the scouts, including Fisk, rode on and camped at midnight.

On June 3, Steele's force moved out at dawn and about 10:00 a.m. rode to the top of a ridge and caught up with Big Bear's retreating band at the narrows of Makwa Lake, sometimes known as Loon Lake. At one point, the pursuit was so close that they caught an Indian making tea over a fire. When the advance scouts came out on a high ridge overlooking Loon Lake, they could see carts and horsemen fording a narrow body of water while others, closer, were striking their lodges and preparing to leave.

Inspector Steele was concerned about the likelihood of an ambush so he had his men dismount and proceed forward slowly. They quickly came under fire from the Indians, directed by Little Poplar, who were trying to surround them. In the ensuing exchange of fire the Indians were driven back but, unfortunately, Sergeant Major William Fury received a bullet through his chest and right lung.[13] Kitty McLean was carrying her baby brother across the ford when the firing started and one bullet passed between her and her brother while another cut her shawl. The Indians got to the peninsula and directed their fire at the pursuers from concealed positions in bush on the high ground. The firing was so intense that the

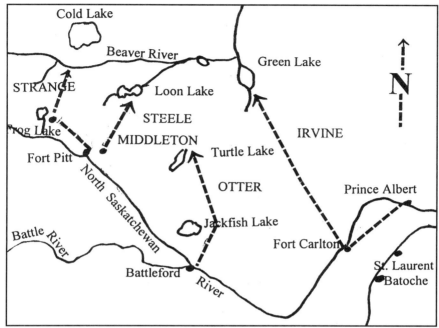

Route Of The Four Columns

Scouts rifles became too hot to handle and were dropped on the ground to cool. It made no sense to try to get across the ford in the face of such heavy fire so Steele pulled his men back to the top of the ridge. Taking Canon McKay with him, he advanced under a white flag to get close enough for McKay to shout in Cree, advising the Indians to give up the prisoners. When the small party was seen, the Indians said "There's only six - let us kill them" and increased their fire.[14] Having virtually exhausted their ammunition and supplies, the Scouts were down to one day's rations and fifteen rounds of ammunition per man. Since there was no sign of the promised support, Steele's only option was to pull back and wait for Middleton's support troops.

At this point, uncertain as to the whereabouts of Big Bear, but knowing the general direction of his flight, General Middleton organized the pursuit in four

The 65th Battalion On The Move To Cold Lake   PAM N-12485

columns which fanned out in an attempt to hopefully cut off any potential escape routes. General Strange, with the Mount Royal Rifles and the Winnipeg Light Infantry, was sent to Frog Lake and then on to the Beaver River. Colonel Otter, with "A" Battery, the Infantry School Corps, the Governor General's Foot Guards and the Queen's Own Rifles, was to go to Battleford then to Jackfish Lake. General Middleton, with all the mounted men, Boulton's Scouts, French's Scouts (now renamed Brittlebank's Scouts), the 90th Winnipeg Rifles, the Grenadiers and the Midlanders, with a few Mounted Police under Superintendent Herchmer, were to follow the lead of Steele's Scouts. Finally, Commissioner Irvine and the Mounted Police from Prince Albert were ordered to proceed to Fort Carlton then to Green Lake.

From Fort Pitt, General Strange's column, less Steele's Scouts, set out for Beaver River about 80 miles away. The terrain was rough, and much of it mud or muskeg, with wagons and especially the 9-pounder gun frequently sinking to the axles and requiring large numbers of men and horses to extricate them. The 65th Mount Royal Rifles often came to the aid of the 9-pounder gun crew. The rough trails, mud and muskeg sometimes made the route appear impassable. The soldiers of the 65th would pull on ropes attached to the gun's hubs, shove on wheels and somehow keep the 9-pounder moving so it maintained momentum and did not sink in the mud or muskeg. This often required the men to work in water and mud up to their waists and, on at least one occasion, the barrel had to be dismounted from the carriage and the gun extricated from the mire in pieces. On another occasion, near the end of the trail, the gun was dismounted and transported, with the ammunition, across a marshy lake a quarter of a mile wide. Despite all this effort and activity, there was no sign of Big Bear so, after waiting at Beaver River until June 25, the force was ordered to return to Fort Pitt.

Colonel Otter's force had been ordered to patrol the Squirrel Plains, northeast of Jackfish Lake to cut off Big Bear should he retreat in that direction. His column moved to Fort Carlton where they crossed the South Saskatchewan River on the *Baroness* and marched off in hot weather. In three days, they reached Stoney Creek then scouted Turtle Lake and patrolled the plains. They captured a few members of Big Bear's band and picked up an old trail of Little Poplar, but did not find Big Bear and, in due course, they also returned to Fort Pitt.

General Middleton left Fort Pitt with a mixed column of mounted troops and infantry, including the Mounted Police and scouts under Herchmer. Sergeant William Parker said he was present when Middleton arrived at General Strange's headquarters near Frenchman Butte and learned that Sam Steele and his scouts had gone after the Indians. He said that when Strange asked Middleton to send his mounted men to assist Steele, Middleton was adamant that no men would be sent.[15] When a courier brought news of a skirmish at Loon Lake, Middleton advised that he was "going to take Major Steele and his men with me and try and catch Big Bear. I am sending all my infantry back as the roads are too bad. I have sent Major

175

First Ford At loon Lake   NAC C-018957

Steele's three wounded men into Fort Pitt."[16] One of the wounded men was Scout Fisk who had his arm bandaged after being wounded then rode on 45 miles with the Scouts. Eventually, when he was evacuated to Fort Pitt, the shattered bone was repaired.

When Middleton arrived at the ridge above Loon Lake, his troops found abandoned equipment and a note saying the prisoners were well. The Indians had crossed on rafts so the soldiers did the same while swimming their horses across. After crossing the first narrows, the force found a recently abandoned campsite and the body of an elderly Indian woman. At the north end of the lake they encountered a large stretch of muskeg in front of them with no apparent way around it. The Indians had jettisoned a large amount of baggage before crossing. Two of Steele's men got through and returned with the information that the trail continued northward. When General Middleton tried to cross, his horse hit a bad patch and sank in to the saddle girth. He immediately ordered the force to return to camp so he could ponder the next move.

Some of the scouts were not impressed with this performance. One member left a description of how the staff dealt with the problem. "At the general's tent is gathered a solemn conclave considering the weighty responsibility of risking our valuable lives in attempting this bottomless morass over which hundreds of Indians and ponies have crossed within two days. And a brilliant and most intelligent lot they are: a major-general, a captain of the Royal Engineers, an infantry lieutenant, an Indian Department official, and a major of militia, each knowing less than the other, offering suggestions and advice *ad nauseum*. Herchmer and Steele are not asked for opinions for our disposer does not admire the police, and the council, after much deliberation, having little brains to guide them, evolve [the plan]."[17] It was believed that "had Herchmer with the mounted men once got across the muskeg, as he could have crossed, he would have been on top of the Indian camp while his commander was wondering whether there was any jam for dinner or not."[18]

General Middleton was not well liked. When extra food and delicacies were sent from Eastern Canada, he ordered that none were to be given to the western troops. The Scouts solved this problem by appropriating part of Middleton's ample personal supply. Their officers not only condoned their activities, but shared in the spoils.

The next morning, when Inspector Steele and Major Charles Boulton were leading the way through the muskeg, General Middleton halted the operation and called them back. He did not want a major obstacle like the muskeg between him and his base. Steele wanted to continue and he went with his scouts to examine the muskeg which "upon careful examination, I found to be a swamp with a solid bottom 2 feet below the surface." It was not impassable. "The staff, however, would not listen to any representations made by members of the Mounted Police, nor to the evidence of their own senses, but leaned on those who had no experience to guide them, with the usual results."[19]   One observer, obviously not an admirer of his general, related that ". . . our Great I Am, with over two hundred and fifty men and two Gatlings, seems afraid to overtake these same Indians." [20] Middleton ordered a return to base at Fort Pitt.   The Mounted Police later commemorated the impassable muskeg by naming a drink the Middleton Muskeg.[21] Soon after crossing the muskeg, the Indians divided into three groups. The Wood Crees, travel weary and unwilling participants, kept going north with the few prisoners that remained, and once they crossed the Beaver River released the last of the captives. The Chippewayans went west, while Big Bear and the Plains Cree went to the east.

With the fall of Batoche, Commissioner Irvine assumed that the military phase of the campaign was over and that the Mounted Police would be given the task of pursuing Big Bear, a task which he considered they "were eminently qualified to perform." He was highly disappointed when General Middleton initially told him to stay in Prince Albert with his men. Irvine commented that "Like myself, every member of the police force was most anxious to secure active employment, and here was work to be done, the nature of which was familiar to us in every detail - such work in fact, as we had been successfully performing for years."[22]   His surprise and disappointment were understandable since his men were much more mobile than the militia, they knew the country, they were familiar with Indians and most of them would recognize the wanted Indians on sight.

Eventually, on June 8, Commissioner Irvine was ordered by General Middleton to take as many of the Mounted Police as possible via Fort Carlton to patrol to Green Lake. Irvine had just sent some rebel prisoners south with an escort commanded by Inspector Gilbert Sanders and he now needed the men involved so the column was recalled.   To get his force across the North

Saskatchewan River, he sent Inspector Frederick Drayner and some men to repair the ferry and when the main body arrived at Fort Carlton, they had assistance from the steamer *Baroness* in making the river crossing. Irvine left a small detachment at Fort Carlton under Sergeant William Smart then took the rest of his force, consisting of four officers and 136 men, with 127 horses and 19 wagons, northward through the Touchwood Hills toward Green Lake.

The column travelled through extremely rough country and had to build corduroy roads over the muskeg in places. One member recalled that they ran out of provisions, but rabbits were plentiful and they ate boiled rabbit three times a day. On June 19, Commissioner Irvine's diary recorded that there had been "nothing to eat for the last two days except tea and 'hard tack.'"[23] Their culinary problems were solved when Constable Herman Des Barres went more than 100 miles to Sandy Plains and returned with 4,000 pounds of provisions.[24] When the party reached the south end of Green Lake they established a base camp and left the wagons near the pillaged Hudson's Bay Company post. Irvine then moved further northward to the head of the lake, having to raft his supplies and swim his horses across waterways en route. Contact was established between his scouts and those of Otter's column.

Finding no trace of Big Bear at Green Lake, Commissioner Irvine returned to his wagon camp and started south sending scouts in every direction through the swamps and muskeg. On June 23, they encountered a Wood Cree who said he could lead them to Big Bear. Irvine, with the old scout Louis Léveillé, started to follow the trail south toward Fort Carlton, arresting a member of Big Bear's band and recovering a Mounted Police horse stolen from Fort Pitt by the Indians. Supplies were still a problem and Irvine was highly annoyed when the Inspector Drayner did not turn up at a rendezvous with supplies because he heard reports that Big Bear was south of him.[25] Irvine learned that Big Bear was headed south toward the Saskatchewan River on a parallel course and when he arrived at Shell

Big Bear's Surrender   PAM N-14577

River, fifty-five miles from Fort Carlton, he was told that Big Bear had been apprehended.

Big Bear was captured on July 2 by Sergeant William Smart, Constable Warren Kerr, Constable Alfred Sullivan, and Constable Frederick Nicholls.[26] He was accompanied by his twelve year-old son, Mistatim Awassis or Horse Child, and Head Man Nanasoo. The Mounted Police detachment was on the north side of the river at Fort Carlton and Mr. Garson of the Hudson's Bay Company was located on the south side. At 3:00 a.m. Garson shouted there were Indians on his side of the river. Kerr, Sullivan and Nichols crossed and found an Indian boy. Constable Kerr found an Indian crouching behind a tent and, having been at the "Craig Incident" at Poundmaker's Reserve the previous summer, immediately recognized him as Big Bear and arrested him.[27] As General Strange described it, "After evading all the columns sent to intercept him, by turning in his tracks, travelling almost alone, and covering his own trail he was arrested by Sergeant Smart . . . about the only man in the Force who had never gone after him. . . ."[28]

The campaign was now finished and the whole sorry mess at an end, although the effects would linger for many years. Canada had fought a totally unnecessary war with citizen soldiers who acquitted themselves well, considering their lack of experience and training. The Métis, despite grandiose plans, had done little except defend their holdings on the South Branch and had no realistic expectation of victory. They appear to have believed that the Canadian government would negotiate rather than fight and they were probably shocked both by the decision to send troops and the numbers and speed with which they mobilized. The Indians did not rise in large numbers and join the Métis. Those who did become involved probably believed they had nothing to lose.

For the North-West Mounted Police the Rebellion was a critical point in the history of the force, with their continued existence threatened by the efforts of General Middleton to have the force abolished. The Mounted Police emerged from the Rebellion with their reputation badly damaged as a result of setbacks such as Duck Lake and the unwarranted criticism of leaders such as Middleton.

A list of the North-West Mounted Police members who were present at the engagement at Frenchman Butte can be found at Appendix "K." A list of the members of the North-West Mounted Police in Steele's Scouts who were present at the engagement at Loon Lake can be found at Appendix "L."

- 14 -
The Aftermath of the Rebellion

As soon as Big Bear was captured and the prisoners released, the majority of the Militia troops were returned to their homes as quickly as possible. The day after their arrival back at Fort Pitt, following the pursuit of Big Bear, the Mounted Police members under General Strange were instructed to return to Fort Macleod and ceased to be part of the Alberta Field Force. On their departure, Strange thanked them "for their valuable services and invariably excellent conduct." He said he had "never commanded better soldiers. Their double duties as horse artillery and, when required, scout cavalry, have been performed to his entire satisfaction. In bringing a 9-pr gun from Fort Macleod to Beaver River, through most difficult country, including the passage of the Red Deer River, the march of some 800 miles, with every horse and man in his place, reflects great credit, not only on Major Perry, but on every noncommissioned officer and man."[1] By the time the detachment returned to Fort Macleod, they had travelled 1,398 miles without the loss of a man or horse, in marked contrast to the march west of the Mounted Police in 1874 with its high losses in horses, especially those assigned to pull the 9-pounder guns.[2]

At the end of the campaign, General Middleton ordered the Mounted Police members of Steele's Scouts to remain at Fort Pitt under Sergeant Albert McDonnell.[3] The immaculate policemen who drew the ire of General Middleton in Prince Albert were no longer immaculate. John S. Macdonald, the telegraph operator, commented that they "had been scouting the woods in quest of Big Bear for some weeks, until both inner and outer garments were reduced to tatters. For shirts, they wore discarded flour sacks through which openings had been made for heads and arms, while what uniforms they possessed were mostly rags."[4] Inspector Steele took the rest of the scouts home to Calgary where they were paid off and disbanded. Steele said the Mounted Police in the Alberta Field Force "were in every way superior to all others in physique, discipline and efficiency. They are collectively the best body of men I have ever had anything to do with."[5]

With the end of hostilities, the Mounted Police were kept busy escorting and guarding those rebel prisoners who were moved to Battleford or Regina and detained in custody while awaiting trial. In Regina, Superintendent R. Burton Deane had to enlarge the guard room accommodation to provide additional cells. On May 23, Louis Riel arrived on a special train. On July 6, 1885, a formal charge of high treason was laid against him. In June, an additional forty prisoners arrived from Prince Albert, with an escort under Inspectors White-Fraser and Sanders. On July 10, Superintendent Herchmer arrived with an additional 22 prisoners, followed on July 17, by Big Bear and fourteen others.

As the rebellion ended, the citizens in the areas most affected started to review what had happened. In Battleford, Inspector William Morris, who was not overly popular with the people who had been crowded into the fort, was criticized for not trying to protect the stores in the old town. The men who had been in the fort kept asking to be allowed to go out and secure the supplies but Morris kept refusing.[6] General Middleton thought the looting at Battleford was largely due to the timidity of Morris, of whom he had a very low opinion. The Indian Department Sub-Agent at Battleford, J. Ansdell Macrae complained to Dewdney that he considered "it a matter of regret that it was impossible to induce the commanding officer to allow messengers to leave camp as there is little doubt that many who have since been forced to join Big Bear might have been brought into communication with us."[7] In defence of Morris, P.G. Laurie, in the *Saskatchewan Herald*, said that had he allowed men to go to the rescue of the houses being looted and a disaster had befallen them the blame would have fallen on one person - Morris. If an attack on the looters had failed and the rebels had gained entry to the fort and carnage followed "the terrible responsibility for it all would never have been lifted from the head of Colonel Morris."[8]

183

Following the Rebellion, a town meeting was held at Battleford on June 6, 1885. At this meeting, those present passed a motion, expressing dissatisfaction with the way the surrender of the Métis and Indians involved in the rebellion was handled. Concerned with their safety, the citizens of Battleford were critical that proper steps had not been taken "to ascertain the number or names of Indians who actually surrendered, nor the number of firearms known to be held back and still in their possession." They referred to freedom of Indians to roam as "a serious drawback to settlement, as well as a standing menace to the peace of the community" and moved that no Indians be allowed off their reserves without a pass, and that they be prohibited from owning horses or possessing arms and ammunition. The citizens concluded with a motion to give the members of the North-West Mounted Police their "sincere thanks for their many acts of kindness during the troublous times from which we have but now emerged."[9] It is interesting that every motion was moved or seconded by former members of the Mounted Police.

During the so-called siege, everyone in the fort was under military discipline which was accepted only because most of them were frightened and had no viable alternative, but it did nothing to endear Inspector Morris to his refugee guests.[10] Morris wrote a report on Mounted Police activities in Battleford during the Rebellion which was subsequently published in the Annual Report of the Commissioner. Like many reports of this type, it made heavy use of the first person and could be construed as intimating that Morris was the only competent person in the Mounted Police barracks and had personally done almost everything. In his report, he stated that he had saved all the goods he could in the town, organized a volunteer company, organized the Home Guard and built the defences, all "without a brother officer to afford assistance or relief." He also stated that "in one instance, when an important message was to be forwarded, I could not secure a man on any terms." When he called for volunteers, Constable Storer alone responded.[11]

The Aftermath Of The Rebellion

In due course, the published report in the Sessional Papers was read by the good citizens of Battleford who must have been woefully short of reading material. The report created so much indignation that the residents held another town meeting to discuss it. This meeting also passed a series of resolutions which, *inter alia*, denied that Inspector Morris had saved all the goods he possibly could, expressed disapproval of his not having paid messengers the amount they were promised and "denounced Morris' report as reflecting on the character of the citizens and the police and the manner in which they discharged their duty." The meeting also placed on record that had Morris "called for volunteers, as he said he did, he would have had not one or two, but dozens for any service," and also denied that Morris had organized either the volunteer company or the Home Guard.[12]

This matter came to the attention of Ottawa and Morris was asked for an explanation. Somewhat chastened, he tried to extricate himself. When it was clear that the men had never been asked to volunteer for the missions where he claimed he could not secure a man on any terms, and that Constable Storer, was the first and only man asked, Morris shifted the blame to the Sergeant Major, who had been given the task of finding volunteers. This debacle did nothing to enhance the reputation of Inspector Morris. It is interesting that, once again, the local citizens who moved and seconded the motions condemning him included some ex-members of the force.

Despite these problems, there was no question of the bravery of Constable Storer who continued to act as a courier and take part in patrols. One unexpected benefit of Inspector Morris' report was that it brought Storer's name to the attention of the hierarchy in Ottawa and Commissioner Irvine was told that it was "the desire of the Honourable the Minister, that Constable Storer . . . should receive recognition by promotion, unless there are special reasons to the contrary."[13] Constable Storer was promoted to Corporal and shortly thereafter to Sergeant.

A Trying Time

With a large number of alleged rebels awaiting trial, General Middleton ordered that the property of half-breeds at Battleford who came from the rebel camp be held until the innocence or guilt of the owners could be established. This was taken as *carte blanche* to liberate virtually anything that was not nailed down and wholesale looting resulted. While most of the alleged looting involved soldiers, the reputation of the Mounted Police was also harmed by rumours of members "liberating" or looting property, although they do not seem to have gone at this as enthusiastically as some soldiers, especially General Middleton. In preparing a claim for damage suffered during the rebellion, the Commissioner of the Hudson's Bay Company pointed out to his superiors in London "that serious accusations are made against the police." Showing the business acumen which has kept the Company in business for more than three hundred years, he advised that "The Company are at present on excellent terms with that force and hold the bulk of their contracts. It would be well therefore if possible to keep back those declarations which reflect upon them." He pointed out, however, that "it is true that both Police and Troops returned laden with furs which were well known to have been the property of the Company."[14]

The trials of the prisoners got underway very quickly, with the Mounted Police providing guards, escorts, witnesses and, in at least one case, an interpreter.[15] The trials were presided over by Colonel Hugh Richardson in Regina, and Charles B. Rouleau in Battleford, with Inspector Francis Dickens acting as a Justice of the Peace. It is interesting that prior to these trials, General Middleton, exercising a power which he may or may not have legally held, discharged a number of prisoners, including Adolphus Nolin, charged with treason felony. Middleton's apparent reason was Nolin's efforts, along with John Pritchard, on behalf of Mrs. Gowanlock and Mrs Delaney.

On July 6, a charge of high treason was laid against Louis Riel and his trial started on July 22, just over two weeks later. On July 31, after an hour of

186

The Trial Of Big Bear & Poundmaker   PAM NWReb-2

deliberation, the jury returned a verdict of guilty and he was sentenced to hang. Corporal John Donkin, who was a member of the squad guarding Riel when he was exercising one day in the area between the Orderly Room and the Guard Room at Regina, said that Riel had looked at a newly erected structure and asked whether it was the scaffold. On receiving an affirmative reply, he said, "Thank God, I do not fear the scaffold."[16] On November 16, Louis Riel was led to this scaffold. As he recited the Lord's Prayer, the trap was sprung.

The members of the Métis Council were charged with treason-felony rather than high treason, which carried a death penalty. Of the 18 persons charged, eleven were sentenced to seven years imprisonment, three received three years each, and four were handed one year terms. Not everyone was pleased, since there were many in western Canada who thought the death penalty was appropriate for anyone involved in the rebellion. Big Bear and Poundmaker each received a three-year sentence. Not impressed with the way justice was being meted out, the *Saskatchewan Herald* commented that "Big Bear was found guilty with a recommendation for mercy. He gets three years board at Stony Mountain, unless

187

his admirers can induce the Government in the meantime to transfer him to a first class hotel in Winnipeg."[17]

The only white supporters of Riel who came to trial were William Jackson and Thomas Scott. Jackson was found not guilty by reason of insanity and Scott was acquitted on the grounds that he had remained loyal. A number of white settlers had been involved in getting Louis Riel to Saskatchewan and were said to have financed his return. Lord Melgund predicted that following the rebellion "much white sedition would be discovered." He was of the opinion that Louis Riel and Gabriel Dumont were depending on the continued support of the whites in addition to the Métis and Indians but they had been badly let down. "Riel put his fighting men in the first line, but in his second line we may perhaps find the disappointed white land shark, the disappointed white farmer. There have been much bigger interests at stake than Métis claims."[18] George A. Flinn, a correspondent, noted that "the white advisers of Louis Riel now took to the woods in great alarm, leaving him to his own devices."[19] There were allegations that as the rebellion ended documents which incriminated some leading local citizens in Prince Albert were spirited out of William Jackson's files and burned.

Judge Rouleau, who had departed hastily under the threat of an Indian rising now returned to preside over the trials at Battleford. Those responsible for the murders at Frog Lake and in the Battleford area, including Wandering Spirit, were sentenced to death. Louison Mongrain, charged with the murder of Constable Cowan at Fort Pitt, was tried by a jury which included some men whose houses had been burned down by the rebels. He too was sentenced to hang. Rouleau, a Roman Catholic, who lost his impressive house and library of law books to arson during the siege of Battleford, now dealt with charges of arson, theft and possession of stolen goods. He handed out sentences for these offences, stiffer than Judge Richardson in Regina was giving for treason-felony. Four Sky Thunder, who had torched the Roman Catholic Church at Frog Lake, was given a fourteen-year sentence. Hayter Reed, a year previously, had described Rouleau as "too lenient." He would have been pleased with the change.[20]

To the amazement of westerners in general, and the Mounted Police in particular, Louison Mongrain's death sentence for the murder of Constable Cowan was commuted to life imprisonment, but the eight Indians convicted of murder were hung simultaneously in a mass hanging at Battleford on November 27, 1885. The gallows was in a hollow square with 150 Mounted Police forming three sides. A large number of local residents and Indians were brought in to witness the execution. The prisoners were marched in about 8:15 a.m. by a police escort. The procession was led by Deputy Sheriff Forget, followed by the Executioner, Robert Hodson, who had been the cook for William McLean at Fort Pitt and, finally, the prisoners. The prisoner's hands were tied behind their backs and they wore black caps with veils to cover their faces.[21] The prisoners sang aboriginal songs, mounted the gallows and stood on the trap doors facing the crowd. After all had a chance to speak, the black caps, veils and nooses were adjusted, the hangman pulled the bolt and all eight dropped to their deaths. After 15 minutes they were declared dead by J. Widmer Rolph, the Mounted Police Assistant Surgeon who had been at Fort Pitt. The eight bodies were buried in a mass grave.

Other than those who fled to the United States, few, if any, of the Indians who were accused of any kind of involvement in the rebellion escaped the legal system. The Métis appear to have fared somewhat better than the Indians, since many were released from custody and others were never charged. With the exception of the token charges against Thomas Scott and William Jackson, there was never any real attempt to prosecute any of the white settlers involved. None of those convicted served their full sentences. Poundmaker was released in March 1886 and died four months afterward while visiting Crowfoot. Big Bear was released in January 1887 and died less than a year after his release. To bring a degree of closure to matters, Lieutenant Governor Dewdney declared an amnesty to all those who had taken part in the rebellion, with the exception of "Little Poplar, I-Mesis, Twin Wolverine, Lone Man, May-may-qua-slew, Pas-co-qua-you and any who committed murder." Nobody would be arrested as long as they behaved.[22]

For many, little really changed as a result of the rebellion, except for the fact that the Indian Department was able to impose firmer control on the Indian bands. By administrative processes, they were able to introduce a system of rewards and punishments beyond any imposed by the courts. The Indian bands were arbitrarily classified by the extent to which they were viewed as having been loyal or disloyal during the rebellion. Those deemed disloyal had their annuity payments stopped for up to five years. When the Cree surrendered to General Middleton at Fort Pitt, they were required to give up their weapons, ammunition, horses, cattle and carts. The work for rations policy was reinstituted.

The Mounted Police sent patrols to Indian reserves seeking those wanted for offences committed during the rebellion. Sergeant Frederick Bagley led one such patrol to the Stoney reserve and arrested four Indians involved in the murder of Barney Tremont. Sergeant Thomas Lake took a patrol to the Thunderchild Reserve to arrest and disarm rebels there, while Superintendent Herchmer, with forty men, went to Poundmaker's Reserve to round up and disarm rebels who remained there.

Although the rebellion had been suppressed and most of the troops had gone home, there was still a great deal of unrest and both the Indians and the Métis were unsettled and disturbed. For the Métis nothing had been gained and in many cases they had lost homes, horses, cattle and livelihood, although many who were involved were never charged or tried for their part in the rebellion. Louis Riel was the only Métis to receive a death sentence. The Indians involved did not avoid punishment nearly as easily as the Métis. The Indian Department used the rebellion as an excuse to impose harsher controls and decided, often arbitrarily, which bands were loyal and which were not. Individuals with no involvement in the rebellion were often punished along with the relatively small numbers who had actually taken an active part. Starvation continued to be a problem and the Mounted Police resumed their efforts to ensure the Indians were adequately fed, often in the face of opposition from the Indian Department.

Due to the unrest in Métis settlements and on Indian reserves following the suppression of the rebellion, the expanded North-West Mounted Police were deployed in the areas where trouble was most likely to occur. General Middleton and Adolphe Caron considered it would be sufficient to keep about 300 men in the territory temporarily until the strength of the Mounted Police could be increased. Dewdney agreed that more policemen should be recruited since he believed the troops were "unaccustomed to Indians and are more likely to get us into trouble if brought in contact with them. . . ."[23] There were suggestions that soldiers be used in addition to policemen and the Governor General suggested the power of the government be demonstrated by having a flying column of police, artillery and mounted infantry go through "Indian country" in the Spring of 1886.[24] This did not happen but some troops remained until the large number of newly recruited policemen were ready to take their place on the force. Writing to Sir John A. Macdonald, Lieutenant Governor Dewdney felt that it would be well if the troops "were kept here until the summer was well advanced, by which time Herchmer will have the police in better shape - the fact is the recruits don't know much and the young officers less."[25]

Life became very difficult for both the Métis and Indians. In January 1886, Inspector A. Ross Cuthbert of the Mounted Police was sent to investigate rumours of starvation in the Duck Lake area. He found acute deprivation in the Métis community and reported the Indians were "miserable beyond description . . . . poorly clothed and huddled in their huts like sheep in a pen." He noted that the previous summer "they lived on gophers and this winter on rabbits . . . they can't go far because they have no clothes. . . ." He left a few old horse blankets with the

Indians and was rewarded with a reprimand from Dewdney.[26] In the final analysis, despite all that had happened, little had changed for those on the verge of starvation on the reservations.

North West Mounted Police Barracks Regina 1885   PAM N-18372

- 15 -
Perilous Times For The Force

At the end of the rebellion there were three groups, the victors, the vanquished and the victims. The victors included the Government of Canada which had overcome several problems, the Canadian Militia, which had turned defeats into victories and the Indian Department, which enjoyed the satisfaction, in their eyes, of seeing the Indians punished, intimidated and, hopefully, brought under control. The vanquished are traditionally considered the Métis and the Indians, although it can be argued that, with the exception of Louis Riel and those who lost their lives in the fighting, the majority of the Métis who were involved escaped relatively unscathed. The Indians, on the other hand, received punishment out of proportion to their actual involvement. The part played by the white settlers who provided the financial and other support to bring Louis Riel back from Montana in the first place was barely recognized and, almost without exception, they were never called to account for their actions.

One of the real losers in the rebellion was the North-West Mounted Police who came out of the insurrection with their reputation badly mauled and were often unfairly maligned by those in authority who should have known better, especially General Middleton. During the years just prior to the troubles, the force was dogged by problems of poor pay, run-down equipment, a constant and serious shortage of horses and other difficulties. "Neglected by the government and beset with internal problems, the Force's condition, but for the outstanding example of a few individuals, was at a low ebb by 1885."[1]

Some of the Mounted Police were under military command as subunit and fought alongside the Militia in actions such as Cut Knife Hill. Others formed the nucleus of units such as Steele's Scouts, composed of a mixture of policemen and civilian volunteers, which had an outstanding record in action at Frenchman Butte and Loon Lake. With the exception of Duck Lake, the piecemeal use of the force

193

never allowed the Mounted Police to go into action as a single unit and gain full credit for their achievements. Throughout the rebellion the policemen who had not been assigned a military role continued to carry out their usual police tasks.

The Mounted Police were fortunate to have survived the North-West Rebellion without many more casualties. They were highly vulnerable on a number of occasions but rebel leaders did not take advantage of their chance to inflict serious damage. A large portion of the force could have been successfully attacked during the retreat from Duck Lake to Fort Carlton, during the evacuation from Fort Carlton to Prince Albert, during the trip of the Fort Pitt Detachment down the ice-choked North Saskatchewan River, and the withdrawal from Cut Knife Hill to Battleford.

With the defeat of Superintendent Crozier and his men at Duck Lake, the force suffered a great loss in prestige. The situation called for strong support by the government and a chance for the Mounted Police to recoup their loss. Unfortunately, the newly arrived Commander of the Canadian Militia, General Middleton, had for some reason brought a highly-developed contempt for the Mounted Police and most of its officers with him. He was not reluctant to give voice to his feelings and his disdain was quickly communicated downward through the ranks of the Militia and to the correspondents of the nation's newspapers. The Mounted Police could take some solace in the fact that they were not the only objects of Middleton's derision. They shared it with the Indians and Métis.

General Middleton had two main targets for his disdain and contempt, Commissioner Irvine at Prince Albert and Inspector Morris at Battleford. By the end of the campaign, this low esteem was matched or exceeded by the low opinion many of Middleton's own troops had for him, but in the early days his comments were accepted as gospel. Middleton referred to the Mounted Police in Prince Albert as "gophers," comparing them to prairie rodents who run for their burrows at the first sign of danger.[2] Fifty years later, one of the so-called "gophers," Colonel Gilbert

Sanders, who was an Inspector at Prince Albert in 1885, wrote that Middleton had ordered the Mounted Police to remain in Prince Albert. He noted that ". . . poor old Colonel Irvine I'm afraid was rather weak and I understand was persuaded not to make use of the order contained in the telegram in defence of himself against the unjust charges General Middleton made against the police."[3]   Sanders, who was among those collectively alleged to be cowards and hiding in Prince Albert, was later recommended for a Victoria Cross during the Boer War in South Africa and received a Distinguished Service Order - some "gopher." After the action against Poundmaker at Cut Knife Hill the troops involved were labelled "otters" because they were allegedly scared to leave their holes in Battleford.[4]

Middleton was annoyed at pressing requests that his forces move to relieve Prince Albert and Battleford since he did not want to change his plan for an attack on Batoche. He would not accept that Prince Albert had ever been in danger and said that "no attempt was made against it, even by Scouts during the whole affair."[5]   When Middleton eventually arrived at Prince Albert he observed that it had been "hastily and imperfectly fortified at different points," but added that it had been "tolerably safe from attack, as the Half-Breeds and Indians are not in the habit of attacking even slightly protected positions on a level plain without cover."[6]

Superintendent R. Burton Deane, a staunch defender of Commissioner Irvine, ridiculed the contention that any intervention by Middleton was necessary. He wrote that "General Middleton had enough men with him to eat the rebel half-breeds, moccasins and all, but seemed to have some ridiculous ideas about the risking of human life, and hesitated and demurred until Colonel Williams's regiment got tired of being made fools of and rushed the half-breed trenches, out of which the dusky occupants scrambled without any ceremony whatever and were lost to sight."[7]

General Middleton's feelings were not shared by all his staff officers. His Chief of Staff, Lord Melgund, who was later the Governor General of Canada as

Lord Minto, commented that it seemed to him the value of the North West Mounted Police under Commissioner Irvine was always under-rated. He said that the presence of Irvine's force at Prince Albert gave settlers a safe refuge and the combination of the need to protect the civilian population and difficult country had always made the possibility of Irvine joining Middleton doubtful, whereas the moral value of Irvine's force at Prince Albert was certain. R.G. MacBeth expressed the belief that General Middleton "resented the dominance of the Mounted Police in the mind of the west and was more ready to make some slighting remark about them than to take their counsel." [8]

J.S. Macdonald, a telegrapher with the Dominion Telegraph Company, who was on the temporary terminal at Clarke's Crossing and Fort Pitt, was concerned about the treatment given the Mounted Police and based on his personal observations wrote that "the Mounted Police had a much larger share in putting down the Rebellion than they have been given credit for. I speak as one who was in a position to know. General Middleton's attitude towards them was, if not unfriendly, at least not cordial, and this attitude was reflected in some degree in the stand taken by a few of his subordinates. This however was not true of such of the militia as were stationed at Battleford, where the relations of the two forces were at once cordial and appreciated."[9]

While General Middleton had nothing but contempt and disdain for Commissioner Irvine, Inspector Morris and Inspector Dickens, he was full of praise for Superintendent William Herchmer from the very beginning, perhaps being aware of the close connection between the Herchmer family and Sir John A. Macdonald. His messages to Colonel Otter often included flattering remarks about Herchmer or messages for him. He asked Otter to "tell Herchmer I am much obliged for all the assistance he has given, which I shall not forget."[10] Middleton was also high in his praise of Captain John French of French's Scouts, an ex-Sub-Inspector in the North-West Mounted Police and brother of the first Commissioner. During the final attack at Batoche, Captain French ran into a house and up to the second storey. As he appeared in a window, he was shot and killed.

While they were under attack by the general, there was little or no support for Commissioner Irvine and the Mounted Police from their political masters. Frederick White sent Irvine a telegram informing him that "Sir John considers Crozier's report of engagement at Duck Lake very incomplete and wishes detailed particulars, also explain why he went to Duck Lake knowing you were about to join him." Lief Crozier was now in Sir John A. Macdonald's bad books and effectively *persona non grata,* despite his recent appointment as Assistant Commissioner of the force. Irvine did not escape the scrutiny from Ottawa and White's message continued, "From yourself he wishes full report from time you left Regina till arrival General Middleton at Prince Albert, why you abandoned Fort Carlton, and why you did not go to Duck Lake, why you did not scour country around Prince Albert and why you did not join General Middleton. Also any further particulars you can furnish. He also wishes full report from Dickens and Morris."[11] The influence of Middleton can be seen in this request. He was critical of Irvine, Crozier, Dickens and Morris and their actions are called into question but nothing is asked of the activities of Steele, Perry or Herchmer. There is also an implicit assumption that Irvine had failed to do certain things which, in fact, he had done, e.g., to scour the country around Prince Albert, instead of asking what he had done in this regard.

During the campaign, General Middleton had obviously been giving some thought to the post-rebellion military organization in Western Canada. This was not a new problem. Some years previously, there had been discussion as to whether a police force or a military force was appropriate for the west. In 1873 Alexander Morris, the newly appointed Lieutenant Governor at Fort Garry did not agree that there was a choice between providing police in the North-West Territories or troops at Fort Garry.[12] He wrote to Sir John A. Macdonald pointing

197

out that "the most important matter of the future is the preservation of order in the North-West and little as Canada may like it she has to stable her elephant. In short the Dominion will have to maintain both a military and police force for years to come."[13]

The initial recruiting of the North-West Mounted Police in 1873 and the move of the first contingent to Lower Fort Garry were accomplished with a great deal of assistance from the Department of Militia and Defence. The temporary first Commissioner was the Deputy Adjutant General of Military District 10 in Manitoba, Lieutenant Colonel W. Osborne Smith, an infantry officer. The first actual Commissioner was a Royal Artillery officer, Lieutenant Colonel George A. French, and many of the first officers and noncommissioned officers were serving or had served in the military. Despite the military connection, there were problems. During the planning for the march west when the force deployed in 1874, Commissioner French was adamant that the force should not be dependent on the Militia for supplies. He informed the Minister of Justice that he wished "it to be particularly understood that from previous as well as present experience I object to the Force under my command being dependent on the officials or contractors of the Militia Department for their supply."[14] In 1874, the Toronto *Mail*, referring to relations between the recently formed North-West Mounted Police and the Department of Militia and Defence, noted "it is true that a jealousy as to the organization prevented the latter from giving cooperation and assistance to the former, at the expense of the poor fellows now lying unsupported and half provided, in the middle of the boundless prairie."[15]

For the first decade or more after its formation the North-West Mounted Police was the focal point for stories of intrepid courage on the plains. The Militia, on the other hand, was rarely west of Fort Garry and was not involved in the kind of activities that produce heroes or even good war stories. At this time the permanent military force of about 850 full-time soldiers was going to be smaller than the North-West Mounted Police which, by the end of the rebellion, had a strength of 1,039 men. If the North-West Mounted Police could be absorbed, the number of full-time soldiers would virtually double overnight and more soldiers meant more generals and it was probably easy for garrison-bound soldiers to imagine that active duty in the west would put them in a seemingly romantic role similar to that of the United States cavalry.

After availing himself of every opportunity to cast the North-West Mounted Police generally and Commissioner Irvine in particular in the worst possible light, General Middleton told Adolphe Caron that the Mounted Police had "completely lost all prestige with whites, breeds and Indians." He suggested instead, "a corps of a thousand infantry, khaki-clad, with carefully chosen officers and proper arms and equipment - no red coats, lace and long boots." He wanted this to be a military force and said "there is no doubt that if the thousand men are still called police and left under Irvine, and with the same organization, people will be uneasy . . . ."[16] Even while he was caught up in conducting the campaign, Middleton continued to lobby for the abolition of the North-West Mounted Police. While at Fish Creek on May 2, he sent a message to Caron, saying, "If I understand rightly that you propose to establish a mounted force for the North-West. It should be distinctly mounted infantry, dressed properly for the duty required - no red coats, lace and long boots but khaki coloured uniforms with Winchesters and sword bayonets." This was followed by his advice that "these forces should be permanent and formed under a military organization and should supercede the Mounted Police altogether." He repeated the allegation that the Mounted Police, "since late events has completely lost all prestige with Whites, breeds, and Indians; but I should recommend that their formation should not be attempted until these troubles are over as the corps should be organized with great care, so that men like Morris and others could not find place in it . . . ."[17] In response Caron said he agreed ". . . about the organization of the Mounted Force, it should be as you say, we shall not organize it for present."[18]

Despite General Middleton's efforts to ensure that Inspector Morris had no place in the post-rebellion force, he continued to serve in the North-West Mounted Police. His consuming interest after the rebellion appears to have been to get himself promoted. When he had a Member of Parliament intercede on his behalf, the response from Ottawa was that nobody junior to him had been promoted "but he seems to have an idea that by using political influence he can step over the heads of some who are senior to him."[19] This is not the way to influence your superiors in a military organization.

On May 16, the vendetta continued when Caron told Middleton "I want you to make searching enquiry into the conduct of Irvine, Morris, Crozier and Colonel of the 65th Battalion. I want you to give these matters your personal attention. . . ."[20] Middleton, who had a campaign to conduct, responded that he was "enquiring into Police affairs, have not much time - statements contradictory and unsatisfactory but am convinced the present police organization is bad."[21] A month later, on June 22, Middleton had more time and in a message to Caron, returned to the theme of somehow abolishing the Mounted Police, repeating his opinion that " . . . there is no doubt that if the thousand mounted men are still called Police and left under Irvine, and with the same organization, people here will be uneasy as without doubt, the Police as a body have lost prestige, and justifiably so I fear . . . "[22]

There were also occasional outside pressures for the government to incorporate the force completely into the Canadian military system. Such suggestions usually emanated from individuals associated with the Militia. Shortly after the North-West Rebellion, a former Minister of Militia & Defence, Senator L.F.G. Masson, suggested to Sir John A. Macdonald that the Mounted Police should be placed under the control of the Militia Department on the model of the French Gendarmerie.[23]

The idea of abolishing the Police and increasing the number of troops in the west did not sit well with the Indian Department. Despite their differences about the treatment of Indians, the Department could exercise a certain amount of influence with the Mounted Police. The Mounted Police and Indians were used to each other and this was not the time to increase tension by introducing soldiers into the equation. Cecil Denny pointed out that "the Indians are used to the police going into their camps for prisoners, but do not understand men dressed in another uniform doing this duty."[24] Lieutenant Governor Dewdney was concerned that soldiers who were not familiar with Indians were likely to have problems. Sir John A. Macdonald was not enthusiastic about replacing the Mounted Police and slowly the idea faded into the background. Superintendent Richard Burton Deane considered that Middleton overdid his bewailing the supposed inefficiency of the Mounted Police to a point where Sir John A. Macdonald resented his criticisms and decided to keep the force under his personal care, rather than turn it over to the Militia Department.

Commissioner Irvine was finished after the rebellion. Although he was in many respects, a scapegoat, his reputation had been damaged beyond repair by the aspersions cast upon his character and effectiveness by General Middleton which were repeated in the press. One correspondent wrote from Prince Albert that "the need for troops is unquestioned, for I fear the prestige of the Mounted Police is lost. Every Half-breed and Indian speaks in contemptuous terms of the force, and has no more dread of it than they have of gophers."[25] The press attacks had started early and, as far back as April, the Belleville Daily Intelligencer had noted "the grumbling at Col. Irvine and Major Crozier is becoming wide spread now, and it is thought that whatever may be the outcome of the trouble their official heads will be chopped off."[26]

Although he was in favour of retaining the police, Macdonald told Edgar Dewdney in November 1885, "We must get rid of Irvine as soon as possible."[27] Once Macdonald decided that Irvine had to go, he was once more in the position of searching for a Commissioner, a matter that had preoccupied him periodically in the past.[28] Sir John A. Macdonald's track record in selecting Commissioners for the force was not impressive. When Macdonald shuffled James Macleod out of the appointment, he explained in the House of Commons that "Colonel Macleod who formerly commanded them was a very good officer but he was too kindly towards the force. He is now a Stipendiary Magistrate, and Colonel Irvine who is now in command, is, I believe, considerably more of a martinet, and is paying particular attention to the correction of the dissolute habits of some of the men."[29] This did not happen. Commissioner Irvine lived up to the more accurate prophecy of Major General Selby-Smyth who had described him as "almost too good natured to command respect."[30] A force historian later commented that Irvine "gained the affection of his subordinates, but not their respect. He failed to rule his officers who in many cases ran their posts to suit themselves, much to the detriment of the Force's morale and efficiency."[31]

Sir John A. Macdonald discussed the matter of a new Commissioner with Lord Lansdowne, the Governor General with a view to offering the position to Lord Melgund who was Lansdowne's Military Secretary.[32] Lansdowne, in a letter to Melgund, noted some of the "reforms which he thought essential, such as an increase in numbers, and a first-class man in command who could undertake the direction of a 'little war.'"[33] Lansdowne told Macdonald that "Melgund is much tempted but hesitating. I don't think Lady Melgund takes kindly to the idea of Regina."[34] Melgund wrote to Macdonald himself, asking a number of questions about the position which obviously appealed to him. He was curious about whether the Commissioner would have to report through a Comptroller and, among other things, whether "a permanent residence at Regina be absolutely necessary?"[35]

Regina seems to have been too much for the Melgunds and Sir John A. Macdonald looked elsewhere. General Strange, back on his ranch at Strangmuir, read press reports that Commissioner Irvine "had gone to Ottawa with the intention of resigning the Commissionership of the N.W.M.P." He immediately wrote to Sir John A. Macdonald offering his services, noting that "it is for you to decide whether my appointment would be popular in Canada." He added that "during the Rebellion I had under my command bodies of the N.W.M.P. and better officers and men I would not wish to command . . . "[36] Sir Alexander Campbell advised Macdonald that Strange ". . . lacks discretion I think and perhaps good sense somewhat."[37] General Middleton had already maligned General Strange, just as he had Commissioner Irvine, and Cecil Denny was highly critical of his activities in relation to the Blackfoot. Strange told Macdonald that he had "friendly relations with both Indians and white settlers."[38] This did not fit with the opinion of Denny that "General Strange is utterly unfit to handle Indians."[39] Nothing came of Strange's application but it would have been an interesting appointment. Strange was blunt, direct and almost totally politically incorrect, but he may have been a better choice than the one that Macdonald ultimately made.

Eventually the Commissioner's appointment went to Lawrence Herchmer, son of a close friend and neighbour from Kingston, who had been promised a commission in the Mounted Police prior to its formation.[40] He had some military experience but was totally lacking in Police experience. His brother, Superintendent William Herchmer, was serving in the force. Richard Burton Deane, who believed he was on the short list for the appointment, along with Major George Hatton and Lawrence Herchmer, credited Herchmer's success to his being "the bosom friend of the Hon. Edgar Dewdney" who had the ear of the Prime Minister.[41] Commissioner Irvine resigned on March 31, 1886 and Herchmer replaced him. At this point, Sir John A. Macdonald, who created the North-West Mounted Police and kept it under his wing, had presided over the demise of three of the first four Commissioners.

The North-West Mounted Police may have survived as an organization but General Middleton was not finished with his attempts to belittle them. In a bizarre decision, the government ruled that members of the North-West Mounted Police would not be eligible for the North-West Canada Medal to be awarded to those who saw service in the rebellion. The somewhat incredible rationale for this decision was that the policemen were only doing their normal duty, while the militia had left home and hearth at a considerable disruption to their personal lives. This meant that militia personnel in the rear areas, who never saw action, were awarded the medal while members of the Mounted Police who fought the rebels face to face were denied the same recognition. If this logic was followed precisely, it should also have meant that the relatively small number of full-time soldiers who served in the campaign and were only doing their normal duty should also have been denied the medal, including General Middleton!

This ludicrous decision was, of course, masterminded by General Middleton who was accused of making petty excuses so that he would not have to acknowledge the considerable contribution of the Mounted Police during the rebellion. Middleton's attitude toward the force caused a great deal of resentment in the west where, unlike their eastern counterparts, newspapers often defended the Police. P.G. Laurie wrote that Middleton's "sentiments concerning that body were well known before he left Ottawa" and he "took good care to keep up the impression that the Mounted Police was an inefficient, useless body . . . " Obviously not a great admirer of Middleton, Laurie went on to explain that the Mounted Police were kept away from the rebels as much as possible since "if he gave them an opportunity they would make Canada ring with their gallant deeds, and this was more than the pompous Englishman could stand." Warming up to his attack, Laurie described Middleton as "prejudiced against the police in the first

The North West Canada Medal

place, he could not forgive them for having taught him how to fight Indians and half-breeds, and now he continues to vent his spite by refusing to recommend them for the medal."[42]

There was widespread negative reaction to this exclusion of members of the Mounted Police and the regulations were amended by an Order-in-Council of July 10, 1886 to allow the award of medals to those members who had actually been under fire. This meant the majority of members still did not qualify and the government received hundreds of requests that all who served in the Rebellion be equally honoured. In December 1886, approval was given for a clasp reading "Saskatchewan" to be issued to those who took part in the engagements at Fish Creek, Batoche, Cut Knife and Frenchman Butte.

A Trying Time

General Middleton suggested a separate clasp be issued for "Batoche" which he described as "the decisive and final engagement of the campaign."[43] The idea that Batoche had been the final engagement of the campaign would have come as a surprise to those in the Alberta Field Force who were under fire at Frenchman Butte and Loon Lake. In any case, the decision was made to have one clasp, for issue to those who were at Fish Creek, Batoche, Cut Knife Hill, and Frenchman Butte.[44] This ignored those who came under fire at Duck Lake and Loon Lake, presumably because these engagements involved the Mounted Police. Sergeant Frederick Bagley, who had taken the Battleford reinforcements to Fort Carlton at the time of the Duck Lake clash, headed the patrol that scouted Poundmaker's position at Cut Knife Hill, led the pursuit of Little Poplar and captured four Indians involved in the killing of Payne, had his application for a medal denied. Frederick White informed Commissioner Herchmer that the authority for medals to the Police was distinctly limited to those who were "actually under fire," and was "intended to include only those who were present and took part in recognized engagements." White added that there was "no report on record here of skirmishes near Battleford with Indians and Halfbreeds from Poundmaker's Camp during which Sergt. Bagley states he was under fire and two Indians were killed."[45]

The battle raged on and eventually, after fifteen years, the bureaucrats in Ottawa capitulated and all members who served in the North-West Rebellion were made eligible for the campaign medal.[46] Ex-Sergeant Major Frederick Bagley, Staff Sergeants Hooper and Raven, had their medals forwarded to them at the port of embarkation in Halifax in 1899, fourteen years after the rebellion, as they were sailing for a new war in South Africa with the Canadian Mounted Rifles.[47]

Many of those who served in the rebellion were disappointed when the only recognition went to General Middleton, who was given a purse of $20,000 by Canada and a knighthood by the Queen. There was widespread criticism of

206

Staff Sergeant Frederick Bagley   SAB-235

Middleton by those who felt slighted at being overlooked for honours and awards and every indication that recommendations for recognition by General Strange, including citation of Inspector Steele and Sergeant William Parker, did not get past Middleton's headquarters. General Strange had recommended Sergeant Hamilton, who acted as Supply Officer for the Alberta Field Force, and Sergeant Fury, who acted as Sergeant Major for Steele's Scouts, for promotion and James Oswald and John Corryell, the officers under Steele in Steele's Scouts, for commissions in the Mounted Police. Nothing came of these efforts.[48]

Those who considered themselves ignored could take some solace when a Bresaylor Métis, Charles Bremner, charged Sir Frederick Middleton, C.B., K.C.M.G., with stealing furs. Middleton had appropriated some valuable furs belonging to Bremner, who was a prisoner at the time, on suspicion of being a rebel. Middleton divided the furs between himself, Hayter Reed and Samuel Bedson. Reed and Bedson instructed Staff Sergeant Sandy Warden, the Mounted Police quartermaster at Battleford, to bundle up the furs. The furs were packed by Constable Arthur Dorion, who had them delivered to a steamer where they were promptly stolen by somebody else.[49] When he was freed, Bremner turned up at Battleford demanding his furs, which Warden no longer had. Bremner persisted in his efforts to seek justice and eventually, after five years, forced an investigation by the House of Commons. Middleton's actions were found to be illegal and effectively ended his career in Canada.[50]

General Middleton did not reserve his contempt for the Mounted Police. He had a poor opinion of the Militia, the Métis and the Indians. He surrounded himself with British officers, placing them in all key staff appointments. He was condescending and patronizing toward Canadians, a characteristic of many British Army officers up to the present day. It is interesting to note that the only major scandal to emerge from the campaign involved a British Army officer, Middleton, an ex British soldier, Bedson, and Hayter Reed, who seemed to wish he was British.

208

Perilous Times For The Force

Many of the Mounted Police and Militia officers who took part in the rebellion rose briefly to prominence and then faded from view. It is an interesting commentary on our history that, while most Canadians would recognize the names of Louis Riel and Gabriel Dumont, few would know Strange, Irvine, or Crozier. The only North-West Mounted Police officer of that time who is well-known today is Sam Steele.

In addition to those who suffered death or wounds, others succumbed to illness during or just after the Rebellion. Sergeant William McMinn and Constable Alexander Dyre, who served in Steele's Scouts, both died of typhoid at Battleford shortly after the Rebellion. Sergeant Charles Chasse, who was at the Craig Incident and Duck Lake, also died of typhoid in 1885, as did Corporal Richard Routledge, who steered the Fort Pitt scow down the ice-choked North Saskatchewan River. Corporal Thomas Gilchrist, who was wounded at Duck Lake but survived, died of a heart attack a few months later in December 1885.

The end of the rebellion marked a turning point in the development of the west and also in the history of the North-West Mounted Police. The Indians and Métis, who had been the numerically dominant group in the west, were now being outnumbered by settlers and were no longer regarded as a threat. The North-West Mounted Police had survived the efforts of those who wished to see it abolished and now faced new challenges. The new Commissioner, Lawrence Herchmer, introduced many badly needed organizational changes and measures to increase the efficiency of the force but, unfortunately, his stewardship of the force was marred by continuous acrimonious disputes with his officers and men as well as others outside the force. The Mounted Police doubled in size within a year and the large influx of raw recruits taxed the ability of the seasoned officers and noncommissioned officers who remained. Fortunately, a number of new officers of considerable ability were appointed at this time, such as Charles Constantine, Cortland Starnes and Zachary Wood, while outstanding officers such as Samuel Steele and Aylesworth Bowen Perry were promoted. The North-West Mounted

A Trying Time

Police now entered a new era, ready for the challenges of rapid settlement of the west while, still unknown to them, the different challenges of bringing law and order to the Yukon and fighting a war in South Africa was barely a decade away.

APPENDICES

The following appendices contain lists of members of the North-West Mounted Police who were present at specific locations and engagements during the North-West Rebellion. The lists have been compiled from a variety of sources and cross-checked wherever possible. An early list was published in T. Arnold Haultain, "History of Riel's Second Rebellion and How It Was Quelled," *Souvenir Edition, Canadian Pictorial & Illustrated War News*, Toronto: Grip Printing, 1885. This list was reproduced in *Scarlet & Gold*, 16th Edition, pp. 9-10. Where information came largely from one main official source, that source is indicated on the specific appendix.

Readers are cautioned that the available research sources have numerous differences in regimental numbers, spelling of names and initials. Where possible, differences have been reconciled by reference to individual service files. Despite the care taken in the compilation of these lists the potential for error exists.

APPENDICES

MEMBERS OF THE NORTH-WEST MOUNTED POLICE AT
THE CRAIG INCIDENT - 1884

	Supt	Crozier	Lief Newbury Fitzroy
285	Insp	Antrobus	William Denny
	Surg	Miller	Robert
27	Sgt Major	Kirk	Michael John
367	S/Sgt	Mackay	Alexander Bryan
507	S/Sgt	Warden	Stephen
247	Sgt	Bagley	Frederick Augustus (1)*
318	Sgt	Brooks	William Alfonse (2)
301	Sgt	Keenan	Henry
264	Cpl	Chasse	Charles
492	Cpl	McNeill	John Edward James McDougall (2)
565	Cpl	Sleigh	Ralph Bateman
619	Const	Allen	Charles
615	Const	Anderson	William (1)*
620	Const	Armour	Samuel D
517	Const	Casault	Godfrey
642	Const	Cole	Archibald (1)*
646	Const	Cole	Charles
605	Const	Colebrook	Colin Campbell
521	Const	Collins	John Jack (2)
802	Const	Cookson	Wilfred (1)
813	Const	DeGear	Jacob Cicero
324	Const	Dorion	Arthur
525	Const	Dowsley	Richard (2)
657	Const	Dufresne	Ovila
652	Const	Duncan	John A
484	Const	Fontaine	Louis
467	Const	Fowler	Frederick (1)
966	Const	Fraser	George
672	Const	Garton	Frederick Holtby*
1247	Const	Grahame	George M (2)*
679	Const	Grogan	Charles (1)
1008	Const	Guthrie	John
682	Const	Halbhaus	William Theodore*
869	Const	Hayne	Murray Henry Edward
538	Const	Hobbs	Robert
995	Const	Hynes	John (2)

Appendices

695	Const	Ince	Robert
887	Const	Kerr	Warren
999	Const	Knight	Charles
707	Const	Leduc	Ferriol
925	Const	Loasby	Clarence McLean
542	Const	Loscombe	Henry Clifton (1)
710	Const	Lunnin	William W
303	Const	MacDermot	Joseph Augustin
37	Const	MacDonald	John A (1)*
544	Const	McAlister	Thomas (1)
724	Const	McQuarrie	William
429	Const	Millar	Malcolm Tanner (2)
717	Const	Millward	Thomas
487	Const	Montgomery	Albert Ernest Garland (2)
993	Const	Morrow	Edward
425	Const	Murray	Arthur Thomas*
733	Const	Murray	William
744	Const	Pembridge	George
747	Const	Potter	William Henry
863	Const	Prior	Frederick Edward
1004	Const	Redmond	Thomas John
884	Const	Roberts	John Jones*
763	Const	Rummerfield	John
762	Const	Rutledge	Richard (1)
764	Const	Scott	David
768	Const	Simons	James Arthur
769	Const	Simons	Percy William
568	Const	St. Denis	Odilon
779	Const	Stevenson	George Vicars
776	Const	Storer	John Harold
994	Const	Straton	William
766	Const	Sullivan	Daniel (1)
841	Const	Williams	William P
391	Const	Wilmot	John Hibbert (2)
788	Const	Worthington	Orlando (2)
610	Const	Yelland	John
864	Const	Young	Campbell (2)
	Interp	Laronde	Louis
	Civ.	Finlayson	Rory

213

Notes: (1) Assigned to Bastion No. 1 on June 18, 1884.

           (2) Assigned to Bastion No. 2 on June 18, 1884.

          *   Remained at Cut Knife Creek (Poundmaker's and Little Pine's Reservation until Big Bear left for Fort Pitt in September 1884.

Appendices

Appendix " B "

MEMBERS OF THE NORTH-WEST MOUNTED POLICE AT THE ENGAGEMENT AT DUCK LAKE, MARCH 26, 1885.

	Supt	Crozier	Lief Newbury Fitzroy
	Surg	Miller	Robert
	Insp	Howe	Joseph
649	Sgt Major	Dann	Frederick G
318	Sgt	Brooks	William Alfonse
773	Sgt	Smart	William Crawford
400	Sgt	Stewart	Alfred
101	Sgt	Pringle	James
947	Cpl	Davidson	Hugh James Alexander
264	Cpl	Chasse	Charles
467	Cpl	Fowler	Frederick
521	Cpl	Collins	John Jack
532	Cpl	Gilchrist	Thomas Haddon
1065	Const	Arnold	George Pearce
516	Const	Carter	Robert
897	Const	Cochrane	Thomas
611	Const	Craigie	Thomas Campbell
642	Const	Cole	Archibald
1034	Const	Des Barres	Herman
525	Const	Dowsley	Richard
1082	Const	Edwards	John
850	Const	Fleming	Thomas Crivers
454	Const	Fontaine	Louis
852	Const	Garrett	George Knox
672	Const	Garton	Frederick Holtby
1003	Const	Gibson	Thomas James
1117	Const	Gordon	Stanley F
462	Const	Gribble	F J
682	Const	Halbhaus	William Theodore
1099	Const	Hammond	Harold B
981	Const	Hoyland	Thomas H
1076	Const	Hetherington	Henry Ashton
1079	Const	Jackson	William
1015	Const	Jamieson	Robert Walter
710	Const	Lunnin	William W
1045	Const	Manners-Smith	Alfred
935	Const	Miller	August

215

1009	Const	Mountain	Albert Charles Glover
487	Const	Montgomery	Albert Ernest G
993	Const	Morrow	Edward
425	Const	Murray	Arthur James
491	Const	McDonald	Alexander
730	Const	McMillan	Andrew Hugh
433	Const	MacPherson	David Hamilton
1012	Const	Nunn	William Charles
854	Const	Perkins	William
1004	Const	Redmond	Thomas John
763	Const	Rummerfield	John
764	Const	Scott	David
1087	Const	Smith	William
596	Const	Street	John
916	Const	Woodman	Alfred Harry
1048	Const	Wood	John Jones
788	Const	Worthington	Orlando

Source: Annual Report 1885, pp. 48-49.

Appendices

SPECIAL CONSTABLES OF THE PRINCE ALBERT
VOLUNTEERS PRESENT AT DUCK LAKE - MARCH 16, 1885.

Capt	Moore	H Stewart
Capt	Morton	John
Sgt	Powers	Thomas
Sgt	Campbell	Thomas Nelson
Sgt	Wilson	Justus
Sgt	McNab	Alexander
Cpl	Ramsay	W C
Cpl	Dixon	W
Cpl	Napier	William
Pte	Anderson	Joseph
Pte	Bakie	James
Pte	Brown	James
Pte	Burns	Robert
Pte	Byrne	Charles
Pte	Drain	William
Pte	Duck	George
Pte	Elliott	Skeff Connor
Pte	Fisher	Alexander
Pte	Flett	James
Pte	Hamilton	Charles
Pte	Markley	Arthur W B
Pte	McGinn	Richard
Pte	McKenzie	Daniel
Pte	McPhail	Daniel
Pte	Nelson	George
Pte	Nelson	Henry
Pte	Newett	Charles
Pte	Sutherland	George
Pte	Tait	William
Pte	Kelly	Henry
Pte	Laurie	William
Pte	Thibault	M
Pte	Wymerskirch	John
Pte	Middleton	Robert
Pte	Stewart	Alexander
Pte	Barker	William
Pte	McKay	Donald
Pte	Haslam	William
Pte	Giveen	Charles

Pte	Clarke	Lawrence
Pte	McKay	Thomas
Pte	Mitchell	Hillyard

Source: Annual Report 1885, p. 49.

Appendices

MEMBERS OF THE NORTH-WEST MOUNTED POLICE
FROG LAKE DETACHMENT - MARCH 1885

565	Cpl	Sleigh	Ralph Bateman
538	Cpl	Hobbs	Robert
515	Const	Carroll	James W
707	Const	Leduc	Ferriol
737	Const	MacDonald	John A
604	Const	Rowley	George W

MEMBERS OF THE NORTH-WEST MOUNTED POLICE
IN THE FORT PITT DETACHMENT - APRIL 1885.

	Insp	Dickens	Francis J
1083	S/Sgt	Rolph	J Widmer
41	Sgt	Martin	John Alfred
565	Cpl	Sleigh	Ralph Bateman
615	Const	Anderson	William
858	Const	Ayre	Henry Thomas
515	Const	Carroll	James W
661	Const	Edmonds	Herbert A
538	Const	Hobbs	Robert
695	Const	Ince.	Robert
707	Const	Leduc	Ferriol
822	Const	Lionais	George
925	Const	Loasby	Clarence McLean
737	Const	Macdonald	John A
739	Const	O'Keefe	Laurence
748	Const	Phillips	Charles T
751	Const	Quigley	Joseph
865	Const	Robertson	Brenton Haliburton
381	Const	Roby	Frederick Cochrane
604	Const	Rowley	George W
762	Const	Rutledge	Richard
866	Const	Smith	Walter William
781	Const	Tector	John W
942	Const	Warren	Falkland Fritz-Mauritz

Appendices

MEMBERS OF THE NORTH-WEST MOUNTED POLICE
IN COLONEL OTTER'S COLUMN - 1885

	Supt	Herchmer	William M
2	Supt	Neale	Percy Reginald
594	Sgt Major	Wattam	Thomas
560	Vet S/Sgt	Riddell	Robert
670	Sgt	Gordon	John Cristie
606	Sgt	Macleod	George
899	Sgt	Richards	John
56	Sgt	Piercy	William T
36	Sgt	Ward	John Henry
633	Cpl	Blake	Samuel M
1074	Cpl	Eales	Cyril John
902	Cpl	Lowry	William Hay Talbot
545	Cpl	McCounsell	William P
469	Const	Bond	Stanislas
1102	Const	Brooke	Arthur Frederick M
973	Const	Elliot	Frank Orlando
528	Const	Forde	William Herbert
931	Const	Gilpin	William
671	Const	Glasford	Edward S
958	Const	Goodwin	Frank
996	Const	Halenback	John
921	Const	Harstone	John Christopher
988	Const	Hyles	Frank
347	Const	Jarvis	Stephen Murray
350	Const	Kerr	John William
999	Const	Knight	Charles
355	Const	Latimer	William
917	Const	Lawder	John Beverly Robertson
713	Const	Lewis	William
706	Const	Lloyd	Richard Wood
934	Const	Miller	John
431	Const	Moody	Arthur Ralph
554	Const	Morgan	William
886	Const	McLeod	Torquil
496	Const	Percival	Samuel
992	Const	Perrin	William
863	Const	Prior	Frederick Edward

221

036	Const	Purchess	George
969	Const	Racey	Edmond Ford
756	Const	Ritchie	William James
800	Const	Ross	James
932	Const	Routledge	William Henry
561	Const	Royce	Joseph Robert
754	Const	Rumball	Alfred Hersey M
1077	Const	Shaw	William Mansfield
768	Const	Simons	Percy William
964	Const	Spencer	Henry
983	Const	Spencer	William Isaac
836	Const	Sunderland	William
835	Const	Swinton	William Charles
962	Const	Taylor	Alfred
796	Const	Wright	Joseph
625	Sp/Const	Burnet	Thomas Francis

Appendices

MEMBERS OF THE NORTH-WEST MOUNTED POLICE
IN FORT BATTLEFORD - 1885

	Insp	Morris	William Springfield
27	Sgt Major	Kirk	Michael John
367	S/Sgt	Mackay	Alexander Ryan
286	Sgt QM	Warden	Stephen
16	Vet Sgt	Fraser	George
247	Sgt	Bagley	Frederick Augustus
13	Sgt	Lake	Thomas Horatio
619	Cpl	Allen	Charles
616	Const	Ashbaugh	Thomas
1080	Const	Brown	Richard Jebb
646	Const	Cole	Charles
581	Const	Davis	Daniel (Peaches)
658	Const	Dawson	James
813	Const	DeGear	Jacob Cicero
324	Const	Dorion	Arthur
657	Const	Dufresne	Ovila
334	Const	Fraser	Joseph Lenson
271	Const	Guthrie	Richard
870	Const	Hawkins	Percy
995	Const	Hynes	John
887	Const	Kerr	Warren
1016	Const	Lavoie	Charles Adelaide
357	Const	Lavelley	David
542	Const	Loscombe	Henry Clifton
719	Const	Meredith	Matthew H.
747	Const	Potter	William Henry
1084	Const	Reid	John Alexander
1064	Const	Ross	Charles
776	Const	Storer	John Harold
994	Const	Straton	William
769	Const	Simons	James Arthur
1013	Const	White	Thomas
841	Const	Williams	William P.
402	Trumpeter	Burke	Patrick
	S/Const	Harpur	George

MEMBERS OF THE NORTH-WEST MOUNTED POLICE
AT CUT KNIFE HILL - MAY 2, 1885.

	Supt.	Herchmer	William.
	Supt.	Neale	Percy Reginald
594	Sgt Major	Wattam	Thomas
966	Vet S/Sgt	Fraser	George
560	Vet S/Sgt	Riddell	Robert
36	Sgt	Ward	John Henry
670	Sgt	Gordon	John Cristie
606	Sgt	Macleod	George
56	Sgt	Piercy	William T
899	Sgt	Richards	John
619	Cpl.	Allen	Charles
615	Cpl.	Anderson	William
858	Cpl.	Ayre	Henry Thomas
633	Cpl.	Blake	Samuel M.
402	Cpl.	Burke	Patrick
658	Cpl.	Dawson	James
813	Cpl.	Degear	Jacob Cicero
657	Cpl.	Dufresne	Ovila
1074	Cpl.	Eales	Cyril John
10	S/Cst	Harpur	George
870	Cpl.	Hawkins	Percy
995	Cpl.	Hynes	John
695	Cpl.	Ince	Robert
350	Cpl.	Kerr	John William
907	Cpl.	Lowry	William Hay Talbot
545	Cpl.	McCounsell	William P.
992	Cpl.	Perrin	William
748	Cpl.	Phillips	Charles T.
863	Cpl.	Prior	Frederick Edward
751	Cpl.	Quigley	Joseph
381	Cpl.	Roby	Frederick Cochrane
865	Cpl.	Robertson	Brenton Haliburton
1064	Cpl.	Ross	Charles
762	Cpl.	Rutledge	Richard
1077	Cpl.	Shaw	William Mansfield
565	Cpl.	Sleigh	Ralph Bateman
467	Const.	Bond	Stanislas

Appendices

1102	Const.	Brooke	Arthur Frederick Montford
973	Const.	Elliot	Frank Orlando
528	Const.	Forde	William Hubert
931	Const.	Gilpin	William
671	Const.	Glasford	Edward S.
958	Const.	Goodwin	Frank
996	Const.	Halenback	John.
921	Const.	Harstone	John Cristopher.
988	Const.	Hyles	Frank.
347	Const.	Jarvis	Stephen Murray
999	Const.	Knight	Charles.
355	Const.	Latimer	William
917	Const.	Lawder	John Beverly Robinson.
713	Const.	Lewis	William.
706	Const.	Lloyd	Richard Wood
886	Const.	McLeod	Torquil.
934	Const.	Miller	John
431	Const.	Moody	Arthur Ralph
554	Const.	Morgan	William
496	Const.	Percival	Samuel.
1036	Const.	Purches	George.
969	Const.	Racey	Edmond Ford
756	Const.	Ritchie	William James.
800	Const.	Ross	James
932	Const.	Routledge	William Henry
561	Const.	Royce	Joseph Robert
754	Const.	Rumball	Alfred Hersey M.
769	Const.	Simons	Percy.William.
964	Const.	Spencer	Henry
983	Const.	Spencer	William Isaac
776	Const.	Storer	John Harold
836	Const.	Sunderland	William
835	Const.	Swinton	William Charles
962	Const.	Taylor	Alfred
942	Const.	Warren	Falkland.Fritz-Mauritz.
579	Const.	Wright	Joseph
Interp.		Alexander	Joseph

Source: NAC, RG 18, RCMP Papers, Vol. 1022, File 3094.

MEMBERS OF THE NORTH-WEST MOUNTED POLICE
IN STEELE'S SCOUTS IN - 1885.

	Insp.	Steele	Samuel Benfield
333	Sgt	Fury	William.
28	Sgt	Parker	William.
547	Cpl.	McDonell	Albert Edward Crosby
680	Cpl.	Gould	Henry Vernon
523	Cpl.	Davidson	Alexander L.
549	Cpl.	McMinn	William Robert.
590	Const.	Bell	Ralph Alexander Gascoigne
975	Const.	Bunt	John Porter
474	Const.	Chabot	Joseph Louis
643	Const.	Craig	Thomas.
648	Const.	Davidson	Alexander.
475	Const.	Duberuil	Oscar A.
653	Const.	Dyre	Alexander R.
684	Const.	Hall	E.R.
894	Const.	Hetherington	Samuel.
699	Const.	Jones	George Payse.
704	Const.	Kerr	Peter
716	Const.	McRae	Donald
720	Const.	Morton	Robert
557	Const.	Percival	Ernest.
758	Const.	Richardson	Frederick Henry
759	Const.	Robinson	John Byron.
795	Const.	Walters	John
790	Const.	Waring	Thomas Henry.
784	Const.	Whipps	James

Source: NAC, RG 18, RCMP Papers, Vol. 1022, File 3094. List of Men Who
Served in Steele's Scouts.

Appendices

MEMBERS OF THE NORTH-WEST MOUNTED POLICE
ATTACHED TO THE ALBERTA FIELD FORCE - 1885.

	Supt.	Perry	Aylesworth Bowen
6	S/Sgt	Horner	Samuel H
612	Sgt.	Hamilton	H.
352	Sgt.	Irwin	William Henry
871	Sgt.	O'Connor	William
946	Cpl.	Harper	Arthur Edward
690	Cpl.	Hodder	Eli
534	A/Cpl.	Green	James Douglas
618	Const.	Alexander	Hart O'Hara
631	Const.	Blake	George A
622	Const.	Blake	George Graham
404	Const.	Brown	James H
910	Const.	Diamond	Herbert Caleb
933	Const.	Dodsworth	Frederick Cadwallader Smith
547	Const.	McCarthy	Joseph
721	Const.	Moyers	William H
742	Const.	Parker	Charles
436	Const.	Pickard	James Stephen
774	Const.	Sache	William
780	Const.	Taylor	J.E
505	Const.	Walsh	Robert
575	Const.	Ward.	George Patrick

Source: Annual Report 1885, p. 72.

MEMBERS OF THE NORTH-WEST MOUNTED POLICE
AT THE ENGAGEMENT AT FRENCHMAN BUTTE

Steele's Scouts

	Insp	Steele	Samuel Benfield
333	Sgt	Fury	William
28	Sgt	Parker	William
547	Cpl.	McDonnell	Albert Edward Crosby
680	Cpl	Goold	Henry Vernon
523	Cpl	Davidson	Alexander L
549	Cpl	McMinn	William Robert
590	Const	Bell	Ralph Alexander Gascoigne
975	Const	Bunt	John Porter
474	Const	Chabot	Joseph Louis
643	Const	Craig	Thomas
648	Const	Davidson	Alexander
475	Const	Dubreuil	Oscar A
653	Const	Dyre	Alexander R
684	Const	Hall	E R
894	Const	Hetherington	Samuel
699	Const	Jones	George Payse
704	Const	Kerr	Peter
716	Const	McRae	Donald
720	Const	Morton	Robert
557	Const	Percival	Ernest
758	Const	Richardson	Frederick Henry
759	Const	Robinson	John Byron
784	Const	Whipps	James
795	Const	Walters	John
790	Const	Waring	Thomas Henry

Fort Macleod Detachment

871	Sgt	O'Connor	William
404	Const	Brown	James H
733	Const	Dodsworth	Frederick Cadwallader Smith
742	Const	Parker	Charles
575	Const	Ward	George Patrick

Source: NAC, RG 18, RCMP Papers, Vol. 1022, File 3094, List of Men Who Served in Steele's Scouts 1885, and Annual Report 1885, p. 72.

MEMBERS OF THE NORTH-WEST MOUNTED POLICE WITH STEELE'S SCOUTS IN THE ENGAGEMENT AT LOON LAKE

	Insp	Steele	Samuel Benfield
333	Sgt	Fury	William
523	Cpl	Davidson	Alexander L.
680	Cpl	Goold	Henry Vernon
680	Cpl	McMinn	William Robert
547	Cpl	McDonell	Albert Edward Crosby
590	Const	Bell	Ralph Alexander Gascoigne
474	Const	Chabot	Joseph Louis
643	Const	Craig	Thomas
648	Const	Davidson	Alexander
475	Const	Dubreuil	Oscar A
653	Const	Dyre	Alexander R
894	Const	Hetherington	Samuel
699	Const	Jones	George Payse
704	Const	Kerr	Peter
720	Const	Morton	Robert
557	Const	Percival	Ernest
758	Const	Richardson	Frederick Henry
759	Const	Robinson	John Byron
784	Const	Whipps	James
790	Const	Waring	Thomas Henry
795	Const	Walters	John

Source: NAC, RG 18, RCMP Papers, Vol. 1022, File 3094, List of Men Who Served In Steele's Scouts - 1885 annotated to show participation in specific engagements.

MEMBERS OF THE NORTH-WEST MOUNTED POLICE
KILLED IN THE NORTH-WEST REBELLION - 1885

1013	Const	Gibson	Thomas J.	Duck Lake
1065	Const	Arnold	George Pearce	Duck Lake
852	Const	Garrett	George Knox	Duck Lake
635	Const	Cowan	David Latimer	Fort Pitt
565	Cpl	Sleigh	Ralph Bateman	Cut Knife Hill
907	Cpl	Lowry	William Hay Talbot	Cut Knife Hill
402	Const	Burke	Patrick	Cut Knife Hill
973	Const	Elliot	Frank Orlando	Battleford

Source: Annual Report 1885, Appendix "N", p. 96..

MEMBERS OF THE NORTH-WEST MOUNTED POLICE
WOUNDED IN THE NORTH-WEST REBELLION - 1885

	Supt	Crozier	Lief Newbury F.	Duck Lake
	Insp	Howe	Joseph	Duck Lake
532	Cpl	Gilchrist	Thomas Haddon	Duck Lake
935	Const	Miller	August	Duck Lake
1117	Const	Gordon	Stanley F.	Duck Lake
1048	Const	Wood	John James	Duck Lake
1045	Const	Manners-Smith	Alfred	Duck Lake
925	Const	Loasby	Clarence McLean	Fort Pitt
36	Sgt	Ward	John Henry	Cut Knife Hill
333	Sgt	Fury	William	Loon Lake
716	Const	McRae	Donald	Frenchman Butte

Source: Annual Report 1885, Appendix "N", p. 96.

Notes

Abbreviations

CSP   Canada, Sessional Papers
GAI   Glenbow-Alberta Archives
HBCA   Hudson's Bay Company Archives
HCD   House of Commons Debates
NAC   National Archives of Canada
PAM   Provincial Archives of Manitoba

CHAPTER 1 - CHANGES ON THE PLAINS

1   See Wallace, Jim, *A Double Duty: The Decisive First Decade of the North-West Mounted Police*, Winnipeg: Bunker to Bunker Books, 1997.

2. Morris, Alexander, *The Treaties of Canada With the Indians of Manitoba and the North West Territories,* Saskatoon: Fifth House Ltd., 1991, pp. 210-211.

3. Stonechild, Blair and Bill Waiser, *Loyal Till Death: Indians and the North-West Rebellion*, Calgary: Fifth House Ltd., 1997, p. 29.

4. NAC, RG 10, DIA, Vol. 3609, File 3229, Dickieson to Meredith, April 2, 1878.

5. *Saskatchewan Herald*, March 24, 1879.

6. James Farquharson Macleod, the second Commissioner of the North-West Mounted Police, was a '73 Original and was on the march west in 1874 as Assistant Commissioner. He became Commissioner in 1876 and was replaced in 1880 by A.G. Irvine and remained in Fort Macleod as a Stipendiary Magistrate.

7. NAC, RG 18, RCMP Records, Vol. 1020, File 2479, Report of Superintendent Crozier. Superintendent Lief Newbury Crozier, born in Ireland in 1846, joined the North-West Mounted Police on November 4, 1873 and was on the march west in 1874. He was appointed Assistant Commissioner in 1885 and resigned on June 30, 1886 when not appointed Commissioner, probably due to the Duck Lake engagement.

8. NAC, MG 26A, Macdonald Papers, Vol. 210, pp. 242-43, Dewdney to MacPherson, August 4, 1881.

9. Denny, Sir Cecil E., *The Law Marches West*, Toronto: J.M. Dent & Sons, 1972, p. 145. Inspector Denny was a '74 Original and on the march west. He served until he resigned to become an Indian Agent.

10. Flanagan, Thomas, *Louis "David" Riel*, Toronto: University of Toronto Press, 1996, p. 107.

11. James Morrow Walsh, a '73 Original who brought the first contingent to Lower Fort Garry in 1873, served until September 1, 1883.

12. Dempsey, Hugh A., *Big Bear; The End of Freedom*, Vancouver: Douglas & McIntyre Greystone Books, 1972, p. 94.
13. James Walker, a '74 Original, was appointed a Sub-Inspector in 1874 and was on the march west. He resigned February 1, 1881 to become the manager of the Cochrane Ranch.

CHAPTER 2 - DEFERENCE TO DEFIANCE
1. *Saskatchewan Herald*, February 9, 1880.
2. *Ibid.*, February 14, 1881. Reg. No. 393 George Drew Gopsill served in the North-West Mounted Police from June 14, 1874 to June 26, 1877.
3. *Edmonton Bulletin*, January 10, 1881.
4. *Saskatchewan Herald*, August 11, 1878.
5. Canada, *Sessional Papers* 1881, Annual Report of the Commissioner of the North-West Mounted Police (hereafter referred to as Annual Report) for 1881, p. 10.
6. Inspector Francis J. Dickens joined the North-West Mounted Police on November 4, 1874, retired in March 1886, shortly after the Rebellion and died shortly thereafter. Reg. No. 339 Sergeant Joseph Howe joined the North-West Mounted Police on June 9, 1979 and was at the engagement at Duck Lake. He was made an Inspector on July 1, 1883 and reached the rank of Superintendent before he died suddenly on August 17, 1902.
7. Reg. No. 167 Constable Gilbert Percy Ashe joined the North-West Mounted Police on June 17, 1878 and rose to the rank of sergeant.
8. *Annual Report 1881*, Appx "F," p. 54.
9. Reg. No. 36 Sergeant John Henry Ward joined the North-West Mounted Police on March 29, 1875 and was later seriously wounded during the engagement at Cut Knife Hill.
10. Superintendent John H. McIllree, a '73 Original, joined the North-West Mounted Police in 1873 as a Sub-Constable and was on the march west. He rose to the rank of Assistant Commissioner.
11. NAC, RG 18, RCMP Records, Vol. 1007, File 408, McIllree to Irvine, May 28, 1883.
12. Canada, HCD 1882, p. 542.
13. GAI, M 320, Edgar Dewdney Papers, Box 4, fo. 57, p. 1194, Irvine to Dewdney, June 24, 1882.
14. Ibid., p. 1203, Irvine to White, September 25, 1883.
15. Frederick White was the Comptroller of the North-West Mounted Police in Ottawa, a position similar to a Deputy Minister. Augustus Jukes, the Senior Surgeon of the North-West Mounted Police was appointed January 24, 1882.
16. NAC, RG 10, DIA, Black Series, Vol. 3744, File 29506, Jukes to White, October 7, 1882.

Notes

17. GAI, M 320, Edgar Dewdney Papers, Box 3, fo. 45, pp. 741-42, White to Dewdney, October 17, 1882.
18. NAC, RG 18, RCMP Records, Vol. 1004, File 4, White to Irvine, December 26, 1882.
19. *Edmonton Bulletin*, February 3, 1883. Chiefs Ermineskin, Bobtail and Samson to Sir John A. Macdonald, January 7, 1883.
20. LaChance, V., "The Diary of Francis Dickens," *Queen's University Bulletin*, No. 29, May 1930, p. 4.
21. *Saskatchewan Herald*, February 3, 1883.
22. *Ibid.*, January 20, 1883.
23. Dempsey, *Big Bear*, p. 123.
24. NAC, DIA, Black Series, File 309A, Dewdney to Macdonald, February 12, 1884.

CHAPTER 3 - TENSION RISING.

1. NAC, RG 10, DIA, Vol. 3686, File 13168, Macdonald to Dewdney, May 15, 1884 and Reed to Vankoughnet, May 15, 1884.
2. McKenzie, N.W.M.J., *The Men of the Hudson's Bay Company*, Fort William: Times-Journal Press, 1921, p. 116.
3. *Ibid.*
4. Inspector Richard Burton Deane, a former Royal Marine Light Infantry officer joined the North-West Mounted Police on July 1, 1883 and served until 1915. He was promoted to Superintendent within a year of joining.
5. Deane, Richard Burton, *Mounted Police Life in Canada*, Toronto: Cassel & Co., 1916, p. 141.
6. GAI, M 320, Edgar Dewdney Papers, Box 4, fo. 58, p. 1315, Acting Assistant Commissioner to Superintendent General Indian Affairs, February 27, 1884.
7. NAC, RG 10, DIA, Black Series File 10, 18, Reed to Macdonald, February 27,1884.
8. Reg. No. 66 Sergeant James Murray Bliss joined the North-West Mounted Police on March 3, 1874 and served until June 16, 1884.
9. Superintendent William Herchmer served in the Militia at Fort Garry and entered the North-West Mounted Police in 1876. He died January 1, 1892 while still serving.
10. Deane, *Mounted Police Life*, pp. 145-146.
11. NAC, RG 10, DIA, Black Series, File 10, 181, Herchmer to White, February 26,1884.
12. Deane, *Mounted Police Life*, p. 147.
13. *Ibid.*, p. 149.
14. *Annual Report 1884*, p. 6.
15. McKenzie, *Men of the Hudson's Bay Company*, p. 117.

16. NAC, RG 18, RCMP Records, Vol. 1011, File 773, White to Irvine, March 20, 1884 and Vankoughnet to White, March 18, 1884.
17. NAC, RG 10, DIA, Black Series, Vol. 3710, File 19550-54, Garnet C. Neff, Solicitor at Grenfell, SK., to Superintendent General Indian Affairs, October 14, 1931.
18. GAI, M 320, Edgar Dewdney Papers, Box 2, fo. 37, pp. 483-84, Macdonald to Dewdney, January 11, 1884.
19. *Reminiscences of the Riel Rebellion of 1885 as Told By Old Timers of Prince Albert and District Who Witnessed Those Stirring Days,* Prince Albert: Herald Printing Co., nd, reprinted by *Prince Albert Daily Herald,* 1935.
20. Canada, *Sessional Papers 1886,* No. 43.
21. Jefferson, Robert, *Fifty Years on the Saskatchewan,* Battleford: Canadian North-West Historical Society, 1929, p. 122.
22. *Saskatchewan Herald,* February 23, 1884.
23. *Ibid.,* March 8, 1884.
24. Reg. No. 649 Sergeant Frederick G. Dann joined the North-West Mounted Police on March 28, 1882. Inspector Samuel Benfield Steele was on the Red River Expedition in 1870 and joined the North-West Mounted Police in 1873 and was on the march west in 1874. He had a good career in the Mounted Police and Army, retiring as Major General Sir Samuel Steele.
25. Reg. No. 795 Constable John Walters joined the North-West Mounted Police on April 20, 1882. Reg. No. 350 Constable John William Kerr joined the North-West Mounted Police on June 9, 1879.
26. NAC, RG 18, RCMP Records, Series C-1, File 854, White to Irvine, May 10, 1884, enclosing Vankoughnet to White, May 2, 1884.
27. Dempsey, *Big Bear,* p. 126.
28. NAC, RG 18, RCMP Records, B-3, Vol. 2294, Telegram, Irvine to Richardson.
29. *Ibid.,* Vol. 1015, File 1212, Reed to Irvine, May 18, 1884.
30. GAI, M 320, Edgar Dewdney Papers, Box 2, fo. 37, p. 491, Dewdney to Macdonald, June 12, 1884.
31. NAC, RG 10, DIA, Vol. 3756, File 309B, Rae to Dewdney, June 28, 1884.
32. GAI, M 320, Edgar Dewdney Papers, Box 2, fo. 37, p. 491, Dewdney to Macdonald, June 12, 1884.
33. *Edmonton Bulletin,* June 4, 1884.
34. NAC, RG 10, DIA, Black Series, File 309B, Crozier to Dewdney, June 25, 1884.

CHAPTER 4 - THE CRAIG INCIDENT

1. Inspector William Antrobus joined the North-West Mounted Police on its formation in 1873 and was on the march west in 1874.

2. Reg. No. 565 Corporal Ralph Bateman Sleigh joined the North-West Mounted Police on June 7, 1881 and was killed at Cut Knife Hill on May 2, 1885.

3. Jefferson, *Fifty Years*, p. 109.

4. *Annual Report 1884*, p. 10.

5. Turner, John Peter, *North-West Mounted Police 1873-1893 (2 Vols)*, Ottawa: The King's Printer, 1950, Vol. 2, p. 60.

6. Stonechild & Waiser, *Loyal Till Death*, p. 56.

7. NAC, RG 18, RCMP Records, Vol. 1015, File 1137, Crozier to Irvine, June 20, 1884.

8. Cochin, Louis O.M.I., *The Reminiscences of Louis Cochin*, Battleford: Canadian North-West Historical Society Publications, Vol. 1, No. II, 1927, p. 8.

9. NAC, RG 18, RCMP Records, Vol. 1015, File 1137, Crozier to Irvine, June 20, 1884.

10. *Ibid.*

11. Reg. No. 27, Sergeant Major Michael J. Kirk served in the Royal Irish Constabulary and joined the North-West Mounted Police on April 19, 1874.

12. GAI, M 44, Diary of Regimental No. 247 Trumpeter Fred A. Bagley, Entry for June 18, 1884

13. NAC, RG 18, RCMP Records, Vol. 1015, File 1137, Crozier to Irvine, June 20, 1884.

14. *Ibid.*, Vol. 3335, File SF 724-McQuarrie W. Reg. No. 887 Constable S. Warren Kerr joined the North-West Mounted Police on May 8, 1883.

15. Reg. No. 1008 Constable John Guthrie joined the North-West Mounted Police on February 27, 1884.

16. NAC, RG 18, RCMP Records, Vol. 3335, File SF 724 - McQuarrie W. Handwritten description of events.

17. Cameron, *On the War Trail of Big Bear*, London: Duckworth, 1926, p. 39. Reg. No. 863 Constable Frederick Edward Prior joined the North-West Mounted Police on November 18, 1882.

18. NAC, RG 18, RCMP Records, Vol. 3335, File SF 724 - McQuarrie W. Constable William McQuarrie joined the North-West Mounted Police on April 3, 1882.

19. Jefferson, *50 Years*, p. 113.

20. Reg. No. 247 Sergeant Frederick Augustus Bagley joined the North-West Mounted Police on May 1, 1874 at the age of fifteen and was on the march west in 1874. He served until April 30, 1899, when he went to South Africa with the Canadian Mounted Rifles. He later served in World War I and retired in the rank of major.

21. NAC, RG 18, RCMP Records, Series B-3, Vol. 2294, Crozier to Irvine, nd.

22. *Ibid.*, Vol. 1015, File 1137, Crozier to Irvine, June 20, 1884.

23. *Ibid.*

24. NAC, RG 18, RCMP Records, Vol. 1015, File 1137, Crozier to Irvine, July 27, 1884.
25. *Ibid.*, Vol. 3335, File SF 724 - McQuarrie W.
26. *Ibid.*, Vol. 1015, File 1137, Crozier to Irvine, July 13, 1884.

CHAPTER 5 - RIEL RETURNS

1. NAC, RG 18, RCMP Records, Vol. 1015, File 1137, Crozier to Irvine, July 13, 1884.
2. *Ibid.*, Crozier to Irvine, July 27, 1884.
3. Pope, Sir Joseph, *Correspondence of Sir John A. Macdonald*, Toronto: Oxford University Press, 1924, p. 314.
4. *Saskatchewan Herald*, July 12, 1884.
5. Pope, *Correspondence*, p. 318, Macdonald to Lansdowne, August 12, 1884.
6. NAC, MG 26A, Macdonald Papers, Vol. 107, p. 42829, Rae to Dewdney, July 29, 1884.
7. *Saskatchewan Herald*, August 9, 1884.
8. NAC, RG 18, RCMP Records, Vol. 1015, File 1137, Crozier to Irvine, August 9, 1884 enclosing Brooks to Crozier, August 8, 1884. Reg. No. 318 Sergeant William Alphonse Brooks joined the North-West Mounted Police on June 9, 1879 and was present at the Craig Incident and the engagement at Duck Lake. He was commissioned July 31, 1885 on recommendation of Assistant Commissioner Lief Crozier.
9. NAC, RG 18, RCMP Records, Vol. 1015, File 1137, Crozier to Irvine, August 14, 1884, enclosing Brooks to Crozier, August 10, 1884.
10. NAC, RG 10, DIA, Black Series, Vol. 3697, File 15423, Sub-Agent Macrae's Report on the Meeting of Cree Chiefs and Rebels Held at Fort Carlton, dated August 28, 1884.
11. GAI, M 320, Edgar Dewdney Papers, Box 4, fo. 66, pp. 1398-1401, Hayter Reed to Dewdney, September 4, 1884.
12. Reg. No. 1017 Constable Joseph Augustin MacDermot joined the North-West Mounted Police on May 7, 1875.
13. NAC, RG 18, RCMP Records, Vol. 1015, File 1137, Sergeant Brooks to Crozier, August 5, 1884 and Crozier to Irvine, August 12, 1884.
14. *Ibid.*, Vol. 12, File 20-1885 (Vol. 1), Report of Constable MacDermot, August 16, 1884.
15. *Ibid.*
16. *Saskatchewan Herald*, September 6, 1884.
17. *Annual Report 1884*, p. 6.
18. GAI, M 320, Edgar Dewdney Papers, Box 4, fo. 66, pp. 1398-1401, Hayter Reed to Dewdney, September 4, 1884. Charles B. Rouleau was the Stipendiary Magistrate at Battleford.

19. *Ibid.*, Box 4, fo. 66, pp. 1398-1401, Hayter Reed to Dewdney, September 4, 1884.
20. Turner, *North-West Mounted Police,* Vol. 2, p. 67, Crozier to White.
21. NAC, RG 18, RCMP Records, Vol. 1015, File 1137, Brooks to Crozier, August 5, 1884.
22. *Ibid.*, Keenan to Crozier, September 7, 1884. Reg. No. 301 Sergeant Henry Keenan joined the North-West Mounted Police on October 3, 1873 and was on the March West in 1874. He served until 1903.
23. NAC, MG 26A, Macdonald Papers, Vol. 105, Keenan to Crozier, September 25, 1884.
24. Macleod, R.C., *The North-West Mounted Police and Law Enforcement 1873-1905,* Toronto: University of Toronto Press, 1976, p. 42.
25. Superintendent Sévère Gagnon joined the North-West Mounted Police on April 3, 1874 as a Sub-Inspector and was on the march west in 1874. He served until 1901.
26. NAC, RG 18, RCMP Records, Vol. 1018, File 2164, Keenan to Crozier, October 4, 1884.
27. NAC, RG 18, RCMP Records, File 1844, Dickens to Crozier, October 12, 1844.
28. *Ibid.*, File 2205, Dickens to Crozier, October 27, 1884.
29. NAC, RG 18, RCMP Records, Vol. 1018, File 2205, Dickens to Crozier, October 27, 1884.
30. Cameron, *War Trail of Big Bear,* p. 19.
31. *Ibid.*, p. 17.
32. *Ibid.*
33. *Ibid.*, p. 20.
34. *Ibid.*, Vol. 1020, File 2527, Gagnon to Crozier, December 23, 1884.
35. *Ibid.*
36. *Annual Report 1885,* p. 21.
37. *Ibid.*
38. NAC, RG 18, RCMP Records, Vol. 12, File 20-85 (Vol. 1), Dickens to Crozier, January 12, 1885.
39. NAC, MG 26A, Macdonald Papers, Vol. 107, p. 43001, Dewdney to Macdonald February 14, 1885.
40. Nelson, Hugh S., *Four Months Under Arms: A Reminiscence of Events Prior to and During the Second Riel Rebellion,* New Denver, B.C.: nd, p. 63.
41. NAC, RG 18, RCMP Records, Vol. 12, File 20-85, Report of Inspector Howe, December 31, 1884.
42. GAI, M 320, Edgar Dewdney Papers, Box 2, fo. 38, p. 45, Macdonald to Dewdney, February 20, 1885.
43. NAC, RG 18, RCMP Records, Vol. 12, File 20-85, Gagnon to Crozier, January 26, 1885.
44. *Ibid.*, Vol. 1015, File 1137, Telegram, Gagnon to Irvine, February 21, 1885.

45. *Ibid.*, Gagnon to Irvine, February 24, 1885.
46. NAC, MG 27 I-C-4, Dewdney Papers, Vol. 36-40, André to Dewdney, February 6, 1885.
47. GAI, M 320, Edgar Dewdney Papers, Box 2, fo. 38, p. 529, Dewdney to Macdonald, February 2, 1885.
48. *Ibid.*, Box 2, fo. 38, pp. 546-547, Macdonald to Dewdney, February 23, 1885.
49. NAC, MG 27 I-C-4, Dewdney Papers, Vol. 1, pp. 348-51, Crozier to Dewdney, February 27, 1885.
50. NAC, RG 13, Justice Department Records Relating to the Rebellion, Vol. 2132, p. 606, Richardson to Crozier, March 4, 1885.
51. GAI, M 320, Edgar Dewdney Papers, Box 3, fo. 48, p. 819, White to Dewdney, March 8, 1885.
52. Donkin, John C., *Trooper and Redskin in the Far North West*, London: Sampson Low, Marston, Searle and Rivington, 1889, p. 103.

CHAPTER 6 - DUCK LAKE

1. Pocock, H.R.A., "The North-West Mounted Police," *Chamber's Journal*, Sixth Series, Vol. 1, 1898, p. 11. Reg. No. 1107 Constable Henry Roger Ashwell Pocock joined the North-West Mounted Police on November 2, 1884 and was invalided out on November 13, 1886.
2. NAC, RG 18, RCMP Records, Vol. 1015, File 1137, Gagnon to Irvine, March 10,1885.
3. Inspector William Springfield Morris was a New Brunswick militia officer appointed to the Mounted Police at the age of 36. He was uncomfortable with Indians and Métis and was accused of timidity by General Middleton and some of the people in Battleford. He did not have an illustrious career but served until his retirement in 1920.
4. NAC, RG 18, RCMP Records, Vol. 1015, File 1137, Crozier to Irvine, March 11, 1885.
5. *Ibid.*, Crozier to Irvine, July 13, 1884.
6. NAC, MG 26A, Macdonald Papers, Vol. 107, p. 43108, Dewdney to Macdonald, March 23, 1885.
7. NAC, RG 18, RCMP Records, Vol. 1015, File 1137, Irvine to White, March 13, 1885.
8. *Annual Report 1885*, p. 21.
9. NAC, RG 18, RCMP Records, Vol. 1015, File 1137, Crozier to Irvine, March 17, 1885.
10. NAC, RG 10, DIA, Black Series, Vol. 3715, File 21264, Ballendine to Dewdney, March 16, 1885.

Notes

11. NAC, RG 18, RCMP Records, B-3, Vol. 3545, Letterbook of Commissioner G.A. French, French to Minister of Justice, April 3, 1875. George A. French, the first Commissioner of the North-West Mounted Police, was appointed in 1873 and led the march west. He resigned in 1876.
12. PAM, MG 12, Morris Papers, B-1, Clarke to Morris, July 10, 1875.
13. NAC, RG 18, RCMP Records, B-3, Vol. 2229, Letterbook of Commissioner G.A. French, French to Minister of Justice, August 6, 1875.
14. PAM, MG 12, Morris Papers, B-1 1139, Langevin to Morris, October 25, 1875.
15. NAC, MG 26A, Macdonald Papers, Vol. 107, p. 42779, Clarke to Dewdney, May 11, 1884.
16. HBCA, B332/b/1, Vol. 1, fo. 44, Wrigley to Clarke, March 17, 1885.
17. *Saskatchewan Herald,* March 27, 1885.
18. Turner, *North-West Mounted Police,* Vol. 2, p. 99.
19. NAC, RG 18, RCMP Records, Vol. 1015, File 1137, Crozier to Irvine, March 18, 1885.
20. Deane, *Mounted Police Life,* p. 21.
21. Turner, *North-West Mounted Police,* Vol. 2, p. 100.
22. Braithwaite, Edward A., "Random Recollections by an Ex-Hospital Sergeant," *Scarlet & Gold,* 1, p. 89.
23. Pocock, Henry R.A., *A Frontiersman,* London: Methuen & Co., 1903, p. 5.
24. *Ibid.,* p. 36.
25. *Ibid.,* p. 35.
26. *The Globe,* Toronto: March 25, 1885.
27. NAC, RG 18, RCMP Records, Vol. 1015, File 1137, Crozier to Irvine, March 19, 1885.
28. Reg. No. 463 Ex-Constable John B. Lash joined the North-West Mounted Police on August 21, 1880 and transferred to the Indian Department on October 20, 1883.
29. Turner, *North-West Mounted Police,* Vol. 2, p. 100.
30. NAC, RG 13, Justice Department Records Relating to the Rebellion, Vol. 2332, p. 685.
31. NAC, RG 18, RCMP Records, Vol. 12, File 20-1885 (Vol. 2), Report of Superintendent Crozier, May 29, 1885.
32. *Ibid.*
33. GAI, M 2286, CPR Riel Rebellion Telegrams, No. 82, p. 27, White to Deane, March 29, 1885.
34. GAI, M 1093, Sanders Family Papers, File 152, Diary of S/Sgt Connon, Entry for March 25, 1885.
35. Reg. No. 383 Ex-Constable Harold Aubrey Edward Ross joined the North-West Mounted Police on June 9, 1879, leaving in 1884 to become Deputy Sheriff at Prince Albert.

36. Beale, Bob & Rod Macleod, *Prairie Fire: The 1885 North-West Rebellion,* Toronto: McClelland & Stewart, 1994, p. 154.
37. NAC, RG 18, RCMP Records, Vol. 12, File 20-1885 (Vol. 2), Irvine to Macdonald, April 1, 1885. Reg. No. 400 Sergeant Alfred Stewart joined the North-West Mounted Police on May 8, 1876.
38. Reg. No. 1078 Constable Edward Charles Waite joined the North-West Mounted Police on September 2, 1884 and deserted in 1893. Reg. No. 1015 Constable Robert Walter Jamieson served in the 42nd Royal Highland Regt. in the Ashanti War then joined the North-West Mounted Police on April 14, 1884 and served until 1889.
39. NAC, RG 18, RCMP Records, Vol. 12, File 20-1885 (Vol. 2), Irvine to Macdonald, April 1, 1885.
40. Reg. No. 1067 Constable John Retallack joined the North-West Mounted Police on August 12, 1884 and reached the rank of sergeant. He was a major in the Army in World War I.
41. Black, Norman Fergus, *History of Saskatchewan and the North-West Territories,* Regina: Saskatchewan Historical Company, 1913, pp. 280-282.
42. *Winnipeg Sun,* June 2, 1885.
43. Black, *History of Saskatchewan,* footnote p. 280.
44. PAM, MG 3, C 13, Diary and Memoirs of George A. Flinn.
45. Pocock, *A Frontiersman,* p. 39.
46. NAC, RG 18, RCMP Records, Vol. 12, File 20-1885 (Vol. 2), Report of Crozier, May 29, 1885.
47. *Annual Report 1885,* Gagnon to Irvine.
48. NAC, RG 13, Justice Department Records Relating to the Rebellion, Vol. 2132, pp. 987-90. Reg. No. 773 Sergeant William Crawford Smart joined the North-West Mounted Police on April 17, 1882. Reg. No. 947 Corporal Hugh Davidson joined the North-West Mounted Police in August 1883. Reg. No. 1021 Constable Ernest William Todd joined the North-West Mounted Police on April 26, 1884.
49. NAC, RG 13, Justice Department Records Relating to the Rebellion, Vol. 2132.
50. According to Native oral history Assee-wee-yin, who lived nearby, was on his way home and unfortunately stumbled into the clash between the rebels and the Mounted Police. See Stonechild & Waiser, *Loyal Till Death,* p. 66.
51. McKay, Joseph, "He Didn't Start the War," *Scarlet & Gold,* 12, p. 71-72.
52. Boulton, Charles A., *Reminiscences of the North-West Rebellion,* Toronto: Grip Printing and Publishing, 1896, p. 184.
53. Reg. No. 852 Constable George Knox Garret, son of a Royal Irish Constabulary officer, joined the North-West Mounted Police on July 4, 1882.

54. Reg. No. 484 Constable Louis Fontaine joined the North-West Mounted Police on September 22, 1880. While referred to and signing as Fontaine, his file is in the name of Le Fontaine. He was dismissed on April 12, 1889 for disgraceful conduct.
55. *Montreal Gazette,* May 12, 1885. Reg. No. 1003 Constable Thomas J. Gibson joined the North-West Mounted Police on March 11, 1884.
56. *Regina Leader Post,* December 21, 1938.
57. *Saskatchewan Herald,* April 25, 1885. Reg. No. 1065 Constable George Pearce Arnold joined the North-West Mounted Police on August 11, 1884. He had been a scout in the Cheyenne War in the United States and came to Canada with his friend, Charles Ross, who also enlisted in the force.
58. *Saskatchewan Herald,* April 23, 1885. Reg. No. 1117 Constable Sydney F. Gordon joined the North-West Mounted Police on November 21, 1884. Reg. No. 532 Corporal Thomas Gilchrist joined the North-West Mounted Police on June 7, 1881. He died of a heart attack shortly after the rebellion, on December 10, 1885.
59. Reg. No. 730 Constable Andrew Hugh McMillan joined the North-West Mounted Police on April 20, 1882.
60. *Saskatchewan Herald,* April 23, 1885. Surgeon Robert Miller was appointed on October 25, 1875. He died in 1887 and Ex-Constable Pocock wrote that he committed suicide.
61. NAC, RG 18, RCMP Records, Vol. 12, File 20-1885 (Vol. 2)
62. Nelson, *Four Months Under Arms,* p. 9.
63. Black, *History of Saskatchewan,* p. 279.

CHAPTER 7 - RETREAT FROM FORT CARLTON

1. NAC, RG 18, RCMP Records, Vol. 12, File 20-1885 (Vol. 2), Telegram, Irvine to Macdonald, March 27, 1885.
2. Reg. No. 28 Sergeant William Parker joined the North-West Mounted Police on April 10, 1874 and served until his retirement as a Superintendent in 1912.
3. NAC, RG 18, RCMP Records, Vol. 12, File 20-1885 (Vol. 2), Irvine to Macdonald, April 1, 1885.
4. *Ibid.*
5. HBCA, E.9/29, Evidence Collected at the 1886 Rebellion Claims Commission Hearing at Prince Albert, fo. 88, Statement of Captain Charles F. Young.
6. Griesbach, W.A., *I Remember,* Toronto: Ryerson Press, 1946, pp. 63-64, quoting Lt. Col. Justus Duncan Willson in an address to the Military Institute at Edmonton in November, 1920.
7. HBCA, E.9/29, fo. 5, North-West Rebellion - Evidence Collected at the 1886 Rebellion Claims Commission Hearing at Prince Albert.
8. HBCA, B 332/b/1, fo. 93, Clarke to Wrigley, May 4, 1885.

9. Reg. No. 101 Sergeant James C. Pringle joined the North-West Mounted Police on June 17, 1878 and served until 1903.

10. HBCA, E.9/28, Statements re Property Destroyed During the North-West Rebellion, fo. 282, Statement of Charles N. Garsen.

11. HBCA, E.9/29, Evidence Collected at the 1886 Rebellion Losses Commission Hearing at Prince Albert - Statement of Harold Ross..

12. NAC, RG 18, RCMP Records, Vol. 12, File 20-1885 (Vol. 2), Irvine to Macdonald, April 1, 1885.

13. NAC, RG 13, Justice Department Records Relating to the Rebellion, Vol. 2132, pp. 939-40.

14. NAC, RG 18, RCMP Records, Vol. 12, File 20-85.

15. NAC, MG 26A, Macdonald Papers, Vol. 85, p. 3204, Lansdowne to Macdonald, March 31, 1885.

16. Steele, *Forty Years*, p. 211.

17. Antrobus, Bertie W., "Reminiscences of Fort Macleod in 1885," *The Canadian Magazine*, Vol. VIII, No. 1, Nov. 1896.

18. Morton, Desmond, and Reginald H. Roy, *Telegrams of the North-West Campaign 1885*, Toronto: The Champlain Society, 1972, p. 137.

19. NAC, MG 27, I-C-4, Dewdney Papers, Vol. 3, p. 1189, Macdonald to Dewdney, April 10, 1885.

20. Canada, Department of Militia & Defence of the Dominion of Canada, *Report On the Suppression of the Rebellion in the North-West of Canada and Matters in Connection Therewith in 1885*, Ottawa: May 8, 1886, p. 53.

21. PAM, HBCA, E.9/29, fo. 86, Statement of J. Taylor.

22. Dempsey, Hugh A., "Fort Ostell and the Riel Rebellion," *Alberta Historical Review*, Vol. 2, No. 3, pp. 26-27.

23. NAC, MG 26A, Macdonald Papers, Vol. 107, pp. 43062-66, Scollen to N.W.M.P. Calgary.

24. Dempsey, Hugh A., *William Parker: Mounted Policeman*, Calgary: Glenbow Institute, 1973, p. 69.

25. *Annual Report 1885*, p. 75.

CHAPTER 8 - FROG LAKE AND FORT PITT

1. NAC, RG 18, RCMP Records, Vol. 1019, File 2422.

2. Turner, *North-West Mounted Police*, Vol. 2, p. 130.

3. NAC, RG 10, DIA, Black Series, Vol. 3755, File 30973, Reed to Indian Commissioner, June 8, 1881.

4. Reg. No. 615 Constable William Anderson joined the North-West Mounted Police on April 10, 1882. He was at Fort Pitt, Cut Knife Hill, and the Pursuit of Big Bear. He was invalided out on September 5, 1885 with broken health due to exposure.

5. Boulton, *Reminiscences*, pp. 325-26.

6. Stonechild & Waiser, *Loyal Till Death*, pp. 113-114.
7. *Ibid.*, p. 117.
8. Cameron, *War Trail*, p. 81.
9. Turner, *North-West Mounted Police*, Vol. 2, p. 135.
10. Cameron, *War Trail*, p. 75.
11. Stonechild & Waiser, *Loyal Till Death*, p. 174.
12. *Ibid.*, p. 176.
13. Cameron, *War Trail*, pp. 222-24.
14. McLean, Elizabeth M., "The Siege of Fort Pitt," *The Beaver*, Dec. 45, p. 22.
15. HBCA, E.218/1, p. 5, McLean, William, "Reminiscences of the Tragic Events At Frog Lake and Fort Pitt District, With Some of the Experiences of the Writer and His Family During the North-West Rebellion of 1885.
16. *Annual Report 1885*, Appx. H, p. 78.
17. HBCA, E.9/29, fo. 88, North-West Rebellion - Evidence Collected at the Rebellion Losses Claims Commission Hearing 1886 at Prince Albert, Statement of Charles Quinney.
18. McLean, Reminiscences of the Tragic Events, p. 1B.
19. Reg. No. 41 Sergeant John Alfred Martin joined the North-West Mounted Police on November 3, 1873 and was on the march west. His real name was Martin Malcolm McIntosh.
20. *Annual Report 1885*, p. 78.
21. Reg. No. 381 Constable Frederick Cochrane Roby joined the North-West Mounted Police on June 9, 1879 and was at the engagement at Fort Pitt and Cut Knife Hill.
22. GAI, M 539, Hougham Papers, fo. 20, "The Narrow Escape of the Mann Family from Onion Lake to Fort Pitt 1885."
23. NAC, RG 18, RCMP Records, Vol. 1022, File 3094, Morris to Dickens, April 5, 1885.
24. McLean, "The Siege of Fort Pitt," p. 23.
25. Reg. No. 635 Constable David Latimer Cowan joined the North-West Mounted Police on July 12, 1882 and was killed by Indians at Fort Pitt on April 15, 1885. Reg. No. 925 Constable Clarence McLean Loasby joined the North-West Mounted Police on July 12, 1883 and was seriously wounded at Fort Pitt on April 15, 1885.
26. McLean, Duncan, "On The Twilight Trail of the Fading West," *The Nor'-Wester*, Vol. 100, No. 1, Winnipeg: July 15, 1970, p. 39.
27. McLean, "Reminiscences of the Tragic Events," p. 5.
28. HBCA, E.9/29, Evidence Collected at the Rebellion Claims Commission Hearing 1886 at Prince Albert, fo. 128, Statement of Rev. Charles Quinney.
29. McLean, "Reminiscences of the Tragic Events," p. 5.
30. *Ibid.*, p. 6.
31. *Ibid.*, p. 10.

32. HBCA, E.9/29 Evidence Collected at the Rebellion Claims Commission Hearing 1886 at Prince Albert, fo. 128, Statement of William McLean.
33. Steele, *Forty Years,* p. 218.
34. Mills, J. Wilford, "The Ambushed Patrol," *Scarlet &Gold,* 14, pp. 21-22.
35. PAM, MG 9, A-6, Charette, Guillame, "Biography of Louis Goulet," (original in French), p. 130.
36. Canada, *Sessional Papers 1886,* No. 52a, Rebellion Trials Battleford, p. 11.
37. PAM, MG 9, A-6, Charette, "Biography of Louis Goulet," p. 131.
38. NAC, RG 18, RCMP Records, Vol. 3335, File SF 925 - Loasby CM.
39. McLean, "Reminiscences of the Tragic Events," pp. 12-13.
40. *Ibid.,* p. 13.
41. HBCA, E.9/49, fo. 128, "Statement of William McLean."
42. McLean, "Reminiscences of the Tragic Events," p. 15.
43. Cameron, *War Trail,* p. 111.
44. McLean, "Reminiscences of the Tragic Events," p. 16.
45. McLean, "The Siege of Fort Pitt," p. 25.
46. Reg. No. 762 Constable Richard Routledge joined the North-West Mounted Police on April 3, 1882 and survived the siege of Fort Pitt and engagement at Cut Knife Hill, only to die of typhoid at Battleford, September 10, 1885.
47. *Kingston Daily News,* April 28, 1885.
48. *Annual Report 1885,* Appx. H, p. 80 - Report of Dickens, June 8, 1885.
49. McLean, "Reminiscences of the Tragic Events," p. 56.
50. HBCA, E.218/1, Letter of General Middleton, May 21, 1886 quoted in McLean, "Reminiscences of the Tragic Events," p. 56.
51. McLean, "Reminiscences of the Tragic Events," p. 16.
52. *Ibid.,* p. 23.
53. *Ibid.,* p. 26.
54. *Ibid.,* p. 27.

CHAPTER 9 - BATTLEFORD

1. NAC, RG 18, RCMP Records, Vol. 3776, *North-West Mounted Police Fort Battleford Post Journal 1885.*
2. *Ibid.,* Entry for March 23, - Davies, Hawkins and Wright authorized to return to duty by telegram from Commissioner.
3. NAC, RG 18, RCMP Records, Vol. 3329, File 517, Jukes to Deane, August 22, 1885.
4. Canada, *Sessional Papers 1886,* No. 52, "Rebellion Trials," pp. 297-298.
5. GAI, M 2286, Canadian Pacific Railway Riel Rebellion Telegrams, No. 30, p. 7, Morris to Middleton, March 27, 1885.
6. GAI, M 2111, Horseman's Hall of Fame, Irvine to the officer, NC officer, or man in charge of party enroute to Carlton, March 27, 1885.
7. *Saskatchewan Herald,* April 29, 1885.

Notes

8. GAI, M 2286, CPR Riel Rebellion Telegrams, No. 99, p. 44, J.M. Rae to Indian Commissioner, March 30, 1885.
9. *Saskatchewan Herald,* April 29, 1885. Reg. No. 269 Ex-Constable John D. Finlayson was in the North-West Mounted Police from December 1, 1875 to April 30, 1879.
10 Turner, *North-West Mounted Police,* Vol. 2, p. 124.
11. Canada, *Sessional Papers 1886,* No. 52, Queen vs Poundmaker.
12. NAC, MG 27 I-D-3, Caron Papers, Vol. 199, p. 69, Message received by F. White and passed to Minister of Militia, March 30/31, 1885.
13. GAI, M 2286, CPR Riel Rebellion Telegrams, No. 148, p. 61, Morris to White, March 30, 1885.
14. Arthur Dobbs, who had served in the British Army during the Indian Mutiny was a member of the Battleford Rifles and was killed at Cut Knife Hill.
15. NAC, MG 27 I-D-3, Caron Papers, Vol. 199, Dewdney to White, March 31, 1885.
16. *Ibid.,* Vol. 199, p. 105, Morris to White, March 31, 1885.
17. Letter from Anna E. Alexander (nee Rouleau), *Scarlet & Gold,* 16, p. 67.
18. Reg. No. 271 Harry H. Nash. Reg. No. 278 Anthony Jefferson Prongua. Reg. No. 393 George Drew Gopsill. Reg. No. 202 Joseph H. Price.
19. *Saskatchewan Herald,* April 23, 1885.
20. Reg. No. 282 Robert C. Wyld served in the North-West Mounted Police from April 7, 1874 to June 1881. Reg. No. 263 Frederick A.D. Bourke served in the North-West Mounted Police from June 5, 1877.
21. NAC, MG 27, I-D-3, Caron Papers, Vol. 199, p. 252, Morris to Caron, April 11, 1885.
22. *Ibid.*
23. *Ibid.,* p. 229, Morris to Caron, April 9, 1885.
24. *Ibid.,* p. 243, Morris to Caron, April 10, 1885.
25. *Ibid.,* p. 282, Morris to Caron, April 10, 1885.
26. NAC, RG 18, RCMP Records, Vol. 1024, File 3320, White to Irvine, August 20, 1885.
27. Reg. No. 995 Constable John Hynes joined the North-West Mounted Police on January 14, 1884 and was at the Craig Incident and Cut Knife Hill. Reg. No. 619 Constable Charles Allen joined the North-West Mounted Police on April 26, 1882 and was at the Craig Incident and Cut Knife Hill.
28. NAC, RG 18, RCMP Records, Vol. 3776, Fort Battleford Post Journal, April 22, 1885.
29. NAC, MG 27, I-D-3, Caron Papers, Vol. 199, p. 266, Morris to Caron, April 13, 1885.
30. *Ibid.,* p. 272, Morris to Caron, April 14, 1885.
31. *Ibid.,* p. 77, Caron to Middleton, March 31, 1885.
32. *Ibid.* Middleton to Otter, April 11, 1885.

33. NAC, MG 30, G-14, Otter Papers, Middleton to Otter, (From Camp, 18 mi. from Humboldt). April 12, 1885

34. Middleton, Frederick D., *Suppression of the Rebellion in the North-West Territories of Canada,* Toronto: University of Toronto Press, 1948, p. 22.

35. GAI, M 2286, Riel Rebellion Telegrams, No. 119, p. 51, Deane to White, March 30, 1885.

36. *bid.,* No. 185, p. 74, Shields to Egan, March 31, 1885.

37. NAC, RG 18, RCMP Records, Vol. 1022, File 3094, Herchmer to Irvine, July 27, 1885.

38. *Ibid.,* Vol. 3776, *Fort Battleford Post Journal,* April 14, 1885.

39. NAC, MG 27, I-D-3, Caron Papers, Vol. 199, p. 299, Wrigley to Caron, repeating message from Morris, April 21, 1885 and p. 300, Caron to Wrigley, April 21, 1885.

40. Mulvaney, Charles Pelham, *The History of the North-West Rebellion of 1885,* Toronto: A.H. Hovey and Co., 1885, p. 103.

41. *Ibid.,* p. 104.

42. Reg. No. 1013 Constable Thos. White joined the North-West Mounted Police on March 6, 1884.

43. NAC, RG 18, RCMP Records, Vol. 3776, *Fort Battleford Post Journal,* April 22, 1885.

44. Mulvaney, *History of the North-West Rebellion,* p. 104.

45. NAC, RG 18, RCMP Records, Vol. 3776, *Fort Battleford Post Journal,* April 27, 1885.

46. NAC, MG 30, G-14, Otter Papers, Annotation on telegram, Wrigley to Otter, April 25, 1885.

CHAPTER 10 - CUT KNIFE HILL

1. NAC, MG 27, I-C-4, Edgar Dewdney Papers, Vol. 5, p. 1806, Otter to Dewdney, April 26, 1885.

2. NAC, MG 30, G-14, Otter Papers, Dewdney to Otter, April 26, 1885.

3. *Ibid.,* Middleton to Otter, April 26, 1885.

4. NAC, RG 18, RCMP Records, Vol. 3322, File SF 247 - Bagley F.A. Reg. No. 776 Constable John Harold Storer joined the North-West Mounted Police on April 19, 1882. He was killed in action on March 5, 1917 at the age of 53 while serving in France as a lieutenant with the Royal Winnipeg Rifles. Reg. No. 747 Constable William Henry Potter joined the North-West Mounted Police on April 18, 1882.

5. *Annual Report 1883,* pp. 29-30.

6. NAC, MG 30, G-14, Otter Papers, Otter to Middleton, April 30, 1885.

7. *Ibid.,* Middleton to Otter, April 30, 1885.

8. *bid.,* Otter to Middleton, May 1, 1885.

9. *Ibid., Middleton to Otter,* May 1, 1885.

10. GAI, M 320, Edgar Dewdney Papers, Box 4, fo. 66, pp. 1412-13, Middleton to Dewdney, May 3, 1885.

11. PAM, P-517-2, James Sutherland Chisholm - North-West Rebellion Battleford Camp.

12. Rumball, A.H., "The Relief of Battleford," *Scarlet&Gold*, 3, p. 49.

13. NAC, RG 18, RCMP Records, Vol. 3318, File SF 36 - Ward J.

14. Reg. No. 907 Corporal William Hay Talbot Lowry joined the North-West Mounted Police on June 7, 1883.

15. Mulvaney, *History of the North-West Rebellion*, pp. 134-35.

16. Mackay, D.S.C., (ed.), "The North-West Rebellion of 1885: A Memoir of Colour Sergeant C.F. Winters," *Saskatchewan History*, Vol. XXXV, No. 1, Winter 1982, p. 15.

17. Reg. No. 858 Constable Henry Thomas Ayre joined the North-West Mounted Police on July 26, 1882.

18. Jefferson, *Fifty Years*, p. 143.

19. GAI, M 1949, Diary of Lieutenant R.S. Cassels, p. 41.

20. NAC, RG 18, RCMP Records, Vol. 3438, File O-51, D.S. Curry to Commissioner, September 7, 1939.

21. NAC, MG 30, G-14, Otter Papers, Otter to Middleton, May 6, 1885.

22. HCD, May 29, 1886, Sir Richard Cartwright.

23. Mulvaney, *History of the North-West Rebellion*, pp. 184-85.

24. *Saskatchewan Herald*, June 29, 1885.

25. Reg. No. 594 Sergeant Major Thomas Wattam joined the North-West Mounted Police on August 1, 1881 and was appointed Inspector July 1, 1886.

26. Canada, *Report on the Suppression of the Rebellion*, p. 25.

27. NAC, MG 26A, Macdonald Papers, Vol. 107, pp. 43071-74, Dewdney to Macdonald, May 7, 1885.

28. *Saskatchewan Herald*, May 18, 1885.

29. Brodie, Neil, *Twelve Days With The Indians*, Battleford; Saskatchewan Herald, 1932, p. 3.

30. Strange, Thomas Bland, *Gunner Jingo's Jubilee*, London: Remington & Co., Ltd., 1894, p. 42.

31. Brodie, *Twelve Days*, p. 3.

32. Reg. No. 670 Sergeant John Cristie Gordon joined the North-West Mounted Police on April 12, 1882 and was in the engagement at Cut Knife Hill.

33. Reg. No. 983 Constable William Isaac Spencer joined the North-West Mounted Police on December 21, 1883.

34. Reg. No. 973 Constable Frank Orlando Elliot joined the North-West Mounted Police on November 17, 1883.

35. *Saskatchewan Herald*, May 18, 1885.

36. NAC, RG 18, RCMP Records, Vol. 3776, *Fort Battleford Post Journal*, May 14, 1885.

37. GAI, M 1949, Diary of Lieutenant R.S. Cassels, p. 41.

CHAPTER 11 - FISH CREEK AND BATOCHE

1. *Winnipeg Free Press*, June 1, 1935, p. 8.
2. HBCA, A.12/27, fo. 276-78, Wrigley to Armit, April 13, 1885.
3. GAI, M 539, Hougham Papers, fo. 33, mss by A.N. Mouat, p. 14.
4. Middleton, *Suppression of the Rebellion*, p. 24.
5. GAI, M 1093, File 152, Diary of S/Sgt Connon, Sanders to MacBrien, March 30, 1935.
6. NAC, MG 27, I-D-3, Caron Papers, Vol. 199, p. 270, Middleton to Caron, April 14, 1885.
7. *Kingston Daily News*, April 29, 1885.
8. Middleton, *Suppression of the Rebellion*, p. 29.
9. Prince Albert Historical Society, *The Voice of the People: Reminiscences of Prince Albert Settlement's Early Citizens 1866-1895*, "Mrs. Plaxton's Story," Battleford: Marian Press Ltd., 1984.
10. NAC, RG 18, RCMP Records, Vol. 3318, File SF 10-Harpur G. Harpur to Macdonald, April 21, 1890.
11. Irvine, A.G., *Diary of Commissioner A.G. Irvine, Comd. N.W.M.P. at Prince Albert and Vicinity, March to July 1885, Kept by Serg (or Staff Sergt) Connon,* (hereafter referred to as *Irvine Diary*), p. 12.
12. GAI, M 1093, File 152, Diary of S/Sgt Connon.
13. Minto, Gilbert John E., "The Recent Rebellion in the North-West of Canada," *Nineteenth Century*, XVIII, No. 2, 1885.
14. Chambers, Ernest J., *The Royal North-West Mounted Police*, Montreal: The Mortimer Press, 1906, pp. 90-91.
15. Morris, Edmund, "Lt Col. Irvine and the N.W.M.P.," *The Canadian Magazine*, Vol. XXXVII, No. 6, Oct. 1911, p. 501.
16. Donkin, *Trooper*, p. 148.
17. Middleton, *Suppression of the Rebellion*, p. 58.
18. Donkin, *Trooper*, p. 148.

CHAPTER 12 - THE ALBERTA FIELD FORCE

1. Steele, *Forty Years*, p. 212.
2. Canada, Dept. Of Militia & Defence, *Report of Lieutenant Colonel W.H. Jackson, Deputy Adjutant General*, Ottawa: Maclean Roger & Co., 1887.
3. "Okotoks Old Timer," *Calgary Herald*, April 20, 1935.
4. Steele, *Forty Years, p. 213.*
5. Canada, *Report on the Suppression of the Rebellion*, p. 53.

6. Reg. No. 910 Constable Herbert Caleb Diamond joined the North-West Mounted Police on June 23, 1883.
7. Reg. No. 946 Corporal Arthur Edmond Harper joined the North-West Mounted Police on August 3, 1883.
8. Canada, *Report on the Suppression of the Rebellion,* p. 55.
9. Steele, *Forty Years,* p. 215.
10. Wallace, *A Double Duty,* pp. 41-42.
11. Reg. No. 352 Sergeant William Henry Irwin joined the North-West Mounted Police on June 11, 1879. He was commissioned an Inspector on May 4, 1893.
12. GAI, M 1313, Williams, Milton, "Account of a trip with General Strange During the Riel Rebellion 1885."
13. Reg. No. 46 George Betts Borrodaile served in the North-West Mounted Police from July 17, 1876 to July 17, 1879 and was a sergeant in Steele's Scouts.
14. Williams, J.O.M., "With General Strange's Column in 1885," *Canadian Sagas,* Vol. 1, No. 1, p. 30.
15. *Ibid.*
16. GAI, M 1515, Joseph Hicks, Reminiscences of the Riel Rebellion 1885, p. 4.
17. *Ibid.,* p. 5.

CHAPTER 13 - THE PURSUIT OF BIG BEAR

1. Reg. No. 575 Constable George P. Ward joined the North-West Mounted Police on June 7, 1881. Reg. No. 742 Constable Charles Parker joined the North-West Mounted Police on March 30, 1882 and served to July 31, 1906.
2. While commonly referred to as Frenchman's Butte, the correct name is Frenchman Butte.
3. McLean, "Reminiscences of the Tragic Events," p. 36.
4. Steele, *Forty Years,* p. 221. Reg. No. 173 Joseph Butlin served in the North-West Mounted Police from March 28, 1874 to March 19, 1880 and joined Steele's Scouts when the Rebellion started.
5. GAI, M 515, Hicks, Joseph, Reminiscences of the North-West Rebellion 1885.
6. *Ibid.*
7. NAC, RG 18, RCMP Records, Vol. 3335, File SF 716. Reg. No. 716 Constable Donald McRae joined the North-West Mounted Police on March 29, 1882.
8. Cameron, *War Trail,* p. 184.
9. *Annual Report 1886,* Appx. "F," p. 76.
10. McLean, "Reminiscences of the Tragic Events," p 44.
11. *Ibid.*
12. Strange, *Gunner Jingo's Jubilee,* p. 478.

13. NAC, RG 18, RCMP Records, Vol. 3324, File SF 333-Fury W. Reg. No. 333 Sergeant William Fury, who acted as Sergeant Major in Steele's Scouts, joined the North-West Mounted Police on July 9, 1879.
14. *Saskatchewan Herald*, June 8, 1885.
15. Dempsey, Hugh A., *William Parker*, p. 73.
16. Strange, *Gunner Jingo's Jubilee*, p. 497.
17. Macleod, R.C., ed., *Reminiscences of a Bungle by one of the Bunglers and Two Other North-West Rebellion Diaries*, Edmonton: University of Alberta Press, 1983, p. 80.
18. *Ibid.*, p. 81.
19. Steele, *Forty Years*, p. 228.
20. Macleod, *Bungle*, p. 71.
21. Light, D., *Footprints in the Dust*, North Battleford: Turner-Warwick Publications, 1987, p. 494.
22. *Annual Report 1885*, p. 31.
23. *Irvine Diary*, June 19, 1885.
24. NAC, RG 18, RCMP Records, Vol. 3345, File 1034. Reg. No. 1034 Constable Herman Des Barres joined the North-West Mounted Police on May 31, 1882.
25. *Irvine Diary*, p. 34.
26. Reg. No. 733 Sergeant William Crawford Smart joined the North-West Mounted Police on April 17, 1882, was in the engagement at Duck Lake and later deserted. Reg. No. 971 Constable Alfred Sullivan joined the North-West Mounted Police on November 14, 1883. Reg. No. 1119 Constable Frederick Nicholls joined the North-West Mounted Police on November 29, 1884.
27. *Saskatchewan Herald*, July 13, 1885.
28. Strange, *Gunner Jingo's Jubilee*, p. 506.

CHAPTER 14 - THE AFTERMATH OF THE REBELLION

1. Divisional Order, Major General Strange, Commander Alberta Field Force, Fort Pitt, June 28, 1885.
2. Wallace, *A Double Duty*, p. 105.
3. Reg. No. 543 Sergeant Albert Edward Crosby McDonell joined the North-West Mounted Police on June 7, 1881.
4. Macdonald, J.S., *The Dominion Telegraph*, Battleford: Canadian North-West Historical Society Publications, Vol. 1, No. VI, 1930.
5. NAC, RG 18, RCMP Records, Vol. 1022, File 3094, Steele to Irvine, August 14, 1885.
6. Mulvaney, *A History of the North-West Rebellion*, pp. 109-110,
7. NAC, RG 10, DIA, Black Series, Vol. 3584, File 1130, Pt. 1A, Macrae to Dewdney, June 10, 1885.
8. *Saskatchewan Herald*, May 4, 1885.

9. *Ibid.*, June 8, 1885.
10. Hildebrandt, Walter, "Battleford 1885: The Siege Mentality," *NeWest Review*, Vol. 10, No. 9, May 1985, pp. 20-21.
11. *Annual Report 1885*, pp. 81-82.
12. *Saskatchewan Herald*, April 26, 1886.
13. NAC, RG 18, RCMP Records, Vol. 1023, File 3094, White to Irvine, August 20, 1885.
14. HBCA, A.12.27, fo. 457, Wrigley to Armit, November 4, 1885.
15. Reg. No. 1210 Constable Louis Napoleon Blache joined the North-West Mounted Police on April 29, 1885 and acted as interpreter for Father Cochin at the trial of Poundmaker.
16. Donkin, *Trooper*, p. 189.
17. *Saskatchewan Herald*, September 21, 1885.
18. Melgund, "Rebellion in Canada," p. 315.
19. PAM, MG 3, C 13, Diary and Memoirs of George A. Flinn.
20. GAI, M 320, Edgar Dewdney Papes, Box 4, fo. 66, pp. 1398-1401, Reed to Dewdney, September 4, 1884.
21. NAC, RG 18, RCMP Records, Vol. 3776, *Fort Battleford Post Journal*, November 27, 1885.
22. HBCA, B 165, b/1, Lieutenant Governor Dewdney's Amnesty.
23. NAC, MG 26A, Macdonald Papers, Vol. 107, p. 43169, Dewdney to Macdonald, June 23, 1885.
24. *Ibid.*, Vol. 85, p. 33262, Lansdowne to Macdonald, November 11, 1885.
25. GAI, M 320, Edgar Dewdney Papers, Box 2, fo. 39, p. 613, Dewdney to Macdonald, April 12, 1886.
26. NAC, RG 18, RCMP Records, File 796, Dewdney to Irvine, February 1, 1886.

CHAPTER 15 - PERILOUS TIMES FOR THE FORCE

1. Horrall, S.W., *Pictorial History of the Royal Canadian Mounted Police*, Toronto: McGraw-Hill Ryerson Ltd., 1973, p. 85.
2. Donkin, *Trooper*, p. 149.
3. GAI, M 1093, File 152, Diary of S/Sgt Connon, Sanders to MacBrien, March 30, 1935.
4. Light, *Footprints*, p. 218.
5. Canada, *Report on Suppression of the Rebellion*, p. 5.
6. *Ibid.*
7. Deane, *Mounted Police Life*, p. 23.
8. MacBeth, R.G., *The Making of the Canadian West*, Toronto: William Briggs, 1898, p. 118.
9. Macdonald, *Dominion Telegraph*, p. 43.
10. NAC, MG 30, G-14, Otter Papers, Middleton to Otter, April 28, 1885.

11. NAC, RG 18, RCMP Records, Vol. 12, File 20-1885 (Vol. 2), Telegram, White to Irvine, November 23, 1885.
12. Wallace, *A Double Duty*, p. 15.
13. NAC, MG 26A, Macdonald Papers, Vol. 252, pp. 113998-114008, Morris to Macdonald, January 16, 1873.
14. NAC, RG 18, RCMP Records, A-1, Vol. 1, File 4-74.
15. *Toronto Mail*, September 8, 1874.
16. NAC, MG 27, I-D-3, Caron Papers, Vol. 199, pp. 529-30, Middleton to Caron, June 23, 1885.
17. *Ibid.,* pp. 350-51, Middleton to Caron, May 2, 1885.
18. *Ibid.,* p. 350, Caron to Middleton, May 2, 1883.
19. NAC, RG 18, RCMP Records, Vol. 3438, File O-51 - Morris WS.
20. NAC, MG 27, I-D-3, Caron Papers, Vol. 199, p. 430, Caron to Middleton, May 16, 1885.
21. *Ibid.,* p. 464, Middleton to Caron, May 30, 1885.
22. *Ibid.,* pp. 529-30, Middleton to Caron, June 23, 1885.
23. NAC, MG 26A, Macdonald Papers, Vol. 279, pp. 98855-57, Masson to Macdonald, June 10, 1885.
24. NAC, RG 10, DIA, Black Series, Vol. 3709, File 19550-51.
25. Mulvaney, *History of the North-West Rebellion*, p. 340.
26. *Belleville Daily Intelligencer*, April 7, 1885.
27. GAI, M 320, Edgar Dewdney Papers, Box 2, fo. 38, pp. 587-88, Macdonald to Dewdney, November 1885.
28. Wallace, *A Double Duty*, p. 22.
29. HCD 1881, p. 1327, Sir John A. Macdonald, March 10, 1881.
30. NAC, RG 18, RCMP Records, Vol. 3437, File O-30 - Irvine.
31. Horrall, *Pictorial History*, p. 85.
32. NAC, MG 26A, Macdonald Papers, Vol. 85, p. 33063, Lansdowne to Macdonald, May 19, 1885.
33. Buchan, John, *Lord Minto: A Memoir*, London: Thomas Nelson & Sons Ltd. 1924, pp. 82-83.
34. NAC, MG 26A, Macdonald Papers, Vol. 85, p. 33063, Lansdowne to Macdonald, May 20, 1885.
35. *Ibid.,* pp. 33065-71, Melgund to Macdonald, May 22, 1885.
36. *Ibid.,* Vol. 423, pp. 206107-206110, Strange to Macdonald, February 27, 1886.
37. *Ibid.,* Vol. 198, pp. 83141-142, Campbell to Macdonald, March 7, 1886.
38. *Ibid.,* Vol. 423, pp. 206107-110, Strange to Macdonald, February 27, 1886.
39. NAC, RG 10, DIA, Black Series, Vol. 3709, File 19550-51, Denny to Superintendent General of Indian Affairs, April 27, 1885.
40. Wallace, *A Double Duty*, p. 14.
41. Deane, *Mounted Police Life*, p. 30.
42. *Saskatchewan Herald*, January 18, 1886.

43. NAC, RG 24, Department of National Defence, Vol. 5916, File HQ 51-4-64.
44. *Ibid.*
45. NAC, RG 18, RCMP Records, Vol. 3322, File SF 247, Bagley to Herchmer, June 23, 1891 and White to Herchmer, July 9, 1891.
46. NAC, RG 9, Department of Militia & Defence, II A 1, Vol. 356, File A12089, Order in Council of August 20, 1900.
47. GAI, M 2111, Horseman's Hall of Fame, White to Bagley. Reg. No. 878 S/Sgt H.C.Lewis Hooper. Reg. No. 1128 S/Sgt Charles Cummins Raven joined the North-West Mounted Police on January 9, 1885, became an Inspector on December 1, 1909 and on retirement became an Anglican clergyman at the age of 57.
48. NAC, MG 26A, Macdonald Papers, Reel C1501, p. 16134, Strange to Macdonald, July 29, 1886.
49. Reg. No. 507 S/Sgt Stephen Warden joined the North-West Mounted Police on July 20, 1876 and served to July 10, 1886. Reg. No. 324 Constable Arthur Dorion joined the North-West Mounted Police on June 9, 1879 and had an unspectacular early career. He became a Corporal on February 8, 1912, after nearly 33 years service, a Sergeant on April 1, 1914, a Staff Sergeant on August 6, 1917 and retired on August 31, 1922 with 43 years service.
50 See Stobie, Margaret, *The Other Side of the Rebellion: The Remarkable Story of Charles Bremner and His Furs*, Edmonton: NeWest Press, 1986.

REFERENCES

Abbreviations

AH	Alberta History
AHR	Alberta Histoical Review
CDQ	Canadian Defence Quarterly
CHR	Canadian Historical Review
CGJ	Canadian Geographical Journal
CM	Canadian Magazine
CPA	Canadian Public Administration
CSP	Canada, Sessional Papers
MPQ	Mounted Police Quarterly
S&G	Scarlet & Gold
SH	Saskatchewan History

Adams, Howard, *Prison of Grass*, Saskatoon: Fifth House Publishers, 1989.

_____, "An Opinion of the Frog Lake Massacre," *AHR*, VIII, 3 (1966), pp. 9-15.

Allan, Iris, ed., "A Rebellion Diary," *AHR*, XII, Summer 64, p. 23.

Allan, R.S., "Big Bear," *SH*, Vol. XXIII, Autumn 1970, No. 3, pp. 105-116.

An Old Scout, "Carrying Despatches in the Riel Rebellion," *S&G*, 16, pp. 5-8.

Anderson, F.W., *"1885': The Riel Rebellion*: Calgary: Frontiers Unlimited, 1955.

Anderson, I.S., "Escape From Fort Pitt," *The Beaver*, Spring 1972.

Andrews, Isabel., "Indian Protest Against Starvation: The Yellow Calf Incident of 1884," *SH*, Vol. XXVIII, No. 2, Spring 1975, pp. 41-51.

Antrobus, Bertie, "Reminiscences of Fort Macleod in 1885," *CM*, Vol. VIII, No. 1, Nov. 1896.

Archer, John H., ed., "North-West Rebellion of 1885: Recollections, Reflections and Items, From the Diary of Captain A. Hamlyn Todd, Who Commanded the Guards Company of Sharpshooters in that Expedition," *SH*, Vol. XIII, No. 3, Autumn 1960, pp. 1-18.

Atkin, Ronald, *Maintain The Right*, Toronto: Macmillan, 1973.

Austin, James M., "Some Experience of the Expedition of the North-West Field Force as Copied From a Diary Kept in My Possession," *SH*, Vol. XXXVIII, No. 1, Winter 1985, pp. 26-35.

Barnett, D.C., *Poundmaker*, Don Mills: Fitzhenry & Whiteside Ltd., 1976.

Barron, F. Laurie, "The Indian Pass System in the Canadian West 1882-1935," *Prairie Forum*, 13, 1, (1988), p. 28.

Barron, F. Laurie and James B. Waldram eds., *1885 and After: Native Society in Transition*, Regina: Canadian Plains Research Center, University of Regina, 1986.

References

"Battleford During the Rebellion of 1885," *SH*, Vol. XXXVIII, No. 3, Autumn 1985, pp. 108-117.

Beal, Bob and Rod Macleod, *Prairie Fire: The 1885 North-West Rebellion*, Toronto: McClelland & Stewart, 1994.

Bingaman, Sandra Estlin, "The Trials of Poundmaker and Big Bear, 1885," *SH*, Vol. XXVIII, No. 3, Autumn 1975, pp. 81-94.

_____, "The Trials of the 'White Rebels' 1885", *SH*, Vol. XXV, No. 2, Spring 1972, pp. 44-54.

Black, Norman Fergus, *History of Saskatchewan and the North West Territories*, Regina: Saskatchewan Historical Company, 1913.

Bowsfield, Hartwell, ed., *Louis Riel: Rebel of the Western Frontier or Victim of Politics and Prejudice*, Toronto: Copp Clark, 1969.

Boulton, C.A., *Reminiscences of the North-West Rebellions*, Toronto: Grip Printing & Publishing Co., 1886.

_____, *I Fought Riel: A Military Memoir*, Toronto: James Lorimer & Co., 1985.

Brass, John, *Narrative of John Brass*, Winnipeg: Hudson's Bay Company Archives.

Brathwaite, Edward A., "Reminiscences of a Hospital Sergeant," *AH*, Vol. 39, No. 1, pp. 15-25.

Brodie, Neil, *Twelve Days With the Indians*, Battleford: Saskatchewan Herald, 1932.

Brooks, G.B., "A Chapter from the North-West Rebellion," *CM*, Vol. 1, No. 6, (1893), pp. 473-474.

Buchan, John, *Lord Minto: A Memoir*, London: Thomas Nelson & Sons Ltd., 1924.

Caldwell, R.H., "The Other Side of the Hill: A Tactical Analysis of Indian and Métis Operations in 1885," Ottawa: Paper Presented at the Canadian Historical Association Meeting, 1986.

Cameron, Wm. Bleasdell, *On The War Trail of Big Bear*, London: Duckworth, 1926.

_____, "March on Battleford," *S&G*, 14, pp. 61-66.

_____, "Clan McKay in the West, *The Beaver*, September 1944, p. 5.

_____, "In The Camp of Big Bear," *S&G*, 2, pp. 70-73.

_____, "Rebellion's End," *The Beaver*, September 1952, p. 4.

Canada, *Epitome of Parliamentary Documents in Connection With the North-West Rebellion 1885*, Ottawa: Maclean, Roger & Co., 1886.

Canada, Department of Militia & Defence of the Dominion of Canada, *Report on the Suppression of the Rebellion in the North-West Territories and Matters in Connection Therewith, in 1885*, Ottawa: May 8, 1886.

"Carrying Dispatches in the Riel Rebellion," by An Old Scout, *S&G*, 16, pp. 5-8.

Carter, Sarah A., *Lost Harvests: Prairie Indian Reserve Farmers and Government Policy*, Montreal: McGill-Queen's University Press, 1990.

_____, "Controlling Indian Movement: The Pass System," *NeWest Review*, May 1885, pp. 8-9.

Chambers, Captain Ernest J., *The Royal North West Mounted Police*, Montreal: The Mortimer Press, 1906.

_____, *History of the 65th Mount Royal Rifles*, (translation), Calgary: 1988.Chapman, Evangeline, *Jud Battell's Story of the Early Days of the West*, Moose Jaw: Bowes Publishing, nd.

Charette, Guillaume, *Vanishing Spaces: Memoirs of a Prairie Métis*, Winnipeg: Editions Bois-Brulés, 1976.

Charlebois, Dr. Peter, *The Life of Louis Riel*, Toronto: New Canadian Publications, 1975.

Clink, William L., *Battleford Beleagured 1885*, Willowdale: Published by Author, 1985.

Cochin, Louis, *The Reminiscences of Louis Cochin, O.M.I.*, Battleford: Canadian North-West Historical Society Publications, Vol. 1, No. II, 1927.

Cornish, F.C., "The Blackfeet and the Rebellion," *AHR*, Vol. 1, Spring 58.

Deane, R. Burton, *Mounted Police Life in Canada*, London: Cassel & Co., 1916.

Dempsey, Hugh A., *William Parker: Mounted Policeman*, Calgary: Glenbow-Alberta Institute, 1973.

_____, *Big Bear: The End of Freedom*, Vancouver: Douglas & McIntyre Greystone Books, 1972.

_____, *Crowfoot: Chief of the Blackfeet*, Edmonton: Hurtig Publishing, 1972.

_____, *Red Crow: Warrior Chief*, Saskatoon: Fifth House Ltd., 1980.

_____, "Brisebois: Calgary's Forgotten Founder," in Anthony W. Rasporich (ed.), *Frontier Calgary*, Calgary: McClelland & Stewart, 1975.

Denison, George T., *Soldiering in Canada*, Toronto: George N. Morang and Co., 1901.

Denny, Sir Cecil E., *The Law Marches West*, Toronto: J.M. Dent & Sons, 1972.

Denny, C.D., "In Memory of Mary Rose (Pritchard) Sayer: The Last Witness," *SH*, 24, No. 2, (Spring 1971): 63-72.

de Trémaudan, Auguste-Henri, *Hold High Your Heads*, Winnipeg: Pemmican Publishers, 1982.

Dickason, Olive Patricia, *Canada's First Nations*, Toronto: McClelland and Stewart, 1992.

Donkin, John C., *Trooper and Redskin in the Far North West*, London: Sampson Low, Marston, Searle and Rivington, 1889.

Drolet, J., "A Rebellion Letter," *AH*, Vol. XXX, No. 3, Summer 1982, p. 28.

References

Duncan, H.G., "The Battle of Duck Lake," *Canadian Frontier*, Vol. 2, No. 2, August 1973.

Dunn, Jack, *The Alberta Field Force of 1885*, Calgary: Published by Author, 1994.

Dyck, N.E., "The Administration of Federal Indian Aid in the North-West Territories 1879-1885," Unpublished M.A. Thesis, University of Saskatchewan, 1970.

Fairey, Elaine Louise, "The Roots of Western Discontent: An Interpretation of the White Settlers' Role in theRebellion of 1885."

Fardy, B.D., *Jerry Potts: Paladin of the Plains*, Langley B.C.: Mr. Paperback, 1984.

Ferguson, Charles Bruce, ed., "A Glimpse of 1885," *SH*, Vol. XXI, No. 1, Winter 1968, pp. 24-29.

Fisher, S.T., ed., "An Episode of the North-West Rebellion, 1885," *SH*, Vol. XX, No. 2, Spring 1967, pp. 75.

Fitzpatrick, Frank, *Sergeant 331*, New York: Published by Author, 1921.

Flanagan, Thomas, *Louis "David" Riel*, Toronto: University of Toronto Press, 1996.

_____, *Riel and the Rebellion: 1885 Reconsidered*, Saskatoon: Western Producer Prairie Books, 1983.

Forin, John A., "Riel Rebellion of 1885," *S&G*, 17, pp. 3-6.

Francis, R. Douglas and Howard Palmer, *The Prairie West*, Edmonton: University of Alberta Press, 1992.

Fraser, W.B., "Big Bear: Indian Patriot," *AHR*, Vol. XIV, No. 2, Spring 1966.

Friesen, G., *The Canadian Prairies: A History*, Toronto: University of Toronto Press, 1984.

Fryer, Harold, *The Frog Lake Massacre*, Surrey B.C.: Frontier Books, 1980.

Gaetz, Annie L., *The Park Country: A History of Red Deer and District*, Vancouver: Wrigley Printing, 1948.

Getty, Ian A.L. and Antoine S. Lussier, eds., *As Long as the Sun Shines and Water Flows: A Reader in Canadian Native Studies*, Vancouver: University of British Columbia Press, 1983.

Gilbey, CSM H.M., "Seven Pounders of the Force," *MPQ*, Vol. 37, No. 3, July 1972, pp. 5-9.

Gordon, Daniel M., "Reminiscences of the North West Rebellion Campaign of 1885," *Queen's Quarterly*, Vol. XI, No. 1, January, 1903.

Gowanlock, Mary and Theresa Delaney, "Two Months in the Camp of Big Bear," Parkdale: *TheTimes*, 1885.

Griesbach, W.A., *I Remember*, Toronto: Ryerson Press, 1946.

Hamilton, C.F., "The Canadian Militia: The Northwest Rebellion 1885," *CDQ*, Vol. VII, No. 2, January 1930.

Haultain, T. Arnold, *A History of Riel's Second Rebellion, and How it was Quelled*, Toronto: Grip Printing & Publishing, 1885.

Hayes, E.A., "Okotoks Old Timer," *Calgary Herald,* April 20, 1935.

Henry, J.R., "Sergeant Fury," *MPQ,* Vol. XVIII, July 1973.

Hicks, Joseph, "With Hatton's Scouts in Pursuit of Big Bear," in *AHR,* Vol. 18, No. 3, Summer '70, pp. 14-23.

Hildebrandt, Walter, *Views From Battleford: Constructed Visions of an Anglo-Canadian West,* Regina: Canadian Plains Research Center, University of Regina, 1994.

_____, "Battleford 1885: The Siege Mentality," *NeWest Review,* Vol. 10, No. 9, May 1985, pp. 20-21.

Horrall, S.W., *The Pictorial History of the Royal Canadian Mounted Police,* Toronto: McGraw-Hill Ryerson Ltd., 1973.

Howard, Joseph Kinsey, *Strange Empire - Louis Riel and the Métis People,* Toronto: James, Lewis and Samuel, 1974.

Hughes, Stuart, ed., *The Frog Lake "Massacre": Personal Perspectives on Ethnic Conflict,* Toronto: McClelland & Stewart Ltd., 1976.

Ings, Frederick, *Before the Fences,* Calgary: McAra Printing Ltd., 1980.

Innes, Campbell, ed. *The Cree Rebellion of 1884,* Battleford: Canadian North-West Historical Society, 1929.

Irvine, A.G., *Official Diary of Lt. Col. Irvine, March to July 1885.*

Jamieson, F.C., ed., *The Alberta Field Force of 1885,* Battleford: Canadian North-West Historical Society Publications, 1931.

Jefferson, Robert, F., *Fifty Years on the Saskatchewan,* Battleford: Canadian North-West Historical Society, 1929.

Jeffrys, Charles W., "Fifty Years Ago," *CGJ,* Vol. 10-11, No. 6, June 1935, pp. 258-269.

Jennings, John Nelson, *The North West Mounted Police and Canadian Indian Policy 1873-1896,* Toronto: Ed D Dissertation, University of Toronto, 1979.

_____, "The North West Mounted Police and Indian Policy After the 1885 Rebellion," in Laurie F. Barron and James B. Waldram, eds., *1885 and After: Native Society in Transition,* Regina: Canadian Plains Research Center, University of Regina, 1986.

Kemp, Vernon, A.M., *Scarlet and Stetson,* Toronto: Ryerson, 1964.

Kennedy, Howard Angus, "Memories of '85," *CGJ,* Vol. LXX, No. 5, May 1965, pp. 154-161.

Killough, J.A., "Carrying Despatches in the Riel Rebellion," *S&G,* 16, pp. 5-8.

Kinnaird, G.J., "An Episode of the North-West Rebellion, 1885," *SH,* Vol. XX, Spring 1967, No. 2, pp. 71-75.

Klancher, Donald, *The North-West Mounted Police and the North-West Rebellion,* Kamloops: Mounted Police Research and Consulting, 1997.

Knuckle, Robert, *In The Line of Duty: The Honour Roll of the RCMP Since 1873,* Burnstown: The General Store Publishing House, 1994.

References

Lachance, V., "The Diary of Francis Dickens," *Queen's University Bulletin No. 29*, May 1930.

Lake, I.E.K, (pseudonym for W. B. Cameron), "The Story of the Three Scouts," *S&G*, 2, pp. 65-69.

Lamb, James, B., *Jingo: The Buckskin Brigadier Who Opened Up the Canadian West*, Toronto: Macmillan Canada 1992.

Larmour, Jean, "Edgar Dewdney and the Aftermath of the Rebellion," *SH*, Vol. XXIII, No. 4, Autumn 1970.

_____, "Edgar Dewdney: Indian Commissioner in the Transition Period of Indian Settlement, 1879-1884," *SH*, Vol. XXXIII, No. 1, 1981, pp. 13-24.

Laurie, R.C., *Reminiscences of Early Days in Battleford and With Middleton's Column*, Battleford: TheSaskatchewan Herald, 1935.

Laurie, William, "What I Saw of the North-West Rebellion," *S&G*, 7, pp. 15-32.

Lee, D., "The Métis Militant Rebels of 1885," *Canadian Ethnic Studies*, Vol. 21, No. 3, 1989, pp. 10-12.

_____, "A Victorian Civil Servant at Work: Lawrence Vankoughnet and the Canadian Indian Department, 1874-1893," in Ian A.L. Getty and A.S. Lussier, eds., *As Long as the Sun Shines and Water Flows*, 104-119. Vancouver: University of British Columbia Press, 1983.

Long, Lt-Col. C.E.,, "A Reminiscence of the North-West Campaign," *CDQ*, IV (1), October, 1917.

Light, D., *Footprints in the Dust*, North Battleford: Turner-Warwick Publications, 1987.

Lussier, A.S., ed., *Louis Riel and the Métis*, Winnipeg: Pemmican Publications, 1988.

MacBeth, R.G., *The Making of the Canadian West*, Toronto: William Briggs, 1898.

_____, "With General Strange in the Big Bear Country," *Maclean's Magazine*, Vol. XXVII, No. 12, October 1914.

_____, "General Strange's Column 1885," *S&G*, 14, pp. 83-84.

_____, "Sir Samuel Benfield Steele," *CM*, Vol. LII, No. 5, March 1917, p. 972.

_____, "On The Fighting Line in Riel's Day," *Maclean's Magazine*, Vol. XXVII, No. 4, February 1915, p. 46.

MacDonald, John Stuart., *The Dominion Telegraph*, Battleford: Canadian North-West Historical Society Publications, Vol. 1, No. VI, 1930.

MacGregor, James G., *Father Lacombe*, Edmonton: Hurtig Publishers, 1975.

_____, Senator Hardisty's Prairies 1849-1889, Saskatoon: Western Producer Prairie Books, 1978.

_____, *Edmonton Trader*, Toronto: McClelland and Stewart, 1963.

MacKay, D.S.C., ed., "The North-West Rebellion 1885: A Memoir by Colour Sergeant C.F.Winters," *SH*, Vol. XXXV, No. 1, Winter 1982, p. 15.

Macleod, R.C., ed., *Reminiscences of a Bugle, by one of the Bunglers and Two Other Northwest Rebellion Diaries*, Edmonton: University of Alberta Press, 1983.

_____, *The North West Mounted Police and Law Enforcement 1873-1905*, Toronto: University of Toronto Press, 1976.

_____, *Swords and Ploughshares: War and Agriculture in Western Canada*, Edmonton: University of Alberta Press, 1993.

_____, "Canadianizing the West: The North West Mounted Police as Agents of the National Policy 1873-1905," in *The Prairie West*, edited by Douglas Francis and Howard Palmer, 225-238. Edmonton: University of Alberta Press, 1992.

McCourt, Edward, *Buckskin Brigadier*, Toronto: Macmillan, 1966.

McDougall, John, *George Milward McDougall, the Pioneer, Patriot and Missionary*, Toronto: William Briggs, 1902.

McKay, the Venerable Archdeacon George, *Fighting Parson*, Kelowna: Published by Author, 1966.

McKay, Joseph, "He Didn't Start the War," *S&G*, 12, pp. 71-72.

McKenzie, N.W.M.J., *The Men of the Hudson's Bay Company*, Fort William: Times-Journal Press, 1921.

McLean, Don, *1885, Métis Rebellion or Government Cnspiracy?* Winnipeg: Pemmican Publications, 1985.

McLean, Duncan, "On the Twilight Trail of the Fading West," *The Nor'-Wester*, Vol. 100, No. 1, Winnipeg: July 15, 1970.

McLean, Elizabeth M., "The Siege of Fort Pitt," *The Beaver*, December 1946, pp. 22-25.

_____, "Prisoners of the Indians," *The Beaver*, June 1947, pp. 14-17.

_____, "Our Captivity Ended," *The Beaver*, September 1947, pp. 38-

McLean, William J., "Reminiscences of the Tragic Events at Frog Lake and in Fort Pitt District with Some of the Experiences of the Writer and his Family during the North West Rebellion of 1885.".

McLeod, Corporal D.F., "Fort Carlton 1885," *MPQ*, Vol. 38, No. 2, April 1973, pp. 12-16.

Middleton, Frederick D., *Suppression of the Rebellion in the North West Territories of Canada 1885*, Toronto: University of Toronto Press, 1948.

Mika, Nick and Helma Mika, comps., *The Riel Rebellion 1885*, Belleville ON: Mika Silk Screening, 1977.

Miller, Carman, ed., "Lord Meglund and the North-West Campaign of 1885," *SH*, Vol. XXII, No. 3, Autumn 1969, pp. 81-108.

Miller, J.R., *Skyscrapers Hide The Heavens: A History of Indian-White Relations in Canada*, Toronto: University of Toronto Press,1989.

_____, ed., *Sweet Promises: A Reader in Indian-White Relations in Canada*, Toronto: University of Toronto Press, 1991.

References

Mills, J. Willford, "The Ambushed Patrol," *S&G*, 14, pp. 21-22.

Minto, Gilbert, John E., "The Recent Rebellion in North-West Canada," *Nineteenth Century*, XVIII, (2), 1885.

Mitchener, Alyn E., "William Pearce and Federal Government Activity in Western Canada 1882-1904," *Canadian Public Administration*, Vol. 10, No. 2, June 1967, pp. 235-243.

Morris, Alexander, *The Treaties of Canada With the Indians of Manitoba and the North-West Territories*, Saskatoon: Fifth House Ltd., 1991.

Morris, Edmund, "Lt Col Irvine and the N.W.M.P.," *CM*, Vol. XXXVII, No. 6, Oct 1911, pp. 493-503.

Morton, Desmond, *The Last War Drum*, Toronto: A.M. Hakkert Ltd., 1972.

_____, "Cavalry or Police: Keeping the Peace on Two Adjacent Frontiers, 1870-1900," *Journal of Canadian Studies*, Vol. 12, Spring 77, pp 27-37.

_____, "Reflections on Old Fred: Major General Middleton and the North-West Campaign of 1885," *NeWest Review*, Vol. 10, No. 9, May 1985, pp. 5-7.

_____, and Reginald H. Roy, *Telegrams of the North West Campaign 1885*, Toronto: The Champlain Society, 1972.

Mulvaney, Chas. Pelham, *The History of the North-West Rebellion of 1885*, Toronto: A.H. Hovey and Co., 1886.

Munro, R., "On the March With the 'Little Black Devils,'" *S&G*, 17, p. 55.

Needler, G.H., ed., Middleton, Frederick D., *Suppression of the Rebellion in the North West Territories of Canada 1885*, Toronto: University of Toronto Press, 1948.

Nelson, Hugh S., *Four Months Under Arms: A Reminiscence of Events Prior to and During the Second Riel Rebellion*, New Denver, B.C.: nd.

Normandeau, Louis, "65th Mount Royal Regiment and the Riel Rebels," *AHR*, Vol. 9, No. 4, 1961.

Oppen, William A., *The Riel Rebellion, a Cartographic History*, Toronto: University of Toronto Press,

Pelletier, Joanne (ed.), *The North-West Resistance of 1885*, Regina: Gabriel Dumont Institute of Native Studies and Applied Research, 1995.

Pennefather, John P., *Thirteen Years on the Prairies*, London: Kegan Paul, Trench, Trubner & Co. Ltd., 1982.

Pocock, Henry R., *A Frontiersman*, London: Methuen & Co., 1903.

_____, "The North West Mounted Police," *Chamber's Journal*, Vol. 75, 1898.

Preston, J.A.V., "The Diary of Lieut. J.A.V. Preston," *SH*, Vol. VIII, No. 3, Autumn 1955, p. 107.

Prince Albert Historical Society, *The Voice of the People: Reminiscences of Prince Albert Settlement's Early Citizens 1866-1895*, Battleford: Marian Press Ltd., 1984.

Racey, Ex-Constable E.F., "A Police Patrol Skirmishes With the Indians," *MPQ*, Vol. 12, No. 4, April 1947, pp. 312-316.

_____, "Skirmish on Patrol," *The Beaver*, March 1945.

"Rebellion of 1885," Scrapbook compiled in New Brunswick partly from Maritime Provinces Newspapers, Calgary: Glenbow Library, 1965.

Reminiscences of the Riel Rebellion of 1885 as Told by Old Timers of Prince Albert and District Who Witnessed Those Stirring Days, Prince Albert Herald Printing Co., ud, reprinted by Prince Albert Daily Herald reprint series for Apr. 15, 16, 17, 1935.

Rivett-Carnac, C.E., "Letters from the North-West," *MPQ*, Vol. XVII, July 1952, pp. 13-18.

Ronaghan, Allen, "Three Scouts and the Cart Train," *AH*, Vol. XXV, Winter '77.

_____, "Who Was That Fine Young Man? The Frog Lake Massacre Revisited," *SH*, Vol. 42, No. 2, Fall 1995, pp. 13-19.

Ross, David, (ed.), "The 1885 North-West Campaign Diary of R. Lyndhurst Wadmore, Infantry School Corps," *SH*, Vol. XLII, Spring 1989, No. 2, pp. 62-78.

Ross, Howard E., "A Glimpse of 1885," *SH*, Winter 1968, pp. 24-29.

Roy, R.H., "The Diary of Rifleman Forin," *SH*, Vol. XXI, No. 3, Autumn 1968, pp. 100-111.

_____, "With the Midland Battalion to Batoche," *SH*, Vol. XXXII, Spring 1979, No. 2.

Rumball, A.H., "The Relief of Battleford," *S&G*, 3, p. 47. *Settlers and Rebels: North-West Mounted Police Reports 1882-1885,* Toronto: Coles Publishing Co., 1973.

Shera, John W., "Poundmaker's Capture of the Wagon Train in the Eagle Hills 1885," *AHR*, Vol. 1, No. 1, 1953, pp. 16-20.

Siggins, M., *Riel: A Life of Revolution,* Toronto: Harper Collins Publishers Ltd., 1994.

Silver, A.I., and Marie France Vailleur, *The North-West Rebellion,* Toronto: Copp Clark Publishing Co., 1967.

Silwa, S., "Treaty Day for the Willow Cree," *SH*, Vol. 47, No. 1, Spring 1995.

Sluman, N., *Poundmaker,* Toronto: 1967.

_____, and Jean Goodwill, *John Tootoosis, Biography of a Cree Leader,* Ottawa: Golden Dog Press, 1982.

Smith, Donald B., "William Henry Jackson: Riel's Secretary," *The Beaver*, Spring 1981.

Sprague, D.N., *Canada and the Métis 1869-1885,* Waterloo: Sir Wilfrid Laurier Press, 1988.

References

Stacey, C.P., "The Military Aspects of Canada's Winning of the West," *CHR*, Vol. XXI, March 1, 1940.

Stanley, George F,G,, "An Account of the Frog Lake Massacre," *AHR*, Vol. 4, No.1, 1956, pp. 23-27.

_____, *The Birth of Western Canada: A History of the Riel Rebellions*, Toronto: University of Toronto Press, 1960.

_____, "Gabriel Dumont's Account of the North-West Rebellion," *CHR*, Vol. 30, 1949.

_____, "The Campaign of 1885: A Contemporary Account," *SH*, Vol. XIII, No. 3, Autumn 1960, pp. 100-107.

Stobie, Margaret, *The Other Side of the Rebellion: the Remarkable Story of Charles Bremner and His Furs*, Edmonton: NeWest Press, 1986.

Stonechild, Blair, "The Indian View of the 1885 Uprising," in J.R. Miller, (ed.), *Sweet Promises: A Reader in Indian-White Relations in Canada*, Toronto: University of Toronto Press, 1991, p. 276.

_____, and Bill Waiser, *Loyal Till Death: Indians and the North-West Rebellion*, Calgary: Fifth House Ltd., 1997.

Steele, Samuel B., *Forty Years in Canada*, Toronto: Coles Publishing, 1973.

Strange, Thomas Bland, *Gunner Jingo's Jubilee*, London: Remington & Co. Ltd., 1894.

Thomas, L.H., *Essays on Western History*, Edmonton: University of Alberta Press, 1976.

_____, *The Struggle for Responsible Government in the North-West Territories, 1870-1897*, Toronto: 1956.

Thomas, Lewis G., (ed.), *The Prairie West to 1905*, Toronto: Oxford University Press, 1975.

Titley, E.B., "Hayter Reed and Indian Administration in the West," in R. Macleod, *Swords and Ploughshares: War and Agriculture in Western Canada*, Edmonton: University of Alberta Press, 1993, pp. 109-147.

Tobias, J.L., "Canada's Subjugation of the Plains Cree, 1879-1885," in J.R. Miller (ed.) *Sweet Promises: A Reader in Indian-White Relations in Canada*, Toronto: University of Toronto Press, 1991, pp. 212-240.

_____, "Protection, Civilization, Assimilation: An Outline of Canada's Indian Policy," in Ian A.L. Getty and A.S. Lussier, eds., *As Long as the Sun Shines and Water Flows*, 39-55. Vancouver: University of British Columbia Press, 1983.

_____, "The Origins of the Treaty Rights Movement in Saskatchewan," in F. Laurie Barron and James B. Waldram, eds., *1885 and After: Native Society in Transition*, 241-252. Regina: Canadian Plains Research Center, University of Regina, 1986.

Tolton, Gordon E., *The Rocky Mountain Rangers: Southern Alberta's Cowboy Cavalry in the North West Rebellion - 1885*, Lethbridge: Lethbridge Historical Society Occasional Paper No. 28, 1994.

Treaty 7 Elders and Tribal Council, *The True Spirit of Treaty 7*, Montreal and Kingston: McGill-Queen's University Press, 1996.

Turner, John Peter, *The North West Mounted Police 1873-1893*, Ottawa: King's Printer, 1950.

Upton, Leslie F.S., "The Origins of Canadian Indian Policy," *Journal of Canadian Studies*, Vol. 8, 1973, pp. 51-61.

Waiser, W.A., "Surveyors at War, A.O. Wheeler's Diary of the North-West Rebellion," *SH*, Vol. XXXVIII, No. 2, Spring 1985, p. 50.

Weaver, Sally M., *Making Canadian Indian Policy: The Hidden Agenda 1868-70*, Toronto: 1981.

Whitehead, C., "A Day in Battleford," *S&G*, 5, pp. 90-91.

Wiebe, Rudy, and Bob Beal (eds), *War in the West: Voices of the 1885 Rebellion*, Toronto: McClelland and Stewart,1985.

_____, *The Temptations of Big Bear*, Toronto: McClelland & Stewart, 1973.

Williams, J.O.M., "With General Strange's Column 1885," *Canadian Sagas*, Vol. I, No. 1, pp. 34-35.

Williams, Milton, "Twice Disappointed," *AHR*, Vol. XI, No. 4, Autumn 1963, p.16.

"With General Strange's Column in the Riel Rebellion," *S&G*, 17, p. 28.

Woodcock, George, *Gabriel Dumont, The Métis Chief and his Lost World*, Edmonton: Hurtig Publishers, 1975.

PHOTO CREDITS

Cover: Photograph reproduced and used by permission of the *RCMP Quarterly*

Page   Photograph/Source.

3.   Map of Canada in 1873 courtesy of Royal Canadian Mounted Police. Reproduced with the permission of the Minister of Public Works and Government Services Canada.

37.   Hudson's Bay Company Archives/Public Archives of Manitoba, "Major Crozier, N.W.M.P." North-West Rebellion Collection - 45, N-12374.

46.   Hudson's Bay Company Archives/Public Archives of Manitoba. "Louis Riel," N-5737.

53.   National Archives of Canada / C-014154, "Big Bear Trading Inside Fort Pitt Just Before the North-West Rebellion.

64.   National Archives of Canada / PA-042139, "Commissioner A.G. Irvine, Photographer: W.J. Topley.

67.   University of Saskatchewan Library, Special Collections, Pamphlets LXII-37, "North West Mounted Police on the March," from Frank Leslies Illustrated Newspaper, April 18, 1885, p. 148.

77.   National Archives of Canada / C-033058, "The Fight at Duck Lake 1885," From the Souvenir Number of the Canadian Pictorial and Illustrated War News, July 4, 1885.

80.   National Archives of Canada / PA-117931, "Fort Carlton From The Hill," Photographer: C. Horetzky.

83.   National Archives of Canada / C-018705, "Fort Carlton As It Appears Since Burnt Down By Mounted Police Under Col. Irvine 1885."

97.   Hudson's Bay Company Archives/Public Archives of Manitoba. HBCA 1987/363-R-34/30, N-13504, "North West Mounted Police Detachment at Fort Pitt."

105.   Hudson's Bay Company Archives/Public Archives of Manitoba, N-12395, North-West Rebellion Colllection - 65, "North West Mounted Police Band at Battleford."

111.   National Archives of Canada / PA-042149, "Inspector W.S. Morris," Photographer: W.J. Topley.

114.   National Archives of Canada / C-007523, "The Looting of the Old Town of Battleford."

119.   National Archives of Canada / PA-042142, "Superintendent W.M. Herchmer," Photographer: W.J. Topley.

121.   Hudson's Bay Company Archives/Public Archives of Manitoba, N-12393, North-West Rebellion Collection - 63, "Otter's Column Approaching The South Saskatchewan River."

124.   Hudson's Bay Company Archives of Canada/Public Archives of Manitoba PAM N-12394 "The Relief of Battleford."

129.   Hudson's Bay Company Archives/Public Archives of Manitoba, N-16095, "Poundmaker," Photographer: Hall & Lowe.

131.   Hudson's Bay Company Archives/Public Archives of Manitoba, N-12346 North-West Rebellion Collection - 7, "Battle of Cut Knife Creek."

135.   National Archives of Canada / C-006744, "A Brave Scout's Untimely End," From Canadian Pictorial and Illustrated War News, May 16, 1885.

141.   National Archives of Canada / PA-012197, "Major General Sir Frederick Middleton," Photographer: W.J. Topley.

151.   Hudson's Bay Company Archives/Public Archives of Manitoba N-14582 North-West Rebellion Collection - 199, "Louis Riel Captured By Scouts."

155.   National Archives of Canada / PA-138789, "Major General Thomas Bland Strange R.A."

169.   National Archives of Canada / C-000595, "Camp of Fleeing Indians and White Prisoners."

PHOTO CREDITS

171. Hudson's Bay Company Archives/Public Archives of Manitoba, N-12475 North-West Rebellion Collection - 156, "Big Bear's Band Under Attack."

174. Hudson's Bay Company Archives/Public Archives of Manitoba, N-12485 North-West Rebellion Collection - 158, "65th Battalion on March to Cold Lake."

176. National Archives of Canada / C-018957, "First Ford at Loon Lake - Scene of Steele's Fight," Photographer: Frederic Hathaway Peters.

180. Hudson's Bay Company Archives/Public Archives of Manitoba, N-14577 North-West Rebellion Collection - 194, ""Big Bear's Surrender."

187. Hudson's Bay Company Archives/Public Archives of Manitoba, N-12344 West Rebellion Collection - 2, "Group at Regina Trials 1885."

192. Hudson's Bay Company Archives/Public Archives of Manitoba, N-18372 North West Mounted Police Collection - 16, "North West Mounted Police Barracks Regina 1885."

205. North West Canada Medal. Provided by Publisher.

207. Saskatchewan Archives Board/235, Fort Battleford Collection. Staff Sergeant Frederick A. Bagley.

INDEX

Index

ABOUT THE AUTHOR

Jim Wallace was born and raised in British Columbia and received his early education in that province. He is a graduate of Carleton University and has a Master's in Public Administration from Queen's University at Kingston. He spent most of his adult life in the Canadian Armed Forces and retired as a Lieutenant Colonel. During his time in the forces he served in Canada, Korea, the United States, Germany, Britain and the Soviet Union.

He has had a lifelong interest in history, particularly the history of Western Canada. His previous book, *A Double Duty*, about the decisive first decade of the North-West Mounted Police was also published by Bunker to Bunker Books.

BY THE SAME AUTHOR

A DOUBLE DUTY

The Decisive First Decade of the North-West Mounted Police

This book covers the first decade in the history of the North-West Mounted Police, a decisive and exciting period in the development of Western Canada. During this period the whisky traders were brought under control, Sitting Bull and the Sioux sought refuge in Canada, the buffalo disappeared, important treaties were signed with the plains Indians and the Canadian Pacific Railway was built across the prairies. That this major change took place without widespread bloodshed was largely due to the work of the Mounted Police. As the decade ended, government neglect and regressive policies set the stage for the North-West Rebellion.

A TRYING TIME

The North West Mounted Police In the 1885 Rebellion

This book describes the activities of the North-West Mounted Police during the 1885 Rebellion. To many Canadians the role of the Mounted Police is virtually unknown, being overshadowed by the activities of the large number of troops sent from Eastern Canada. The Mounted Police warned Ottawa that a rebellion would occur unless there was a change in their treatment of aboriginals. When their warnings went unheeded they were caught in a war they had tried to prevent. While the force was occupied with the insurrection, General Middleton, the Commander of the Canadian Militia, was attempting to have the force abolished.

Available From

Bunker to Bunker Books

34 Blue Spruce Crescent

Winnipeg, MB.

R3M 4C2